ASSESSMENT FOR INCLUSION IN HIGHER EDUCATION

Bringing together international authors to examine how diversity and inclusion impact assessment in higher education, this book provides educators with the knowledge and understanding required to transform practices so that they are more equitable and inclusive of diverse learners.

Assessment drives learning and determines who succeeds. *Assessment for Inclusion in Higher Education* is written to ensure that no student is unfairly or unnecessarily disadvantaged by the design or delivery of assessment. The chapters are structured according to three themes: 1) macro contexts of assessment for inclusion: societal and cultural perspectives; 2) meso contexts of assessment for inclusion: institutional and community perspectives; and 3) micro contexts of assessment for inclusion: educators, students, and interpersonal perspectives. These three levels are used to identify new ways of mobilising the sector towards assessment for inclusion in a systematic and scholarly way.

This book is essential reading for those in higher education who design and deliver assessment, as well as researchers and postgraduate students exploring assessment, equity, and inclusive pedagogy.

Rola Ajjawi is Professor of Educational Research at the Centre for Research in Assessment and Digital Learning, Deakin University, Australia, where she has led an extensive programme of research into student failure and success, with particular interest in equity, feedback, and learning cultures.

Joanna Tai is Senior Research Fellow at the Centre for Research in Assessment and Digital Learning, Deakin University, Australia. She researches student experiences of learning and assessment from university to the workplace, including feedback and assessment literacy, evaluative judgement, and peer learning.

David Boud is Alfred Deakin Professor and Foundation Director of the Centre for Research in Assessment and Digital Learning at Deakin University, Australia. He is also Emeritus Professor at the University of Technology Sydney and Professor of Work and Learning at Middlesex University. His current work is in the areas of assessment for learning in higher education, academic formation, and workplace learning.

Trina Jorre de St Jorre is Honorary Fellow at the Centre for Research in Assessment and Digital Learning, Deakin University, and Student Experience Portfolio Manager at the University of New England. Her research and practice is focused on continual improvement of the student experience, with particular interest in graduate employability and student achievement.

ASSESSMENT FOR INCLUSION IN HIGHER EDUCATION

Promoting Equity and Social Justice in Assessment

Edited by Rola Ajjawi, Joanna Tai, David Boud, and Trina Jorre de St Jorre

Routledge
Taylor & Francis Group
LONDON AND NEW YORK

First published 2023
by Routledge
4 Park Square, Milton Park, Abingdon, Oxon OX14 4RN

and by Routledge
605 Third Avenue, New York, NY 10158

Routledge is an imprint of the Taylor & Francis Group, an informa business

British Library Cataloguing-in-Publication Data
A catalogue record for this book is available from the British Library

Library of Congress Cataloging-in-Publication Data
Names: Ajjawi, Rola, editor. | Tai, Joanna, editor. | Boud, David, editor. | De St. Jorre, Trina Jorre, editor.
Title: Assessment for inclusion in higher education : promoting equity and social justice in assessment / Edited by Rola Ajjawi, Joanna Tai, David Boud, and Trina Jorre de St Jorre.
Identifiers: LCCN 2022043883 | ISBN 9781032275031 (hardback) | ISBN 9781032274942 (paperback) | ISBN 9781003293101 (ebook)
Subjects: LCSH: Educational tests and measurements--Evaluation. | Inclusive education. | Education, Higher--Evaluation. | Educational equalization. | Social justice and education. | Multicultural education.
Classification: LCC LB3051 .A7668 2023 | DDC 371.2601/3--dc23/eng/20220930
LC record available at https://lccn.loc.gov/2022043883

ISBN: 978-1-032-27503-1 (hbk)
ISBN: 978-1-032-27494-2 (pbk)
ISBN: 978-1-003-29310-1 (ebk)

DOI: 10.4324/9781003293101

Typeset in Bembo
by KnowledgeWorks Global Ltd.

CONTENTS

SECTION III
Micro contexts of assessment for inclusion: Educators, students, and interpersonal perspectives 165

FIGURES AND TABLES

Figures

Tables

CONTRIBUTORS

Taskeen Adam is Associate Manager at Open Development & Education, a Senior Research Lead at EdTech Hub and a Research Associate at the University of Johannesburg. She specialises in tech-supported teacher professional development, virtual learning environments, justice-oriented open education, Massive Open Online Courses, and decolonising EdTech.

Rola Ajjawi is Professor of Educational Research at the Centre for Research in Assessment and Digital Learning, Deakin University, Australia where she has led an extensive programme of research into student failure and success, with particular interest in equity, feedback and learning cultures.

Allen Baird is language and study-skills adviser to international students at TasTAFE. He previously worked at the University of Tasmania as a teaching academic, and student adviser, on pre-degree (enabling) programmes.

Margaret Bearman is Professor with the Centre for Research in Assessment and Digital Learning (CRADLE), Deakin University, Australia. Her current research investigates feedback, assessment, and digital learning in higher and professional education, with particular interests in sociomateriality and clinical contexts.

David Boud is Alfred Deakin Professor and Foundation Director of the Centre for Research in Assessment and Digital Learning at Deakin University, Australia. He is also Emeritus Professor at the University of Technology Sydney and Professor of Work and Learning at Middlesex University. His current work is in the areas of assessment for learning in higher education, academic formation, and workplace learning.

Roseanna Bourke is Professor of Learning and Assessment at Massey University, Aotearoa New Zealand, and her research focuses on assessment, applied professional ethics, informal and everyday learning, and children's rights and capabilities.

Matt Brett is Director of Academic Governance and Standards at Deakin University. He has a longstanding commitment to student equity spanning roles in research, policy and practice. He has been involved in over $1m of externally funded competitive research grants, convened the 2011 National Summit on the Mental Health of Tertiary Students, and co-edited Student Equity in Australian Higher Education: 25 Years of A Fair Chance For All'.

Penny Jane Burke is Professor and Global Innovation Chair of Equity and Director, Centre of Excellence for Equity in Higher Education, University of Newcastle, Australia. Widely published across the field, Professor Burke is co-editor of the Bloomsbury Gender and Education book series and Global Chair of Social Innovation, University of Bath. She has served as an expert member of the Australian government's Equity in Higher Education Panel and Equity in Research & Innovation Panel.

Nicole Crawford is Senior Research Fellow at the National Centre for Student Equity in Higher Education, Curtin University, Australia. Her research focuses on equity and inclusion in higher education, enabling education, and student and staff mental wellbeing.

Joanne Dargusch is Senior Lecturer at the Centre for Research in Equity and Advancement of Teaching and Education, Central Queensland University, Australia. Her current work includes research in the areas of assessment, equity and participation in higher education and school contexts, and assessment in initial teacher education.

Phillip Dawson is Professor and Associate Director of the Centre for Research in Assessment and Digital Learning, Deakin University, Australia. He researches higher education assessment, with a focus on feedback and cheating.

Janine Delahunty is Honorary Fellow, Arts, Social Sciences & Humanities, University of Wollongong and Adjunct Fellow, National Centre for Student Equity in Higher Education, Curtin University. Her research is equity-focused, motivated by how participation and success can be improved for diverse students, with a recent focus on students from regional and remote areas.

Mollie Dollinger is Senior Lecturer of Learning Futures at Deakin University. Her research interests include student equity, students as partners, and work-integrated learning.

Sherridan Emery is Research Fellow at the University of Tasmania in Australia who is engaged in educational evaluation and research. She is an early career researcher exploring intersections between culture, wellbeing, and education.

Gabrielle Fletcher is a Gundungurra Traditional Custodian from the Blue Mountains of New South Wales, Australia and Professor and Director of the National Indigenous Knowledges Education and Innovation (NIKERI) Institute, Deakin University, Australia. Her current work focuses on Indigenous narrativity, relationality, and Indigenous Knowledge Systems.

Johanna Funk completed her PhD in Open Educational Practices with Indigenous Workforce development. She is applying what she learnt to her work as a research active lecturer in cultural knowledges in the College of Indigenous Futures, Education and Arts at CDU on Larrakia Country, Australia's Northern Territory.

Jessamy Gleeson is a First Nations woman, and an Associate Director (Teaching and Learning) at the National Indigenous Knowledges Education and Innovation (NIKERI) Institute, Deakin University, Australia. Jessamy's current research considers impacts of trauma and use of power in academic and activist spaces.

Lois Harris is Senior Lecturer in the School of Education and the Arts at Central Queensland University, Australia and is affiliated with CQU's Centre for Research in Equity and Advancement of Teaching and Education. Her current research includes work relating to assessment, educational equity, and student engagement in both compulsory and higher education settings.

Andrew Harvey is Professor of Education at Griffith University and Director of the Pathways in Place programme, Logan. He is lead editor of Student Equity in Australian Higher Education.

Neera R. Jain is Postdoctoral Research Fellow at the Centre for Health Education Scholarship at the University of British Columbia Faculty of Medicine, Canada. She researches ableism and disability inclusion, particularly throughout the trajectory of medical training and practice.

Christopher Johnstone is Associate Professor of Comparative and International Development Education at the University of Minnesota and serves as Director of Graduate Studies for the Department of Organizational Leadership, Policy, and Development. His research focuses on inclusive education in global contexts as well as internationalisation of higher education.

Trina Jorre de St Jorre is Honorary Fellow at the Centre for Research in Assessment and Digital Learning, Deakin University, and Student Experience Portfolio Manager at University of New England. Her research and practice is focussed on continual improvement of the student experience, with particular interest in graduate employability and student achievement.

Leanne R. Ketterlin Geller is Professor in the department of Education Policy and Leadership in the Simmons School of Education and Human Development. She holds the Texas Instruments Endowed Chair in Education and is also the director of Research in Mathematics Education unit. Her research focuses on inclusive classroom assessment practices in mathematics education to support teachers' decision-making.

Shannon Krattli is an international student undertaking Honours of Nutrition Science at Deakin University, Australia. Her research interests are biochemical metabolism and chronic diseases. She co-authored a paper with Cancer Council Victoria that is to be published in the Journal of Studies on Alcohol and Drugs.

Sarah Lambert is Honorary Research Fellow at the Centre for Research in Assessment and Digital Learning, Deakin University, Australia. Working remotely on Dja Dja Wurrung country (north of Melbourne), she pursues a body of collaborative international research into social justice in higher education with an interest in critical digital pedagogy.

Jan McArthur is Senior Lecturer in Education and Social Justice in the Department of Educational Research at Lancaster University, UK. Her research focuses on assessment for social justice and rethinking authentic assessment.

Juuso Henrik Nieminen is Assistant Professor at the Academic Unit of Social Contexts and Policies of Education, University of Hong Kong, and Honorary Research Fellow at the Centre for Research in Assessment and Digital Learning, Deakin University, Australia. His current research focuses on student experiences of assessment and feedback, student formation and inclusive assessment.

Geraldine O'Neill is Associate Professor and educational developer in the UCD Teaching & Learning Unit, University College Dublin, Ireland. She has led and researched many national and institutional inclusive assessment and feedback projects. She is recently receiving a national research fellowship for work on assessing work-integrated learning.

Sarah O'Shea is Professor at Curtin University. She is a nationally and internationally recognised educator and researcher who has worked across the Higher, Vocational, and Adult education sectors for nearly 30 years. She has held numerous university leadership positions, which have directly informed changes across the Australian higher education sector, particularly in the field of student access and participation.

Thanh Pham is Senior Lecturer in Education at Monash University in Australia. Her research interests are in higher education, graduate employability, and internationalisation. She is currently researching how international graduates in different contexts negotiate their employability and developing employability teaching programmes at Monash University.

Daniella Prezioso is a student partner, studying Bachelor of Nutrition Science (Dietetics Pathway) at Deakin University, Australia, who also graduated from 2020 Deakin Accelerate Program in Disability, Diversity, and Inclusion with distinctions. She endeavours to advocate and create positive change within tertiary education systems, to facilitate equitable opportunities for diverse students.

Bret Stephenson is Senior Research Fellow within the Data and Analytics (Advanced Analytics) team at La Trobe University, Australia. His work pursues a programme of research and practice in the areas of student equity, success, and retention, and the ethical application of data analytics throughout the university.

Joanna Tai is Senior Research Fellow at the Centre for Research in Assessment and Digital Learning, Deakin University Australia. She researches student experiences of learning and assessment from university to the workplace, including feedback and assessment literacy, evaluative judgement, and peer learning.

Matthew Krehl Edward Thomas is Senior Lecturer in Pedagogy and Curriculum and the Academic Director of Professional Practice at Deakin University, Australia. Matthew lectures in teaching and curriculum and trains postgraduate researchers. In addition, he works internationally leading humanitarian projects through global immersion programmes. He is a former schoolteacher with a background in leadership, strategy, and negotiation. Matthew's research explores time, human rights, initial teacher education and surveillance capitalism.

Martha Thurlow is Senior Research Associate at the National Center on Educational Outcomes, University of Minnesota. Dr. Thurlow's career has emphasised the need to ensure accessible curricula and assessments for students with disabilities, including inclusive education, with the goal of enabling students to leave school ready for post-school success.

Ben Whitburn is Associate Professor of Education at the Southampton Education School, University of Southampton, England. Ben teaches inclusive education, in relation to knowing and relating to difference, interpreting evidence in context, inclusive curriculum and assessment design, as well as applying frameworks of inclusive pedagogy. As a disabled scholar, Ben conducts collaborative conceptually driven research which is orientated toward heightening educational equity, through emphasising diverse experiences and agencies.

INTRODUCTION

Rola Ajjawi

Assessment occupies an important position in higher education. In addition to recognising student achievement, it influences student learning and creates significant work (including bureaucratic and emotion work) for students and staff and therefore, requires scrutiny. Assessment plays a key role in high stakes consequential decisions that can limit or enhance students' choices and directions. Its key non-negotiable feature is determining whether students have met the declared learning outcomes of their courses. Other features, such as particular deadlines or methods of assessment, may be of practical importance, but they are less central to the crucial decision. Not all students may be able to meet the key requirement under the same conditions or with the same time constraints as others, however. Assessment may therefore exclude students who can successfully meet the necessary learning outcomes.

The central unifying value position of this book is that assessment should not disadvantage students because of characteristics or abilities extraneous to the outcomes being judged. While all students must meet the core standards, they may not all be able to do so in the same ways or in the same circumstances. They should therefore not be penalised for reasons beyond their ability to do so. Assessment for inclusion as we discuss in this book seeks to ensure diverse students are not disadvantaged through assessment practices.

We, like our students, have unique careers, personal attributes, and capabilities, that constitute our achievements at work and outside of it. What we produce as part of our work is judged in similar ways to others, but it is also personalised based on our career trajectories, opportunities, roles, and so on. However, in current assessment regimes, students are treated as mostly homogenous, under the erroneous operationalisation of reliability as sameness, fairness or even equivalence. Authors in this book systematically show that assessment based on apparently identical tasks or identical conditions can systematically

DOI: 10.4324/9781003293101-1

discriminate, whether, for example, against students with disabilities, or those from low socio-economic backgrounds. Instead, they suggest that the values of equity and social justice should undergird assessment practices throughout.

This book is a result of an international research symposium hosted by the Centre for Research in Assessment and Digital Learning (CRADLE), Deakin University, Melbourne Australia in October 2021. International experts were invited in the areas of assessment; critical disability studies; social justice, equity, and inclusion; and higher education more generally. The authors in this collection are students, researchers, teachers, equity practitioners, and leaders in higher education. Contributors to the symposium and this volume come from: Australia, New Zealand, UK, USA, South Africa, Hong Kong, Finland, and Ireland.

The chapters here seek to disrupt some taken for granted notions of assessment. They contend that assessment should recognise diversity in student learning, and endeavour to ensure that no student is discriminated against by virtue of features other than their ability to meet appropriate standards.

The book is divided into three sections. These relate to the levels at which considerations about assessment are framed. Assessment is a social practice and therefore involves the complex interplay between individual, relationship, community, and societal factors. To affect sustainable change and mainstream assessment for inclusion such that inclusion becomes an everyday consideration of assessment, we need to pay attention to each level:

1. Macro contexts of assessment for inclusion: societal and cultural perspectives;
2. Meso contexts of assessment for inclusion: institutional and community perspectives; and
3. Micro contexts of assessment for inclusion: educators, students, and interpersonal perspectives.

Section I orients us to a diverse range of theoretical concepts and tools that might help us to conceptualise assessment for inclusion. Each chapter challenges assumptions about assessment seeking to disrupt the taken for granted or norms of practice. The focus then shifts from the procedures of assessment (e.g. fairness) to also include outcomes of assessment that are inclusive and just.

1. Joanna Tai, Rola Ajjawi, Trina Jorre de St Jorre, and David Boud – the editors – outline the ways in which assessment can exclude students, offering a conceptualisation of assessment for inclusion and arguing that assessment needs to be reconsidered to ensure that students are judged on legitimate criteria.
2. Jan McArthur draws parallels between her theorisation of social justice – a broader orientation to assessment – and assessment for inclusion, arguing that both share the same commitment to problematise, challenge and rethink taken-for-granted assessment practices, and assumed guarantees of quality and fairness.

3. Neera Jain takes up assessment for inclusion through the lens of critical disability theory arguing against minor change, seeking instead to disrupt notions of what is regarded as normal. A crip theory lens calls on assessment for inclusion to design from disability and considers how the lived experience of disability can productively inform assessment.
4. Jessamy Gleeson and Gabrielle Fletcher introduce Indigenous perspectives to trouble assessment and Western ways of knowing arguing for the continued expansion and development of the cultural interface such that required structural conditions of assessment can enable collaboration and diverse standpoints for all.
5. Sarah Lambert, Johanna Funk, and Taskeen Adam argue that the decolonisation of education is necessary for assessment for inclusion to flourish. The authors propose three dimensions: *justice-as-content, justice-as-process,* and *justice-as-pedagogy* that would prompt the design of assessment for inclusion.
6. Juuso Nieminen critiques the prevalent approaches to promoting inclusion in assessment, namely those of individual accommodation and universal design from the point of view of their procedural focus. He argues that assessment for inclusion needs to look beyond the institution towards authentically engaging with society through a critical, political stance.
7. Ben Whitburn and Matthew Krehl Edward Thomas adopt an ontological framework to assessment for inclusion, rather than the procedural, and encourage paying attention to the implications of diversity in educational design. They critique the notion that time manifests equally, reminding us of the uneven temporal distributions of assessment.

Section II orients us to specific facets of assessment for inclusion that necessitate reflexivity, accountability, and care. These chapters focus on what communities and/or institutions can and should do to foster more equity in assessment through policy, ethical, legal, and validity frameworks.

8. Penny Jane Burke highlights how unequal power relations and taken-for-granted values and practices shape assessment, which makes inclusivity an ongoing challenge. She introduces the concept of "Communities of Praxis" as a framework to engage with these challenges and work collaboratively towards developing possibilities for inclusive assessment.
9. Matt Brett and Andrew Harvey through an analysis of the higher education assessment policy landscape, identify misalignments and advocate for stronger institutional accountability, monitoring, and regulation as well as education for all staff on the legislative requirements and moral imperatives of inclusion.
10. Phillip Dawson argues that to be more inclusive in assessment we need to re-think cheating, anti-cheating approaches, and inclusion in terms of how they influence validity. If dominant assessment practices entrench exclusion, they are as much of a threat to validity as cheating is.

11. Bret Stephenson and Andrew Harvey examine several examples of Artificial Intelligence-enabled assessment and explore the ways in which each may produce inequitable or exclusionary outcomes for students. They show that technological solutions to equity and inclusion are often of limited value.
12. Christopher Johnstone, Leanne Ketterlin Geller, and Martha Thurlow: track the historical landscape of Universal Design in higher education in the United States. They propose a dialectical approach that considers both accommodations and universal design of assessment as separate approaches that are complementary but also could be influential to one another.
13. Trina Jorre de St Jorre and David Boud critique the ways in which assessment treats students as if they were homogenous and highlight that assessment for inclusion should provide equal opportunities for students to succeed but it also needs to be equally meaningful to them.
14. Thanh Pham critiques how current assessment practices which focus on employability skills disadvantage international students due to taken for granted assumptions about communication and behaviours. The chapter calls for legitimatising marginalised knowledge in assessment for inclusion.

Section III orients us to practice-based approaches to making assessment more inclusive. These chapters foreground research and scholarship that influences changes in curricula and draw recommendations for improving inclusion and equity in assessment as well as warning of potential pitfalls.

15. Sarah O'Shea and Janine Delahunty critique limited notions of success (as simply passing) through empirical research with first in family students. Participant rarely focused on grades alone. They show that assessment for inclusion should reflect varied and relevant notions of success – through de-emphasising grades and engaging students as partners in design.
16. Nicole Crawford, Sherridan Emery, and Allen Baird draw on 51 interviews conducted with regional and remote students to show how the multiple eco-systems of the university serve to exclude students in assessment. Assessment for inclusion should value and draw upon the numerous assets and expertise of students.
17. Roseanna Bourke, through a case study of self-assessment from her own practice, shows that alternative assessment designs are necessary for assessment for inclusion. Whilst these may not be popular initially, they can lead to a greater focus on learning.
18. Geraldine O'Neill showcases her program of research in assessment choice, highlighting the challenge of introducing multiple assessment methods for staff and students, and offering a 7-step process on how to design, implement, and evaluate this approach in practice.
19. Joanne Dargusch, Lois Harris and Margaret Bearman adopt a students-as-partners approach to change assessment practices towards greater inclusion for students with disabilities. To achieve more inclusive assessment,

they argue, universities must overcome a tendency to generalise about student needs and provide many more opportunities to include diverse student voices in assessment design.

20. Shannon Krattli, Daniella Prezioso and Mollie Dollinger also present a students-as-partners project exploring how assessment could be more inclusive and equitable to diverse students. They recommend empathetic relationships between staff and students; ensuring assessment materials are consistent and clear; and that learning resources are located in one place at the beginning of the course unit. This chapter is co-authored and co-researched with students.

Finally, in Chapter 21, Rola Ajjawi, David Boud, Joanna Tai, and Trina Jorre de St Jorre – the editors – close the book with concluding remarks and ways forward, identifying common refrains that persist throughout the chapters, across their various perspectives and foci.

We hope this book prompts all those who are part of the higher education sector to engage in more critical conversations about assessment and reflection on its purposes and designs towards inclusion and social justice, and to make it valid for all students. We also hope that it speaks to academics and professional staff responsible for the design and delivery of assessment to prompt ethical reflexivity, collaboration, and compassion. We hope that any students who are reading this book can draw on ideas presented here to improve their own assessment experiences, to get involved as partners and to advocate for others. And finally, we hope that researchers expand their ways of knowing when researching assessment – taking stronger theoretical understandings and applying critical lenses to assessment. The editors would like to thank all the authors for their generosity and careful scholarship in developing their chapters and engaging in open peer review and revisions.

SECTION I

Macro contexts of assessment for inclusion: Societal and cultural perspectives

1

PROMOTING EQUITY AND SOCIAL JUSTICE THROUGH ASSESSMENT FOR INCLUSION

Joanna Tai, Rola Ajjawi, David Boud, and Trina Jorre de St Jorre

Assessment in higher education is inescapable; it assures competence, drives learning, and shapes learners. It is something that students must undertake if they wish to succeed and graduate. While they might be able to evade other aspects of the higher education experience, they cannot escape assessment (Boud 1995). However, while all students might be required to participate in assessment, their experiences of assessment may differ significantly, particularly if they are from non-traditional backgrounds (Tai et al. 2022b).

In the move from elite to widespread higher education, the diversity of students has increased (Marginson 2016). Different students come with different goals and aspirations: some are primarily career focused, others wish to learn to change the world, yet others want to keep their options open. Thus, equity of opportunity within higher education is important to ensure its purpose is being fulfilled. Efforts to promote equity and social justice have focused mainly on entry and participation and have been successful in increasing the proportion of equity students entering higher education (Department of Education Skills and Employment 2020a). However, evidence suggests that equity students are not as successful as "traditional" students in terms of completion and employment (Department of Education Skills and Employment 2020b; Li and Carroll 2019; Tomaszewski et al. 2019). Given we accept diverse students into universities, it is a moral obligation that universities do not act directly or indirectly to disadvantage those it has enrolled (Burke, Crozier, and Misiaszek 2016). This is not just about avoiding discrimination: universities must value the full range of characteristics of their students, which contributes to the rich fabric of the social and academic world.

Assessments are purposefully developed to judge students' capabilities based on educational criteria and standards represented by explicit learning outcomes. By its very nature, assessment excludes challenges and discomforts. It needs to discriminate between those who have and who have not met the appropriate

DOI: 10.4324/9781003293101-3

outcomes at the requisite level. Underperformance in assessment is frequently positioned as a problem of the student and attributed to student diversity and/or background characteristics. However, the assessment might also be inequitable and therefore excludes students inappropriately. This requires a shift in the way we think about assessment, to become more aware of the disparity in experience and opportunity that students have in present-day assessment, and then, a shift to better assessment systems, designs, and processes, that do have inclusion in mind.

This is important not just for reasons of justice and equity but also to ensure assessment methods maintain their validity: institutions and their staff must be able to evidence that assessment has done its job of determining which students are suitably qualified to progress to the next course, or to graduate, and which students have not sufficiently demonstrated their capabilities. Poor performance is often assumed to be a problem with the student rather than the assessment. This deficit framing meant that the "problem" could be resolved through student-focused measures such as individual accommodations and/or additional support (O'Shea et al. 2016), rather than considering what could be problematic about the assessment. Though accommodations for assessment are required by law in Australia and elsewhere for groups of students with protected characteristics (principally physical disability) (Tai, Ajjawi, and Umarova 2021), this approach ignores the potential for assessment to be made more inclusive from the outset. This may still unintentionally exclude students for reasons other than attainment of the outcomes being judged, which then requires alterations for potentially multiple students. When this does occur, it calls into question the validity and reliability of assessment for all students.

Therefore, we argue here for adopting the concept of assessment for inclusion (Tai, Ajjawi, and Umarova 2021; Tai et al. 2022a, 2022b), which seeks to ensure diverse students are not disadvantaged through assessment practices. We contend that assessment should recognise diversity in student learning and endeavour to ensure that no student is discriminated against by virtue of features other than their ability to meet appropriate standards (Tai et al. 2022a).

Moreover, assessment for inclusion necessarily recognises that:

- Diversity has many dimensions, including overlapping/intersectional qualities.
- Assessment performances and decisions are always made within specific contexts, which has an impact on generalisability.
- There will always be new frontiers on which to make inclusive advances (i.e. into the future, we will not only accept the present reductive categorisations when considering something to be inclusive or not).

Positioning assessment for inclusion within fields of research and practice

Assessment for inclusion builds on a growing consideration of equity and social justice in higher education, and particularly, within assessment. Much of this work has been done since widespread acknowledgement about equality has made its way into national and international legislation and policy (e.g., *Convention on the Rights of Persons with Disabilities (CRPD)* 2006; *Disability Discrimination Act* 1992; *Equality Act* 2010). Early work in higher education assessment focused on the logistics and implementation (Waterfield and West 2006). However, prior to this, the concept of inclusion was already used frequently within the school sector, representing initially the consideration of special needs students, and had also already shifted to considering any student who faced barriers to participation in education (Hockings 2010).

The term "inclusive assessment" has been defined as "the design and use of fair and effective assessment methods and practices that enable all students to demonstrate to their full potential what they know, understand and can do" (Hockings 2010, 34) which speaks mainly to the certification aspect of assessment, rather than considering how assessment interacts and is entangled with curriculum and learning and how assessment may also contribute to future learner trajectories and identities. While a good starting place for assessment design work, a more expansive purpose is required.

McArthur (2016) more recently introduced the concept of *assessment for social justice*, which seeks to achieve the broader purposes of "justice of assessment within higher education, and to the role of assessment in nurturing the forms of learning that will promote greater social justice within society as a whole" (968). She argues that considering social justice in assessment is a necessary move, since previous ideas of justice in assessment focused on fairness of assessment procedure, rather than considering if the outcomes of assessment were just. This constrains possibilities for inclusion, since the greater potential for societal impacts, which are related to just *outcomes* of assessment, are largely ignored. McArthur continues this discussion in Chapter 2, identifying synergies and distinguishing the differences between *assessment for social justice* and assessment for inclusion. Similarly, in this chapter, we take assessment for social justice as a broader philosophy and argue that "assessment for inclusion" might be positioned at the nexus of the procedural and outcome aspects of assessment, through which social justice might be achieved. This is to say, we are focusing on the specific and overall design of assessments, albeit framing assessment design more broadly than just the task, to also consider interactional processes, policy, people, spaces, and materials (Bearman et al. 2017).

Within the broader philosophical notions of social justice, we already see two conceptualisations of assessment for inclusion in the literature. Nieminen (2022) calls for "radical inclusion" of marginalised groups of students. He positions assessment for inclusion as reflexively drawing on individual accommodations and inclusive assessment design. Assessment for inclusion is positioned as "a critical and resistive approach to assessment: it recognises the prevalent socio-cultural, -historical and -political positioning of marginalised students in assessment and, if needed, explicitly disrupts such positioning by promoting student agency" (5–6). Nieminen's conceptualisation comes from a program of research underpinned by social justice and critical theories (see also Chapter 6). Our own positioning for assessment for inclusion is more pedagogical in flavour, seeking to mainstream assessment for inclusion for all students, by making inclusion an everyday lens of assessment design. Student agency should certainly be a key pillar of any assessment design, but we are perhaps more pragmatic. We suggest "'assessment for inclusion' captures the spirit and intention that a diverse range of students and their strengths and capabilities should be accounted for, when designing assessment of and for learning, towards the aim of accounting for and promoting diversity in society" (Tai et al. 2022a, 3). There is room for both conceptualisation in overcoming the entrenched nature of structural inequality and traditional practices in our assessment regimes.

We now turn to contemplate how inclusion should be considered. Within the higher education literature, inclusion can refer to both disability inclusion and social inclusion. Stentiford and Koutsouris (2021) remind us that "inclusion is an elusive concept, intertwined with difficult to resolve tensions" (2245). Inclusion can refer to many equity groups that are usually named in relation to disability access (including physical disabilities, learning disabilities, and mental and physical health conditions) and widening participation initiatives (including students from low socio-economic backgrounds, Indigenous peoples, and mature age students). Thus, we adopt the word inclusion in all its meanings. While there may be an ever-growing list of categorisations to consider when thinking about assessment, students are not just the groups they belong to, and they may consider themselves as belonging to several groups and sub-groups (Willems 2010). Therefore, we should focus not so much on whether students are members of any given equity group (which may be a heuristic that deflects attention from specific structural issues), but on the underlying issues commonly represented within these groups. That is, assessments as currently constructed do not lead to equitable assessment processes, experiences, and outcomes.

Being "fair" in assessment might have once been about ensuring that all students face equal – that is, the same – conditions. However, with an inclusion and equity lens, what is considered "fair" in assessment is the subject of ongoing discussion (O'Neill 2017; Riddell and Weedon 2006). Fairness can also depend significantly on the perceptions of individuals. Even students themselves are concerned that accommodations or adjustments give students with disabilities or other conditions some kind of "unfair" advantage (Grimes et al. 2019a). Addressing one disadvantage might be seen by a different student as inappropriately advantaging another. Though accommodations and adjustments are deliberately made to construct as level a playing field as possible, they can only respond to existing barriers or impediments which can be readily identified. An equity and social justice focus calls on us to do more than identify barriers, instead, we should design assessment proactively to enable all students to demonstrate their learning in suitable ways without the need to reveal personal characteristics which may not be apparent and gain reactive accommodations. "Fairness" may then not be enacted through equal treatment – rather, it can take advantage of and draw strengths from diverse student backgrounds, goals, and capabilities.

How assessment can exclude

Contemporary assessment tends towards solo, unaided performance with few opportunities to work with others (Lipnevich et al. 2021). Further, it removes students from the normal resources (e.g., Internet access, the advice of colleagues) that graduates would typically access in everyday practice. These unchallenged limitations are likely to have more of an impact on the success of those who might gain the most from an inclusive approach to assessment. The lack of authentic scaffolds, those that would be available in the real world, such as use of a calculator or an Internet search engine, or even a keyboard and screen, is itself a threat to validity (see Chapter 10).

The various assumptions we hold dear about assessment practices may prove exclusionary. For example, the predominance of closed book exams that advantages those who can recall information quickly under pressure. These may not be characteristics necessary to demonstrate the specific outcomes being judged (Tai et al. 2022a). Further, strict timed exams advantage students who can concentrate immediately, maintain focus for the duration of assessment, perform the task quickly, and/or perform well under stress. Students who have physical or cognitive conditions that prevent them from doing so are disadvantaged, as are students that have not been schooled in undertaking such tasks. Rigid deadlines disadvantage students with multiple demands on their time including caring and work commitments, or students with fluctuating chronic medical conditions. Ironically, the procedures, designed to afford students accommodations, are likely to add greater burdens on time-poor students, who must usually disclose personal information, submit additional paperwork, and demonstrate proof of a special condition (Grimes et al. 2019b). Restrictions around time and access to resources were traditionally thought to level the playing field by creating equal conditions for all students to perform. However, these types of restrictions ignore intrinsic characteristics of students as well as contextual factors outside of assessment, and so may form actual threats to validity. Our focus on assuring reliability through uniform conditions should not be allowed to undermine the validity of assessment.

These and other problematic notions related to assessment design that may lead to failure and exclusion persist for three key reasons (see Tai et al. 2022a, for a detailed explanation). First, assessment design often draws on tradition rather than recent evidence and scholarship. Research shows that there are entrenched practices and fixed perspectives that perpetuate these types of assessment design (Ashworth, Bloxham, and Pearce 2010). Second, standards such as learning outcomes are beholden to a transparency agenda where learning outcomes can easily become rigid, fragmented, and inflexible. This cements particular assessment practices in place when it is the learning outcomes themselves that need to be challenged. Third, the near-hysteria and reverence within which a specific view of assessment security is held within the academy has flow on effects to poor and discriminatory assessment practices. For example, remote proctored exams have been criticised as ableist due to features like eye tracking that expect to see unobstructed neurotypical eye movements (Logan 2020).

What this brief tour through common assessment practices shows is that educators and assessment designers need to be more critical of their assessment practices and see them in a wider context. In turn, universities need to create critical appraisal mechanisms of common assessment practices, and how they act to exclude and to identify alternatives. In the next section, we identify current practices that seek to promote inclusionary practices of assessment.

Perspectives on assessment for inclusion

Research in assessment about inclusion is growing. The many different lines of enquiry which could be pursued under assessment for inclusion include assessment design, assessment outcomes, and even broader work on the decolonisation of curriculum (incorporating the decolonisation of assessment). However, alongside this, we suggest that the relationship between theory and practice needs to be challenged. Rather than holding the two in a dichotomy, a spectrum of praxis should be considered, to suit particular aims in particular contexts. One thing that is clear in previous work is that there is unlikely to be a single solution that will solve all problems with inclusion, since both assessment and inclusion always occur within a context, with particular people, involving specific interactions (Tai, Ajjawi, and Umarova 2021; Tai et al. 2022a, 2022b).

Enactments of inclusion in assessment have so far taken two main paths: drawing on Universal Design for Learning principles within assessment design (termed Universal Design for Assessment, UDA (Ketterlin Geller, Johnstone, and Thurlow 2015)), or seeking to make accommodations for individual students (Kurth and Mellard 2006). UDA is defined as an integrated system with a broad spectrum of possible supports to provide the best environment in which to assess students' capabilities (Ketterlin Geller 2005). UDA aims to support proactive designs of assessment that allow students choice and flexibility, but these have not been widely adopted (Tai, Ajjawi, and Umarova 2021). Meanwhile, accommodations tend to be personalised and take an assessment design as a given. They typically are marginal and procedural including changes to timing, duration, or rooms for students completing the assessment. These approaches could function together to improve inclusion overall, as Johnstone et al. (Chapter 12) argue. This can occur through increased adoption and formalisation of UDA through institutional policy, strategy, and evaluation, and supporting teachers to provide more latitude for accommodations, both in terms of who can access them, and the types of accommodations themselves.

It is worthwhile to consider what else could be drawn upon to improve the inclusivity of assessment. The review by Tai, Ajjawi, and Umarova (2021) identified that several published inclusive assessment endeavours focused on mitigating language-based differences. Here, students were able to negotiate or choose different formats of assessments, or even the language in which they completed the task. The option to choose the assessment format has been perceived positively by most students (Chapter 18; Tai, Ajjawi, and Umarova 2021). However, careful consideration of how these options align with learning outcomes is necessary, both within a unit/module of study, and across the entire program/course. Consideration could also be extended to what types of capabilities students may require beyond university and this may lead to an emphasis on, for example, authentic assessments (Chapter 6) or assessments that encourage and celebrate distinctiveness (Chapter 13).

A programmatic approach to assessment (Schuwirth and Van der Vleuten 2011) is also likely to be helpful when explicitly used, to establish a shared understanding of when and how learning outcomes will be assessed, across a collection of assessments which have been subject to wider and deeper scrutiny. Programmatic assessment design teams should involve those who know about the exclusionary effects of various assessments, so that the needs of all perspectives are met. When assessment is supported appropriately (i.e. scaffolded tasks with increasing complexity/difficulty), this certainty may also allay anxiety, stress, and pressure which many students report (Craddock and Mathias 2009). This may be especially important in light of the prevalence of mental health conditions amongst students (Grimes et al. 2017).

However, to genuinely disrupt current notions of assessment, we need to look to broader theoretical perspectives which interrogate the taken-for-grantedness of much assessment discussion and the hegemony of ableist, positivist discourses. Philosophical and sociological examinations of the purposes of assessment for inclusion may help to open new ways of thinking, for example critical disability perspectives such as Jain (Chapter 3), and Whitburn and Thomas's ontological perspective (Chapter 7), the decolonial approaches posed by Lambert, Funk, and Adam (Chapter 5), Indigenous ways of knowing by Gleeson and Fletcher (Chapter 4), or Burke's invocation of timescapes (Chapter 8). In order to see how assessment may have inappropriately exclusionary effects, it is useful to have conceptual and metaphorical levers to draw sharp attention to the effects of taken-for-granted assessment practices and ways in which alternatives might be imagined.

Action on inclusion should not be left to individuals and their good will and commitment. Understanding how policy at different levels shapes the way that assessment does or does not serve inclusive purposes also sheds light on what might be refined (Chapter 9). Meanwhile, limited regulatory and ethical frameworks around artificial intelligence in assessment might be leading to exclusion and bias (Chapter 11). We also need to privilege research and development with students to understand their needs and mobilise their agency to effect change. For example, we need to understand students' needs and experiences in more nuanced ways (Chapters 14–16) and as genuine partners in this endeavour of education (Chapters 19 and 20). Finally, we need further exploration and evidence generation in naturalistic settings to consider what works, and what does not work, how and why, to promote inclusion (Chapters 17 and 18).

Conclusion

Inclusion looks different in different contexts, for different people in different cultures. A constant reminder that there is no "one size fits all" approach is necessary to continue work in this space. Shutting down possibilities, or not exploring potential avenues for inclusion too early, is likely to lead to a similar situation to that which we find ourselves in currently: where we have settled on one approach (accommodations and adjustments) which leaves assessment practices unexamined and unchanged, without seeking alternative paths which may serve more students – and indeed universities – better. Instead, what we are calling for with the concept of *assessment for inclusion* is not just a pragmatic fix. By interrogating assessment, we begin to view the whole curriculum differently through considering what may promote inclusion, equity, and participation. What we hope to achieve is to open new challenges to ways in which we think about not just assessment but higher education practices broadly, and the implications that choices in adopting theory, designs, or practices of assessment have for diverse learners, both now and into the future.

References

Ashworth, M., Bloxham, S., and Pearce, L. 2010. "Examining the Tension between Academic Standards and Inclusion for Disabled Students: The Impact on Marking of Individual Academics' Frameworks for Assessment." *Studies in Higher Education* 35 (2): 209–223. https://doi.org/10.1080/03075070903062864.

Bearman, M., Dawson, P., Bennett, S., Hall, M., Molloy, E., Boud, D., and Joughin, G. 2017. "How University Teachers Design Assessments: A Cross-Disciplinary Study." *Higher Education* 74 (1): 49–64. https://doi.org/10.1007/s10734-016-0027-7.

Boud, D. 1995. "Assessment and Learning: Contradictory or Complementary." In *Assessment for Learning in Higher Education*, edited by Peter Knight, 35–48. London: Kogan Page.

Burke, P. J., Crozier, G., and Misiaszek, L. I. 2016. *Changing Pedagogical Spaces in Higher Education*. Abingdon: Routledge. https://doi.org/10.4324/9781315684000.

Convention on the Rights of Persons with Disabilities (CRPD). 2006. United Nations. https://www.un.org/development/desa/disabilities/convention-on-the-rights-of-persons-with-disabilities.html.

Craddock, D., and Mathias, H. 2009. "Assessment Options in Higher Education." *Assessment and Evaluation in Higher Education* 34 (2): 127–140. https://doi.org/10.1080/02602930801956026.

Department of Education Skills and Employment. 2020a. "2019 Section 11 Equity Groups." https://www.dese.gov.au/higher-education-statistics/resources/2019-section-11-equity-groups.

Department of Education Skills and Employment. 2020b. "Completion Rates of Higher Education Students – Cohort Analysis, 2005–2019." https://www.dese.gov.au/higher-education-statistics/resources/completion-rates-higher-education-students-cohort-analysis-2005-2019.

Disability Discrimination Act. 1992. Commonwealth of Australia. https://www.legislation.gov.au/Details/C2018C00125.

Equality Act 2010. 2010. United Kingdom. https://www.legislation.gov.uk/ukpga/2010/15/contents.

Grimes, S., Scevak, J., Southgate, E., and Buchanan, R. 2017. "Non-Disclosing Students with Disabilities or Learning Challenges: Characteristics and Size of a Hidden Population." *Australian Educational Researcher* 44 (4–5): 425–441. https://doi.org/10.1007/s13384-017-0242-y.

Grimes, S., Southgate, E., Scevak, J., and Buchanan, R. 2019a. "University Student Perspectives on Institutional Non-Disclosure of Disability and Learning Challenges: Reasons for Staying Invisible." *International Journal of Inclusive Education* 23 (6): 639–655. https://doi.org/10.1080/13603116.2018.1442507.

Grimes, S., Southgate, E., Scevak, J., and Buchanan, R. 2019b. "Learning Impacts Reported by Students Living with Learning Challenges/Disability." *Studies in Higher Education* 46 (6): 1146–1158. https://doi.org/10.1080/03075079.2019.1661986.

Hockings, C. 2010. "Inclusive Learning and Teaching in Higher Education: A Synthesis of Research." *EvidenceNet, Higher Education Academy*. www.heacademy.ac.uk/evidencenet.

Ketterlin Geller, L. R. 2005. "Knowing What All Students Know: Procedures for Developing Universal Design for Assessment." *Journal of Technology, Learning, and Assessment* 4 (2). https://ejournals.bc.edu/index.php/jtla/article/view/1649.

Ketterlin Geller, L. R., Johnstone, C. J., and Thurlow, M. L. 2015. "Universal Design of Assessment." In *Universal Design in Higher Education: From Principles to Practice* (Rev. ed.), edited by Sheryl Burgstahler, 163–175. Cambridge, MA: Harvard Education Press.

Kurth, N., and Mellard, D. 2006. "Student Perceptions of the Accommodation Process in Postsecondary Education." *Journal of Postsecondary Education and Disability* 19 (1): 71–84. http://ahead.org/publications/jped/vol_19.

Li, I. W., and Carroll, D. R. 2019. "Factors Influencing Dropout and Academic Performance: An Australian Higher Education Equity Perspective." *Journal of Higher Education Policy and Management* 42 (1): 14–30. https://doi.org/10.1080/1360080X.2019.1649993.

Lipnevich, A., Panadero, E., Gjicali, K., and Fraile, J. 2021. "What's on the Syllabus? An Analysis of Assessment Criteria in First Year Courses across US and Spanish Universities." *Educational Assessment, Evaluation and Accountability* 33 (4): 675–699. https://doi.org/10.1007/s11092-021-09357-9.

Logan, C. 2020. "Refusal, Partnership, and Countering Educational Technology's Harms." *Hybrid Pedagogy*. https://hybridpedagogy.org/refusal-partnership-countering-harms/.

Marginson, S. 2016. "The Worldwide Trend to High Participation Higher Education: Dynamics of Social Stratification in Inclusive Systems." *Higher Education* 72 (4): 413–434. https://doi.org/10.1007/s10734-016-0016-x.

McArthur, J. 2016. "Assessment for Social Justice: The Role of Assessment in Achieving Social Justice." *Assessment and Evaluation in Higher Education* 41 (7): 967–981. https://doi.org/10.1080/02602938.2015.1053429.

Nieminen, J. H. 2022. "Assessment for Inclusion: Rethinking Inclusive Assessment in Higher Education." *Teaching in Higher Education*. http://doi.org/10.1080/13562517.2021.2021395.

O'Neill, G. 2017. "It's Not Fair! Students and Staff Views on the Equity of the Procedures and Outcomes of Students' Choice of Assessment Methods." *Irish Educational Studies* 36 (2): 221–236. https://doi.org/10.1080/03323315.2017.1324805.

O'Shea, S., Lysaght, P., Roberts, J., and Harwood, V. 2016. "Shifting the Blame in Higher Education – Social Inclusion and Deficit Discourses." *Higher Education Research and Development* 35 (2): 322–336. https://doi.org/10.1080/07294360.2015.1087388.

Riddell, S., and Weedon, E. 2006. "What Counts as a Reasonable Adjustment? Dyslexic Students and the Concept of Fair Assessment." *International Studies in Sociology of Education* 16 (1): 57–73. https://doi.org/10.1080/19620210600804301.

Schuwirth, L. W. T., and Van der Vleuten, C. P. M. 2011. "Programmatic Assessment: From Assessment of Learning to Assessment for Learning." *Medical Teacher* 33 (6): 478–485. https://doi.org/10.3109/0142159X.2011.565828.

Stentiford, L., and Koutsouris, G. 2021. "What Are Inclusive Pedagogies in Higher Education? A Systematic Scoping Review." *Studies in Higher Education* 46 (11): 2245–2261. https://doi.org/10.1080/03075079.2020.1716322.

Tai, J., Ajjawi, R., Bearman, M, Boud, D., Dawson, P., and Jorre de St Jorre, T. 2022a. "Assessment for Inclusion: Rethinking Contemporary Strategies in Assessment Design." *Higher Education Research and Development*. https://doi.org/10.1080/07294360.2022.2057451.

Tai, J., Ajjawi, R., Bearman, M, Dargusch, J., Dracup, M., Harris, L., and Mahoney, P. 2022b. *Re-Imagining Exams: How Do Assessment Adjustments Impact on Inclusion?* Perth: National Centre for Student Equity in Higher Education. https://www.ncsehe.edu.au/publications/exams-assessment-adjustments-inclusion/.

Tai, J., Ajjawi, R., and Umarova, A. 2021. "How Do Students Experience Inclusive Assessment? A Critical Review of Contemporary Literature." *International Journal of Inclusive Education*. https://doi.org/10.1080/13603116.2021.2011441.

Tomaszewski, W., Perales, F., Xiang, N., and Kubler, M. 2019. Beyond Graduation: Long-Term Socioeconomic Outcomes amongst Equity Students. https://www.ncsehe.edu.au/wp-content/uploads/2019/08/Tomaszewski_UQ_Final_Accessible_9_8.pdf.

Waterfield, J., and West, B. 2006. *Inclusive Assessment in Higher Education: A Resource for Change*. Plymouth: University of Plymouth. https://www.plymouth.ac.uk/uploads/production/document/path/3/3026/Space_toolkit.pdf.

Willems, J. 2010. "The Equity Raw-Score Matrix – A Multi-Dimensional Indicator of Potential Disadvantage in Higher Education." *Higher Education Research and Development* 29 (6): 603–621. https://doi.org/10.1080/07294361003592058.

2

REFLECTIONS ON ASSESSMENT FOR SOCIAL JUSTICE AND ASSESSMENT FOR INCLUSION

Jan McArthur

Introduction

Assessment for social justice (McArthur 2016, 2018) was conceived as a broad concept to encapsulate the multi-faceted ways in which assessment attitudes, values, and practices can nurture greater social justice within and through higher education. Key to the early development of assessment for social justice was a challenge to largely procedural views of justice as fairness in assessment. These deeply ingrained, socially embedded views emphasise fair procedures as the foundation of just assessment: get the right procedures in place and we can be assured that our assessment practices are fair. Such thinking underpins many of the taken-for-granted assessment practices that are still common today: students must do exams in a time-limited way; students should be assessed in the same way; assignments should be submitted at the same time; students should undertake exams at the same time and place; and the same rules should apply to everyone (albeit with largely charitable exceptions for exceptional circumstances).

Assessment for social justice does not disregard the importance of fair procedures, nor the importance of equitable treatment and academic integrity, but it does shift the focus from the procedures to the outcomes of social justice. The other significant change heralded by assessment for social justice, compared with traditional notions of assessment fairness, is that the focus encompasses all those involved in assessment, not simply the students. For assessment to be socially just, it must not cause injustice or misrecognition to those staff who undertake different assessment tasks. Injustice to assessors is becoming an increasing problem in highly regulated higher education systems with increasing workload issues (Shin and Jung 2014). Assessment represents an important moment in the life of a teacher in two ways. Firstly, it can signify a moment of student achievement,

DOI: 10.4324/9781003293101-4

which should be a joyous event when we see some of the outcomes of our students' learning. Secondly, it can signify the necessity for care and commitment, which should be joyful in its own way: this is the moment where we see what our student does not understand, and therefore how we can continue to help them. When staff are denied these moments of joy, it serves as a form of professional misrecognition which is unjust. I'll explain more about this concept of misrecognition later in this chapter.

The third dimension of assessment for social justice is the relationship to society. Higher education serves several socially important roles, including nurturing the professionals who will go on to work in employment/social roles, and the citizens who will help shape the broader character of society. Assessment can, and should, intersect with these social roles, and in assessment for social justice, I argue that this involves enabling positive social change, not just reproducing the status-quo. The overall purpose of assessment needs to be understood by staff, and students, through this social lens. Social justice should shape the nature of assessments and how students are assessed. The goal is for graduates to have knowledge, skills, and dispositions which are orientated towards contributing to a more just society.

Assessment for social justice is therefore both a very broad concept and one which, in my own conceptualisation (McArthur 2018), is framed in a fairly specific way grounded in Frankfurt School critical theory. Assessment for inclusion is a welcome initiative to focus on the development of specific aspects of assessment for social justice. This chapter represents both a reflection on the concept of assessment for social justice, which I first conceived over eight years ago, and a looking forward to the possibilities of understanding and practicing just and inclusive assessment, which are heralded by the exciting initiative of assessment for inclusion. These are different concepts but they serve our joint endeavour of better assessment and a just society.

Reflecting on assessment for social justice

The term assessment for social justice clearly pays homage to the groundbreaking work on assessment for learning, which re-shaped and re-focused our understanding of assessment. We have much to thank the revolutionary higher education scholars who did so much to bring an understanding of assessment's role at the heart of learning to wider attention and acceptance. These include: Sadler (1987, 1989), Hounsell (2003, 2007), Boud and Falchikov (2006, 2007), Knight (1995, 2002, 2006), McDowell and Sambell (1999), and Sambell and McDowell (1998). Perhaps the most important contribution of all the scholarship on assessment for learning is the positive way it re-imagined a student's relationship with the act of assessment:

> Rather than vilifying students for being concerned with 'what was on the exam', this interest became recognized as perfectly reasonable. The notion

> that students should study for a term and then find an exam full of tricks and surprises was unveiled as pedagogically questionable and ethnically unsound.
>
> *(McArthur 2018, 2)*

Assessment for social justice is an idea under which different possible practices, dispositions and beliefs can coalesce and find meaning. My original exploration (McArthur 2016) provides a rationale for the concept. It was a statement of intent: how could we think differently about assessment? I made five proposals. Firstly, that assessment is not only about the procedure of assessing a certain moment, but about the outcome of engagement with knowledge that lasts. Here there are clear resonances with Boud's (2000) sustainable assessment. Secondly, I argued for a new way of dealing with difference which does not make charitable exceptions and the assumption of a single ideal set of student circumstances. This is the thread that is most clear in assessment for inclusion (Tai et al. 2022). Thirdly, I challenged the idea of a perfect mark and the deceptive nature of highly differentiated grading systems. This was a theme picked up again in my book, under the idea of assessment honesty (McArthur 2018). Fourthly, I established that the purposes of assessment cannot involve a disarticulation of the social and economic realms: preparing students for life beyond the institution means more than preparing them for work alone. Finally, I asked, who should make assessment decisions? This question is about more than students as partners in assessment, but rather about deep reflection on in whose interests is assessment undertaken and how do all involved have a voice?

This first exploration of the rationale of assessment for social justice drew on both the capabilities approach of Sen (2010) and Nussbaum (2011) and critical theory, including the older work of Adorno (2005) and the current work of Fraser (2003, 2007). I ended by saying:

> As much as anything else, assessment for social justice is an ongoing commitment to problematising issues of justice and assessment rather than the pursuit of enduring solutions.
>
> *(McArthur 2016, 980)*

I took up my own invitation when I wrote the book *Assessment for Social Justice*, and other colleagues are now taking it up in a different way with *Assessment for Inclusion*. My book was distinct from the original article in many ways, but most obviously I chose to narrow my theoretical lens in order to work through the idea, focusing much more on third generation critical theorist, Axel Honneth. Does this mean you have to buy in to Honneth's critical theory in order to buy in to assessment for social justice? No, but this point does require some explanation.

In *Assessment for Social Justice,* I aimed to bring together what I consider the radical pessimism of the early Frankfurt School with the contemporary work of third generation critical theorist, Axel Honneth. I did so particularly for the multi-faceted understanding of social justice that Honneth offers in his work on mutual recognition (e.g., Honneth 1996, 2004a, 2014). Honneth's social justice can be summarised as the interconnections between mutual recognition of our basic existence as a human being of worth (love recognition); recognition of our universal rights and our abilities to understand and exercise those rights as a member of civil society (respect recognition); and recognition of the contribution we each make to the social whole through our own individual skills, dispositions or knowledge (esteem recognition). None of these can be separated from the other, but it is through the dimension of esteem recognition that the links to assessment can be most easily seen. Esteem recognition focuses on the knowledge, skills or dispositions we each have as individuals and through which we make a contribution to society as a whole: to the wellbeing of others. But what is essential is that each individual is recognised by others for this, and that they recognise it in themselves. In this way, individual and social wellbeing are fundamentally intertwined.

Our students suffer misrecognition if they are not given opportunities to develop, display, and be recognised for the traits and abilities through which they contribute to social wellbeing; be it a more efficient form of energy or a piece of beautiful music. Not every assessment task will do this; it is perfectly OK to sometimes assess the building blocks of knowledge. But at some point in their higher education experience, students must have an opportunity for this form of recognition, and assessment is a key arena for this. This links to my earlier point about staff misrecognition. If assessment processes are so stressful and overwhelming that staff never get to feel recognition for their professional expertise, the same issue of misrecognition, and hence injustice, occurs.

My intention was to demonstrate how one could take an understanding of social justice and follow through those principles into the realm of assessment; as such it was to act as an exemplar rather than the final word. Other scholars could embrace assessment for social justice using a different theoretical lens, equally committed to progressive social justice, such as the capabilities approach of Sen or Nussbaum. One issue we may debate, however, as academics jointly committed to social justice, is the extent to which different theoretical lenses to underpin assessment for social justice offer a truly transformative possibility for higher education.

In the book on assessment for social justice, I offered five values, or ways of thinking about the world, which should inform how we think about and design assessment: trust, honesty, responsibility, forgiveness, and responsiveness. Each highlights a different dimension of assessment for social justice: trusting pedagogical relationships; honesty about all aspects of the assessment process; opportunities for students to take responsibility for their own assessment experiences; forgiveness in the sense of assessment that does not destructively punish the errors and mistakes that are integral to the process of learning; and, a sense of responsiveness to the world around but also what students themselves bring into an assessment experience (McArthur 2018). These are exemplars of ways into thinking differently about assessment: they are not a fixed, nor exclusive, list.

The key to beginning to realise assessment for social justice is being prepared not only to think differently, but to talk openly in different ways: to bring new words into faculty meetings, course team meetings or even corridor chats. Words like joy, compassion, adventure, care and kindness: all of these belong in our assessment discussions, and in using these to demonstrate our thinking differently, we can foster change.

New understandings of assessment for social justice

At the end of the original article on assessment for social justice, I stated that the aim was to promote conversations about assessment. In the time since I wrote both earlier works, my thoughts have developed and moved on. Both the article and the book fit Connell's (2007) just criticism that "most theoretical texts in the social sciences are written in the global North, and most proceed on the assumption that this does not matter" (50). Since writing those texts, I have directly confronted the relevance of critical theory in our age of decolonisation (McArthur 2021a). Here I argue that the Frankfurt School's failure to explore issues of race and colonialism (particularly the first two generations) cannot be excused. But there are other elements of critical theory that can equip non-Indigenous scholars with ideas and understandings that can help them, in Denzin and Lincoln's (2008, 8) words, be "fellow travellers of sorts" with Indigenous scholars who share a fundamental commitment to greater social justice. One of these, which has become more and more central to my work, is the interrelationship between individual and social wellbeing in Frankfurt School critical theory, one of the few dimensions that arguably runs through all generations (Honneth 2004b). This places critical theory as travelling on the same plane as Indigenous philosophies with their various emphasis on self and others. The southern African idea of Ubuntu – I am because you are – is perhaps the most well-known expression of this. Phrased in different ways, however, the same idea runs through Indigenous thought. Dei (2011, 4) explains "Indigenous knowledge speaks of the inseparability and inter-dependence of selves and the collective".

The interconnection between individual and social wellbeing has therefore become central to my more recent work to ensure assessment for social justice is placed within the contemporary decolonial context. For example, it framed my work taking assessment for justice into empirical research on students' beliefs and experiences of assessment (part of a larger project within the Centre for Global Higher Education[1]). An initial study of first year Chemistry and Engineering students explored whether they thought the purposes of assessment were linked to making a social contribution (McArthur 2020a). Unsurprisingly, but still disappointing, I found no evidence of these students seeing such a link; however, they did display a very strong sense of the link between assessment and learning. Within the same project, a larger comparative and longitudinal study (McArthur et al. 2021) also confirmed fears that realisation of the ultimate dimension of assessment for social justice, the sense of inter-relation between individual student achievement and social wellbeing, will take some time and considerable cultural change to achieve. In this study, we looked for instances where student discussions of assessment displayed an orientation to self, discipline/profession or society. Out of 427 interviews, we found only a handful of instances where students articulated a connection between their assessment activities and broader society: and most of these were "fleeting or tangential" (McArthur et al. 2021, 8). Of those orientations to society that we did find, most were in South Africa, rather than our other two locations of England and the USA, possibly reflecting the prominence of social justice issues in South African everyday culture and discourse. On the other hand, that observation makes our outcome even more disappointing: why did not more students in South Africa see this social connection?

Two examples from this study exemplify the challenges facing assessment for social justice. The first is demonstrated by the story of a student with the pseudonym Scarlet, who is going to be the focus of further research as we continue this longitudinal project to its eighth and final year. Scarlet's first year interview transcript is a joy to read. It is resounding with quotes about saving the world and making South Africa a better place. But by second year these thoughts are hard to find. And by third year they have disappeared altogether, and Scarlet's only connection between assessment and the wider world is ensuring she gets employed by a company. Clearly it is not for us to criticise Scarlet's focus and ambitions, however, if we return to the interconnection of individual and social wellbeing, we are potentially seeing a diminution of Scarlet's individual wellbeing as her focus on that of others appears to diminish.

A second lesson comes from a cluster of students at another South African university who provided many of our examples of an orientation to society. They were part of a cohort of students who did an assessment task exploring solutions to water shortages (at the time some parts of South Africa were experiencing extreme water shortages). Water shortages are closely linked to issues of social justice, racial justice and poverty in South Africa. But these issues did not really feature in the "fleeting or tangential" connections these students made between their assessment and society. Nor did other students undertaking the same assessment task make any such connection at all. The same phenomenon was also apparent in the earlier study of first year students, where an assessment on environmentally sustainable transport did not give rise to any statements of connection to society (McArthur 2020a). What we learn here is that having an assessment topic that has a social justice dimension, may not actually ensure that students make connections between their own assessment achievements and social wellbeing. Indeed, in this study of Chemistry and Chemical Engineering the importance of transformative curriculum and assessment design, in conjunction with one another, becomes clear. In the very crowded curriculum typical of these disciplines, and the assessment design which emphasises a fast pace of moving from one assessment to another, there is little time or room for the reflective space to consider one's achievements that is needed for assessment for social justice to get a foothold.

The other direction I am taking assessment for social justice involves greater connection with work on epistemic (in)justice. Here I would very much like to connect the idea of assessment for social justice with Ashwin's (2020) recent work on reclaiming the educational purposes of higher education: namely, transformative engagement with knowledge. This would then extend to consider more issues of epistemic injustice (Fricker 2007) in an assessment context.

Finally, the implication of assessment for social justice led to my rethinking of authentic assessment and arguing for a reframing of what authenticity means in terms of a student as a whole person (McArthur 2020b, 2022). I challenge the conflation of the concepts of "real world" and "world of work" which underpins a great deal of assessment literature. Work is, of course, an important way in which many people achieve esteem recognition, but this is not necessarily the case and there are other avenues. Hence, shackling assessment purely to a narrow idea of work significantly reduces the opportunities for genuine esteem recognition. In addition, focusing on the task, as a source of authenticity, and not the reason for doing a task or who the student doing it is, could lead to profoundly unjust outcomes.

The term authentic assessment is very popular at the moment, and there are some excellent examples of authentic assessment practices (e.g., Sambell and Brown 2021), but this does not deny the necessity to reflect, challenge, and rethink. Assessment for social justice requires a socially situated approach to assessment that is prepared to challenge the taken-for-granted and habitual practices, even those done in good faith. It is just such a challenge that assessment for inclusion offers, with its focus on diversity and assessment design.

The significance of assessment for inclusion

In this final section, I consider the significance of assessment for inclusion to the broader concept of assessment for social justice. In their article on assessment for inclusion, Tai et al. state:

> Drawing on the general philosophy of assessment for social justice, and noting the importance of outcomes, we suggest 'assessment for inclusion' captures the spirit and intention that a diverse range of students and their strengths and capabilities should be accounted for, when designing assessment *of* and *for* learning, towards the aim of accounting for and promoting diversity in society. In introducing this new term, we hope to better negotiate praxis: that is, joining together theory and practice, to act as a lever to achieve change in assessment but also through assessment.
>
> *(2022, 3)*

The approach of these authors is to focus on assessment design to achieve the overall aims of assessment for justice, mindful that design is about more than the immediate task but also includes the broader course context, and institutional context (Dawson et al. 2013). In their focus on inclusion, such authors bring to the fore issues of student diversity and the importance of assessment design that celebrates difference rather than disadvantages students who fall outside some fictional norm. The focus therefore is on students, but not in such a way that is disarticulated from their relationships with assessors and with wider society. Most importantly, assessment for inclusion shares the same commitment to problematise, challenge, and rethink taken-for-granted assessment practices and assumed guarantees of quality and fairness.

The significance of assessment for inclusion, from my perspective, is that it demonstrates the value of an approach that focuses close-up on particular assessment issues, and which nevertheless has very broad consequences for assessment integrity, student wellbeing, and broader social justice. Assessment for social justice was always meant to be an expansive umbrella, and none of us can do everything all the time. This zooming in and out from broad philosophical perspectives to everyday practices is vital, and assessment for inclusion is an important demonstration of how that can be done. At the same time, it demonstrates how different lenses and normative values can be brought into a common endeavour. Those writing on assessment for inclusion do not share a specific lens or indeed world view: they certainly don't adhere to the very specific way in which I used critical theory to work through the possibilities of assessment for social justice. This is a very good thing, and such diversity is essential.

The challenge we face, however, is to ensure diversity and a plurality of voices rethinking assessment, without this drifting away from the core goal of thinking through how assessment should be considered central to achieving the social justice purposes of higher education. What is important here, I believe, is not that we all think the same, but that we understand when we are thinking differently. When we bring our objectives and assumptions to the surface, we move the conversation on productively and avoid the dangers of hidden forms of distortion or domination.

Assessment for inclusion also heralds a holistic approach to both inclusion and diversity, as such it resonates with my own work to rethink inclusion in higher education (McArthur 2021b). But "holistic" is another one of those buzzwords that take off in higher education discourse. The challenge in my own work and for assessment for inclusion is to retain the integrity of what we mean by holistic. It is a complex word and practice that is too easily peppered through academic literature without a real examination of what it means and the implications for practice. To think of our students holistically involves, among other things, temporal, spatial, interpersonal and cultural aspects. We have to not only understand where our students have come from but also allow them to bring those identities into university and to flourish not because they have adapted to the prevailing stereotype, but because they have challenged it.

Thinking differently is at the core of social justice. From a critical theory perspective, it provides a guard against passively accepting injustices that are not easily seen, or even hidden in plain sight. For example, the broadly accepted social norm of past decades where women were expected to remain in the home and perform domestic duties was a case of injustice hidden in plain sight. Many of the issues raised by assessment for inclusion are the same: injustice hidden in plain sight. A clear example of this is the one already mentioned; using exceptional circumstances to adjust patently unjust traditional assessment systems to make them seem inclusive.

From a critical theory perspective such as my own, the greatest harm comes from leaving issues below the surface and unchallenged. The more open our acknowledgement of issues and problems, and the more open our exchange of different – even incompatible – views and solutions, the better. The strength of assessment for inclusion is that, by focusing on a particular dimension of the broader idea of assessment for social justice, academics can converge in one clear place to continue this work of rethinking assessment. My hope is that others will also take up the invitation, focusing on different dimensions that also complement, but vitally extend, the broader plane of assessment for social justice.

Conclusion

Assessment for social justice began as a challenge to ingrained assumptions about assessment and as a commitment to realise the social justice potential of assessment that was inherent in the work of early pioneers of assessment for learning. It was a concept developed on the foundations of many other higher education scholars, and yet it was also something that emerged in relative isolation for me personally. The purpose was always for other scholars, researchers, and teachers to take it up in their own ways. In assessment for inclusion, colleagues have done just this with their focus on diversity and assessment design. The important challenges inherent in the emerging work on assessment for inclusion more than meet the call to action in assessment for social justice.

Note

1 See https://www.researchcghe.org/research/2015-2020/local-higher-education-engagement/project/knowledge-curriculum-and-student-agency/

References

Adorno, T. W. 2005. *Critical Models*. New York: Columbia University Press.

Ashwin, P. 2020. *Transforming University Education: A Manifesto*. London: Bloomsbury Publishing.

Boud, D. 2000. "Sustainable Assessment: Rethinking Assessment for the Learning Society." *Studies in Continuing Education* 22 (2): 151–167. https://doi.org/10.1080/713695728.

Boud, D., and Falchikov, N. 2006. "Aligning Assessment with Long-term Learning." *Assessment and Evaluation in Higher Education* 31 (4): 399–413. https://doi.org/10.1080/02602930600679050.

Boud, D., and Falchikov, N. 2007. "Introduction: Assessment for the Longer Term." In *Rethinking Assessment in Higher Education: Learning for the Longer Term*, edited by David Boud, and Nancy Falchikov, 3–25. London: Routledge.

Connell, R. 2007. *Southern Theory*. Crows Nest: Allen and Unwin.

Dawson, P., Bearman, M., Boud, D., Hall, M., Molloy, E., Bennett, S., and Joughin, G. 2013. "Assessment Might Dictate the Curriculum, but What Dictates Assessment?" *Teaching and Learning Inquiry: The ISSOTL Journal* 1 (1): 107–111. https://doi.org/10.2979/teachlearninqu.1.1.107.

Dei, G. J. S. 2011. "Introduction." In *Indigenous Philosophies and Critical Education: A Reader*, edited by George J. Sefa Dei, 1–13. New York: Peter Lang.

Denzin, N. K., and Lincoln, Y. S. 2008. "Introduction: Critical Methodologies and Indigenous Inquiry." In *Handbook of Critical and Indigenous Methodologies*, edited by Norman K. Denzin, Yvonna S. Lincoln, and Linda Tuhiwai Smith, 1–20. Thousand Oaks: SAGE Publications Inc.

Fraser, N. 2003. "Distorted Beyond All Recognition: A Rejoinder to Axel Honneth." In *Redistribution or Recognition: A Political-Philosophical Exchange*, edited by Nancy Fraser, and Alex Honneth, 198–236. London: Verso.

Fraser, N. 2007. "Re-framing Justice in a Globalised World." In *(Mis)Recognition, Social Inequality and Social Justice*, edited by Terry Lovell, 17–35. London: Routledge.

Fricker, M. 2007. *Epistemic Injustice*. Oxford: Oxford University Press.

Honneth, A. 1996. *Struggle for Recognition*. Cambridge: Polity Press.

Honneth, A. 2004a. "Recognition and Justice: Outline of a Plural Theory of Justice." *Acta Sociologica* 47 (4): 351–364. https://doi.org/10.1177/0001699304048668.

Honneth, A. 2004b. "A Social Pathology of Reason: On the Intellectual Legacy of Critical Theory." In *The Cambridge Companion to Critical Theory*, edited by Fred Rush, 336–360. Cambridge: Cambridge University Press.

Honneth, A. 2014. *The I in We: Studies in the Theory of Recognition*. Cambridge: Polity Press.

Hounsell, D. 2003. "Student Feedback, Learning and Development." In *Higher Education and the Lifecourse*, edited by Maria Slowey, and David Watson, 67–78. Maidenhead: Society for Research into Higher Education and Open University Press.

Hounsell, D. 2007. "Towards More Sustainable Feedback to Students." In *Rethinking Assesment in Higher Education*, edited by David Boud, and Nancy Falchikov, 101–113. London: Routledge.

Knight, P. 1995. "Introduction." In *Assessment for Learning in Higher Education*, edited by Peter Knight, 13–23. London: Kogan Page.

Knight, P. 2002. "Summative Assessment in Higher Education: Practices in Disarray." *Studies in Higher Education* 27(3): 275–386. https://doi.org/10.1080/03075070220000662.

Knight, P. 2006. "The Local Practices of Assessment." *Assessment and Evaluation in Higher Education* 31 (4): 435–452. https://doi.org/10.1080/02602930600679126.

McArthur, J. 2016. "Assessment for Social Justice: The Role of Assessment in Achieving Social Justice." *Assessment and Evaluation in Higher Education* 41 (7): 967–981. https://doi.org/10.1080/02602938.2015.1053429.

McArthur, J. 2018. *Assessment for Social Justice*. London: Bloomsbury Publishing.

McArthur, J. 2020a. "Assessment for Social Justice: Achievement, Uncertainty and Recognition." In *Changing Higher Education for a Changing World*, edited by Claire Callender, William Locke, and Simon Marginson, 144–156. London: Bloomsbury Publishing Plc.

McArthur, J. 2020b. "Student Involvement in Assessment: Involving the Whole Student in Pursuit of Social Justice and the Social Good." *RELIEVE*, 26 (1). http://doi.org/10.7203/relieve.26.1.17089.

McArthur, J. 2021a. "Critical Theory in a Decolonial Age." *Educational Philosophy and Theory*. https://doi.org/10.1080/00131857.2021.1934670.

McArthur, J. 2021b. "The Inclusive University: A Critical Theory Perspective Using a Recognition-Based Approach." *Social Inclusion* 9 (3): 6–15. https://doi.org/10.17645/si.v9i3.4122.

McArthur, J. 2022. "Rethinking Authentic Assessment: Work, Wellbeing and Society." *Higher Education*. https://doi.org/10.1007/s10734-022-00822-y.

McArthur, J., Blackie, M., Pitterson, N., and Rosewell, K. 2021. "Student Perspectives on Assessment: Connections between Self and Society." *Assessment and Evaluation in Higher Education*. https://doi.org/10.1080/02602938.2021.1958748.

McDowell, L., and Sambell, K. 1999. "Fitness for Purpose in the Assessment of Learning: Students as Stakeholders." *Quality in Higher Education* 5 (2): 107–123.

Nussbaum, M. C. 2011. *Creating Capabilities*. Cambridge, MA: Belknap Press of Harvard University Press.

Sadler, D. R. 1987. "Specifying and Promulgating Achievement Standards." *Oxford Review of Education* 13: 191–209. https://doi.org/10.1080/0305498870130207.

Sadler, D. R. 1989. "Formative Assessment and the Design of Instructional Systems." *Instructional Science* 18 (2): 119–144. http://dx.doi.org/10.1007/BF00117714.

Sambell, K., and Brown, S. 2021. "Covid-19 Assessment Collection." Accessed July 19, 2021. https://sally-brown.net/kay-sambell-and-sally-brown-covid-19-assessment-collection/.

Sambell, K., and McDowell, L. 1998. "The Construction of the Hidden Curriculum: Messages and Meanings in the Assessment of Student Learning." *Assessment and Evaluation in Higher Education* 23 (4): 391–402. https://doi.org/10.1080/0260293980230406.

Sen, A. 2010. *The Idea of Justice*. London: Penguin.

Shin, J. C., and Jung, J. 2014. "Academics Job Satisfaction and Job Stress across Countries in the Changing Academic Environments." *Higher Education* 67 (5): 603–620. https://doi.org/10.1007/s10734-013-9668-y.

Tai, J., Ajjawi, R., Bearman, M., Boud, D., Dawson, P., and Jorre de St Jorre, T. 2022. "Assessment for Inclusion: Rethinking Contemporary Strategies in Assessment Design." *Higher Education Research and Development*. https://doi.org/10.1080/07294360.2022.2057451.

3

WHY *CRIP* ASSESSMENT? CRITICAL DISABILITY STUDIES THEORIES TO ADVANCE ASSESSMENT FOR INCLUSION

Neera R. Jain

Introduction

Theory offers a strong starting place to develop assessment for inclusion. Theory unveils current ways of thinking and doing, examines them, and identifies alternatives. Freire's (2000) call to *praxis* for social change puts theory to work in academic spaces. Praxis requires critical reflection on current conditions and prompts transformative action, through theory. Theory that reveals taken for granted power dynamics offers academic changemakers a starting place to interrogate and revise practice to move towards inclusion.

In this chapter, I argue that critical disability theory is a necessary lens to develop assessment for inclusion. Disability is frequently overlooked in liberatory pedagogies and associated assessment theory (Kryger and Zimmerman 2020; Waitoller and Thorius 2016). When disability is included, such as in Universal Design for Learning research, it often fails to disrupt "the desirability of the normate[1] or normative curriculum itself" (Baglieri 2020, 63). That is, traditional efforts towards inclusive practice often seek to include disabled people into existing systems with minor changes. In contrast, critical disability praxis demands fundamental transformation that disrupts notions of normalcy to create more just worlds through and with disability. Any approach to assessment for inclusion must seek to disrupt notions of normal and, therefore, requires engagement with critical disability theory. To this end, I offer three interconnected theoretical movements from critical disability studies that are necessary to problematise and reframe assessment for inclusion: studies in ableism, crip theory, and critical universal design. Pollinated with principles from disability justice (Sins Invalid 2019), these movements advance ways of thinking from disability that help to develop assessment for inclusion and build its case.

DOI: 10.4324/9781003293101-5

A critical disability studies lens begins from "the vantage point of the atypical" (Linton 1998, 5) to identify how assessments exclude and how such exclusion could be addressed. This way of looking assumes that disability can be desirable and creates productive friction to imagine assessment anew (McRuer 2006). Critical disability studies, however, does not stop with a disability-focused analysis; it goes further by engaging intersectionality, identifying linkages across axes of marginalisation, and challenging normalcy (Goodley 2017; McRuer 2006). Critical disability studies theories, then, offer assessment for inclusion a lens that begins from disabled peoples' experiences to broadly question the assumptions built into assessments and their impacts. These tools demand reaching beyond mere inclusion to *cripping* (McRuer 2006), a creative disability-led approach that dismantles exclusionary arrangements. In the following sections, I introduce studies in ableism, crip theory, and critical universal design. From each theoretical move, I identify provocative questions to advance assessment for inclusion. These critical disability lenses aid reconsideration of factors that construct assessment practices at multiple levels: from university structures (e.g., semester timescape, rigid assessment word-lengths by course level), to program-level expectations (e.g., uniform assessment across all program courses), to individual course design. Thus, readers who occupy different university roles (leadership, learning designers, course leaders) will find examples that activate critical disability principles within their spheres of influence. I invite readers to activate provoking questions in their own work and bring them to collegial discussions to spark collective contemplation.

Studies in ableism

Studies in ableism (Campbell 2009, 2017) conceptualise the foundational problem of social exclusion as a system that continually (re)instantiates a false dis/ability binary wherein those coded as "disabled" are excludable and those that approximate hegemonic norms of physical and mental ability are privileged. Campbell (2017) explains that this hierarchical system is formulated and upheld through dividing practices, which she outlines as differentiation, ranking, negation, notification, and prioritisation. Scholars and activists have demonstrated that ableism is intwined with other marginalising systems, such as white supremacy, capitalism, and cis/hetero/patriarchy, which inform and reproduce norms of physical and mental ability (Annamma, Connor, and Ferri 2013; Lewis 2022). Bailey and Mobley (2019), for example, explain that "Notions of disability inform how theories of race were formed, and theories of racial embodiment and inferiority (racism) formed the ways in which we conceptualize disability" (27). To undo this damaging system of ableism, the false binary of abled/disabled must be dismantled. With notions of intersectionality and co-constitution in mind, ableism must be dismantled in concert with other marginalising forces.

The university is deeply rooted in ableist practices. Dolmage (2017) explains that academia, figuratively and literally, maintains "steep steps" to enter, succeed in, and exit that persist despite claims of widening participation, access, and equity. In fact, Mitchell (2016) argues that maintaining ableism appears fundamental to the business of the academy. Assessing ability and certifying mastery are core functions of the university as we know it. Assessment can be understood as a chief dividing practice of academic ableism. Differentiating and ranking students by their ability to meet markers of academic success creates insiders and outsiders. In this sense, the notion of "assessment for inclusion" creates a paradox: because assessment is a central feature of an ableist system it precludes inclusion. If we want to undo damaging systems of exclusion, ought we not dispense with assessment altogether? Are anti-ableist assessments even possible in the academy as it currently operates? Further work to explore these questions is necessary, in concert with a larger examination of academic ableism, to interrogate the purpose and mechanisms of assessment.

Undoing academic ableism requires a reckoning with the academy's purpose in modern life. Studies in ableism demands, first, a critical examination of the purpose of assessments and what is deemed necessary to assess. To begin, we might consider the following questions:

- How do assessment practices create and reinforce division/hierarchies?
- Why must assessment occur and what must be assessed?

Taking this line of thinking further, an examination of how enablement and disablement occur in assessment practices is needed.

- How does assessment (re)construct a "normal" learner in form and function?
- What assumptions underlie this construction of normality and who does it disadvantage?
- Can assessment function in a way that does not marginalise some people? How?

If assessment must continue, careful consideration of how assessments are constructed, results interpreted and used, is necessary. Such an analysis may offer clues towards what must be dismantled to approximate a more just system. Given ableism's grip on society, constant consideration of its operation and active resistance towards it are necessary to begin to undo its power.

Crip theory

Crip theory (McRuer 2006) offers a route to rethink the academy and assessment, to dismantle ableism. Building from queer theory's foundations, crip theory declares that disability is a desirable force to disrupt taken-for-granted notions of ability and normality demanded by neoliberal capitalism. This potential, McRuer (2006) argues, exists when we call out, fail, or refuse to meet ableism's demands for compulsory ablebodiedness and mindedness. Crip theory centres disability, critiques dominant formulations of it, and asserts liberatory ways to be and do through and with disability. The theoretical orientation towards desiring disability, rather than seeking to normalise or erase it, calls on us to imagine radical futures with disability that reconceptualise seemingly fixed presents (Kafer 2013). By insisting on radically inclusive futures, possibilities for disabled peoples' presents expand. Never ending with a static notion of disability, a crip theory analysis leads to interconnected critiques of debilitating ideologies (e.g., capitalism, colonialism, hetero/cis/sexism, and white supremacy) and invokes possible worlds that lay beyond (McRuer 2006). Crip theory suggests that in assessment we must bring forth an understanding of ability and quality that assumes and values all kinds of bodies and minds.

A crip theory lens calls on assessment for inclusion to design from disability, to look for ways assessment can resist compulsory ablebodiedness and mindedness. To do so, we must search for existing knowledge that identifies problems and possible solutions, what Johnson and McRuer (2014) call *cripistemologies*, lived knowledge from the critical, social, sensory, political, and personal position of disability. Put more simply, Lau (2021) defines cripistemologies as "ways of knowing that are shaped by the ways disabled people inhabit a world not made for them" (3). Seeking cripistemologies of assessment might begin with considering ways disabled people fail to fit current assessment expectations and redesign from these "failures" (Mitchell, Snyder, and Ware 2014). Crip time and interdependence offer two illustrative examples.

Crip time concerns temporality. It is built through experiences such as pain, differing forms of cognition, communicating with sign language (and through interpreters, assistive technology, and so on), and navigating medical and social systems (Kafer 2013; Price 2011; Samuels 2017; Zola 1993). Disabled students regularly face university expectations that temporally misalign with their embodied experience, resulting in what one disabled medical student described as constantly "battling time" (Jain 2020, 127). Miller (2020) exposed the power of neoliberal temporality to marginalise students who are LGBTQ+ and disabled, including through assessment mechanisms such as attendance, participation, and rigid deadlines that did not account for experiences of disability and regular experiences of anti-LGBTQ+ bias. Such assessment regimes affected students academically and tended to limit their ability to engage in activist work and other community spaces (Miller 2020). Crip time suggests not just a need for more time, but an exploded concept of time that is flexibly managed, negotiated, and experienced (Kafer 2013; Price 2011; Samuels 2017; Wood 2017).

Engaging the notion of crip time requires that assessment assumes learners will operate on varied temporalities. Therefore, we must seek to explode notions of linear, normative time and tempo in assessment design. Beyond those with a formal disability label, assessments built on crip time would produce allied benefits, for example, for learners who are carers, who must work, and for whom English is not a first language. Lau (2021), for example, describes alternative strategies built through an understanding of crip and pandemic time that move away from time-sensitive assessments towards alternative mechanisms such as asynchronous discussion boards, cumulative and semester-long reflective journal assignments, take-home exams with prompts provided well in advance, scaffolded essays with incremental parts and ongoing feedback, and projects with adjustable deadlines.

Disabled peoples' experiences reveal the falsity of the independent, autonomous individual, demanding that we (re)centre interdependence as a core understanding of humans' relational being, knowing, and doing in the world (Sins Invalid 2019). A cripistempology of interdependence is built through, for example, disabled peoples' understanding of the self as cyborg, reliant on technology and other non-human entities to live, communicate, perceive, and/or move, or reliance on other humans to conduct activities of daily living and achieve access to society (Reeve 2012; Wong 2020). Rather than understanding these experiences as reflective of disabled peoples' fundamental dependence, they highlight an understanding of humans as always already interdependent, with some forms socially coded as exceptional while others are made invisible. Consider our reliance on family and friends, municipal garbage collection, bus drivers, supermarket workers, and smartphones as interdependent relationships we are not often called on to recognise as fundamental forces in our lives. A cripistemology of interdependence calls on us to see relationality as a liberating force and to foreground the ways we are connected and reliant on each other (Mingus 2017).

Rather than prioritising knowing and doing alone, activating interdependence in assessment shifts towards knowing and doing with others, objects, and devices. This forces re-evaluation of what is important to assess as individual knowledge or ability, why, the benefits of imagining differently, and how to assess in interdependent ways. Beyond disability, an orientation to interdependence better reflects the realities of living and working in the world, where knowing and doing is collaborative, with other human and non-human actors. Engaging interdependence also aligns with many Indigenous knowledge systems, reflecting a decolonising praxis (Waiari et al. 2021). Enacting interdependence in assessments could include such mechanisms as cycles of peer and instructor formative feedback while producing assessments, open-book and Internet-enabled assessments that dispense with memorisation, assessment platforms with built-in spellcheck and text to speech, and equitable negotiated role-taking in group projects that enacts collective access.

The use of intermediaries in health science education offers another example of interdependence, wherein a disabled learner directs a nonmedical professional to gather information without providing clinical input (Blacklock 2017; Jauregui et al. 2020). Intermediaries are generally used when a learner cannot perform physical or sensory tasks needed to gather clinical information. Assessment of individual clinical competence while using an intermediary enacts interdependence in information-gathering, while continuing to assess clinical decision-making as an independent act. Intermediaries are not universally accepted in medical education (e.g., McCulley v. University of Kansas School of Medicine 2014), perhaps reflecting a lack of understanding of interdependence in the realm of disability and in clinical practice more generally (Sebok-Syer et al. 2018).

A crip theory lens on assessment for inclusion re-centres disabled students and considers how their lived experience can productively inform assessment. To begin rethinking assessment with crip theory, we might consider the following questions:

- How would program requirements and associated assessments shift if we assumed disabled students can be successful learners and future professionals?
- What ways of being, doing, and knowing are brought into question through disabled bodyminds and how can these reconceptualise traditional assessment?
- How can assessment incorporate manifold ways of being, doing, and knowing?

Then, to shift away from ableist assessments that enforce compulsory ablebodiedness and mindedness, we must seek to understand disabled peoples' work-arounds, resistances, or failures to meet current expectations.

- How and why do learners struggle to perform (or fail) on current assessments?
- How do learners work around, or ask for exceptions to, current assessments? How might this inform redesign?

The cripistemologies we identify become clues towards new ways to do assessment and imaginative principles of re-design. In short, crip theory asks that we embrace embodied messiness and resist standardisation in assessment for inclusion.

Critical universal design

Critical universal design offers a way towards a cripped future, not just in crip moments or revised approaches, but in the fundamental fabric of assessment. Originating in architecture, universal design offers a process towards design for maximum inclusivity without the need to retrofit (Center for Universal Design 1997). The concept has since travelled beyond architecture to spaces such as education. Arguing that universal design's radical roots have been defanged and technicised in neoliberal times, some scholars argue for a critical notion of universal design that re-invigorates its radical political origins (Baglieri 2020; Dolmage 2017; Hamraie 2016, 2017). Rather than reducing the process to checklists or a static endpoint, Dolmage (2017) explains that this conception of universal design must be an active, ongoing process, "a way to move" (116). Critical universal design eschews the post-disability ideology that has creeped into universal design practice, which treats disability oppression as a thing of the past and functions to depoliticise disability (Hamraie 2016). In universities, this ideology allows diminished resourcing of the work needed to facilitate a fundamental shift away from ableism (Dolmage 2017). Instead, critical universal design leans into disability politics while attending to intersectionality, treats disability as a valued resource for transformation, and requires deliberate examination of who is imagined within the notion of "universal" (Hamraie 2017). That is, rather than a diffused understanding of universal, critical universal design demands attention to particularity, working with those most marginalised in current systems to design anew. This approach to universal design attends to root causes of disabled peoples' marginalisation in educational environments, taking ableism seriously, in contrast to more "pragmatic", partial approaches that seek to de-centre disability (e.g., Tobin and Behling 2018).

Taking a critical universal design approach to assessment for inclusion would begin prior to developing assessments. The questions posed throughout this chapter provide productive starting points to think about the intention of assessments and their impacts. Stepping back to think about what must be assessed, why, and the potential consequences in the context of a broad conception of the universe of potential learners, forces deliberate contemplation towards inclusive assessment practices. The conceptualisation of potential learners must undergo critique to ensure a bold outlook that seeks to expand the learner profile and engages intersectionality. For example, this must include a broad group of students with disabilities, including those who are also Black, Indigenous, queer, and people of colour. From this intentionally broad base, design would incorporate, from the earliest stages, ongoing consultation with those learners most marginalised by current arrangements to consider pitfalls and possibilities in assessment and build more flexible and inclusive design. Such an approach would also require deep, ongoing work with academic staff to develop a critical universal design habitus, recognise the historical roots of educational exclusion and their contemporary echoes, and cultivate a critical universal design stance towards education, including in assessment. Ensuring that the process is open-ended would build in flexibility and ongoing review on multiple levels: within a single class to a program, school, and university level.

Scholars from disability studies seek more inclusive assessments through practices that align with critical universal design. Their accounts focus on thoughtful design that anticipates heterogeneous disabled students will inhabit the classroom, infuses flexibility as a matter of course, and promotes co-construction such that universal design is treated as a verb (Dolmage 2017). For example, Polish (2017) engages multimodal discussions of assessments via Google doc, in course blogs, or on paper, where students pose questions, note what they would like to change, and indicate aspects they are excited about, offering a route towards further assessment customisation. Others describe similar efforts that engage with students to actively (re)formulate assessments that amplify their strengths and interests (Castrodale 2018; Kryger and Zimmerman 2020; Lau 2021). These negotiations are conducted with all students and without the need to substantiate or justify the desire for change. Another common strategy is to build flexibility into set assessment modes. Castrodale (2018) designs assessment rubrics flexible enough to account for multiple forms of engagement, allowing students to choose the best mode to express their learning, from a written essay to a podcast, video, student-instructor conference, or poster, among other options. Bones and Evans (2021) build in dropped assignments and late passes that may be used without negotiation, as well as a list of assessments students can choose from. Others outline the myriad ways they assess participation beyond speaking in class (McKinney 2016; Stanback 2015).

While our focus here is assessment, it is important to note that stories of larger-scale implementation of critical universal design that move beyond a single course to a program, school, or university remain thin in the literature. Though assessment is a crucial site requiring change, without larger-scale attention, ableist forces will remain central in academic environments and constrain inclusive innovation. For example, Castrodale (2018) indicates the need to query departmental or program grading expectations such as expected averages, curriculum prerequisites, and reporting timelines that may impact what is possible within a classroom.

A critical universal design praxis for assessment reactivates disability politics in design from the start. We might begin with fundamental questions about our learning environments:

- Who are our learners? Who is missing and why?

We seek to understand ways of being, doing, and knowing that are not currently assumed in educational design to consider how current practices might shift. To do so, we might pursue the following lines of inquiry:

- What do learners (in particular, those with disabilities and others most marginalised by educational and social systems) tell us about how they could best demonstrate their learning?
- How can assessments assume diverse bodies and minds from the outset?
- How will we know our assumptions are sufficiently broad?

Embracing intersectionality and crip theory, the practice is alive and iterative. We must consider:

- How do we keep assessment for inclusion moving, as an unsettled concept?

The aim is to dismantle ableism and other co-constituting forces by centring racialised and queer disabled people and acting continually with the aim to include this group as an ethic of practice.

Conclusion

While developed from a disability perspective, the theoretical tools introduced here broadly question how learners and learning have been conceptualised and are critical to furthering assessment for inclusion. Because assessment is rooted in hierarchies of value among minds, critical evaluation of its purpose, form, and function is needed. Examining notions of ability, how they are coded and produced in assessments and more broadly within educational environments, is necessary to develop assessment for inclusion. This examination must unearth the implications of ability constructions for people with disabilities, broadly understood, in addition to (and intersecting with) other groups marginalised in current assessment regimes. An intersectional analysis is crucial to avoid lacuna in the development of just pedagogies of assessment. Critical disability studies praxis seeks to undo this kind of oversight, demanding that disabled bodyminds are centred as expected ways of being and doing in the classroom and that intersectional thinking is deployed to consider experiences beyond those labelled disabled, who are nonetheless disabled by educational arrangements.

If the goal of assessment is to measure students' learning in a disciplinary area, starting with theoretical tools from critical disability studies will propel introspection on how exclusionary norms have shaped dominant notions of learning, the requirements of a profession (and therefore what ought to be assessed), and measurement itself. Cripping assessment is no simple task, it requires deep and ongoing grappling. These theories build a case for cripping assessment for inclusion and pave a route towards an anti-ableist approach to assessment by design, that undoes assessment as we know it and allows students to thrive.

Acknowledgements

The author would like to acknowledge the support of Professor Missy Morton, Professor Christine Woods, and the Imagining the Anti-ableist University project, as well as postdoctoral fellowship funding from Waipapa Taumata Rau the University of Auckland and the Business School's Equity Committee, which contributed to the completion of this chapter.

Note

1 Garland-Thomson (1997, 8) explains that the normate is "the constructed identity of those who, by way of the bodily configurations and cultural capital they assume can step into the position of authority and wield the power it grants them". Similar to, and bound up in, whiteness, the normate is a figure often made invisible that nonetheless dominates the workings of our social worlds. Adopting Price's (2015) argument for bodymind, I consider the normate to include mental configurations.

References

Annamma, S. A., Connor, D., and Ferri, B. 2013. "Dis/Ability Critical Race Studies (DisCrit): Theorizing at the Intersections of Race and Dis/Ability." *Race Ethnicity and Education* 16 (1): 1–31. https://doi.org/10.1080/13613324.2012.730511.

Baglieri, S. 2020. "Toward Inclusive Education? Focusing a Critical Lens on Universal Design for Learning." *Canadian Journal of Disability Studies* 9 (5): 42–74. http://doi.org/10.15353/cjds.v9i5.690.

Bailey, M., and Mobley, I. A. 2019. "Work in the Intersections: A Black Feminist Disability Framework." *Gender and Society* 33 (1): 19–40. http://doi.org/10.1177/0891243218801523.

Blacklock, B. 2017. "Use of an Intermediary as Reasonable Accommodation for Medical Education." *Disability Compliance for Higher Education* 23 (6): 7. http://doi.org/10.1002/dhe.30380.

Bones, P. D. C., and Evans, A. 2021. "Cripping the COVID Classroom: Centering Students through Transformative Disability-Informed Instruction." *Journal of Transformative Learning* 8 (1): 1–9.

Campbell, F. K. 2009. *Contours of Ableism.* Hampshire: Palgrave MacMillan.

Campbell, F. K. 2017. "Queer Anti-Sociality and Disability Unbecoming: An Ableist Relations Project?" In *New Intimacies, Old Desires: Law, Culture and Queer Politics in Neoliberal Times*, edited by Oishik Sircar, and Dipika Jain, 280–315. New Delhi: Zubaan.

Castrodale, M. A. 2018. "Teaching (with) Dis/Ability and Madness." In *International Perspectives on Teaching with Disability: Overcoming Obstacles and Enriching Lives*, edited by Michael S. Jeffress, 187–204. London: Routledge.

Center for Universal Design. 1997. *The Principles of Universal Design*. Raleigh, NC. NC State University. https://projects.ncsu.edu/www/ncsu/design/sod5/cud/about_ud/udprinciplestext.htm.

Dolmage, J. T. 2017. *Academic Ableism.* Ann Arbor: University of Michigan Press.

Freire, P. 2000. *Pedagogy of the Oppressed.* Translated by Myra Bergman Ramos. New York: Bloomsbury.

Garland-Thomson, R. 1997. *Extraordinary Bodies: Figuring Physical Disability in American Culture and Literature.* New York: Columbia University Press.

Goodley, D. 2017. *Disability Studies: An Interdisciplinary Introduction.* Rev. ed. London: SAGE.

Hamraie, A. 2016. "Universal Design and the Problem of "Post-Disability" Ideology." *Design and Culture* 8 (3): 285–309. https://doi.org/10.1080/17547075.2016.1218714.

Hamraie, A. 2017. *Building Access: Universal Design and the Politics of Disability.* Minneapolis: University of Minnesota Press.

Jain, N. R. 2020. "Negotiating the Capability Imperative: Enacting Disability Inclusion in Medical Education." PhD Thesis, University of Auckland.

Jauregui, J., Strote, J., Addison, C., Robins, L., and Shandro, J. 2020. "A Novel Medical Student Assistant Accommodation Model for a Medical Student with a Disability during a Required Clinical Clerkship." *AEM Education and Training* 4 (3): 275–279. http://doi.org/10.1002/aet2.10426.

Johnson, M. L., and McRuer, R. 2014. "Cripistemologies: Introduction." *Journal of Cultural and Disability Studies* 8 (2): 127–148. http://doi.org/10.3828/jlcds.2014.12.

Kafer, A. 2013. *Feminist, Queer, Crip.* Bloomington: Indiana University Press.

Kryger, K., and Zimmerman, G. X. 2020. "Neurodivergence and Intersectionality in Labor-Based Grading Contracts." *Journal of Writing Assessment* 13 (2): 1–12. https://escholarship.org/uc/item/0934x4rm

Lau, T. C. W. 2021. "Access from Afar: Cultivating Inclusive, Flexible Classrooms after COVID-19." *Nineteenth-Century Gender Studies* 17 (1). http://ncgsjournal.com/issue171/PDFs/lau.pdf

Lewis, T. A. 2022. Working Definition of Ableism – January 2022 Update. *Talila A. Lewis (blog).* January 1, 2022. https://www.talilalewis.com/blog/working-definition-of-ableism-january-2022-update

Linton, S. 1998. *Claiming Disability: Knowledge and Identity.* New York: NYU Press.

McCulley v. The University of Kansas School of Medicine. 2014. Case No. 13-3299 (10th Cir. 2014).

McKinney, C. 2016. "Cripping the Classroom: Disability as a Teaching Method in the Humanities." *Transformations: The Journal of Inclusive Scholarship and Pedagogy* 25 (2): 114–127. http://doi.org/10.5325/trajincschped.25.2.0114.

McRuer, R. 2006. *Crip Theory: Cultural Signs of Queerness and Disability.* New York: NYU Press.

Miller, R. 2020. "Out of (Queer/Disabled) Time: Temporal Experiences of Disability and LGBTQ+ Identities in U.S. Higher Education." *Critical Education* 11 (16): 1–20. http://doi.org/10.14288/ce.v11i16.186495.

Mingus, M. 2017. "Access Intimacy, Interdependence, and Disability Justice." *Leaving Evidence (blog).* April 12, 2017. https://leavingevidence.wordpress.com/2017/04/12/access-intimacy-interdependence-and-disability-justice/

Mitchell, D. T. 2016. "Disability, Diversity, and Diversion." In *Disability, Avoidance, and the Academy*, edited by David Bolt, and Claire Penketh, 9–20. Oxon: Routledge.

Mitchell, D. T., Snyder, S. L., and Ware, L. 2014. ""[Every] Child Left Behind": Curricular Cripistemologies and the Crip/Queer Art of Failure." *Journal of Literary and Cultural Disability Studies* 8 (3): 295–313. http://doi.org/10.3828/jlcds.2014.24.

Polish, J. 2017. "Final Projects and Research Papers: On Anti-Ableist Assignment Design." *Visible Pedagogy (blog).* July 12, 2017. https://vp.commons.gc.cuny.edu/2017/07/12/final-projects-and-research-papers-on-anti-ableist-assignment-design/

Price, M. 2011. *Mad at School.* Ann Arbor: University of Michigan Press.

Price, M. 2015. "The Bodymind Problem and the Possibilities of Pain." *Hypatia* (30) 1: 268–284. http://doi.org/10.1111/hypa.12127.

Reeve, D. 2012. "Cyborgs, Cripples and iCrip: Reflections on the Contribution of Haraway to Disability Studies." In *Disability and Social Theory: New Developments and Directions*, edited by Dan Goodley, Bill Hughes, and Lennard Davis, 91–111. London: Palgrave Macmillan.

Samuels, E. 2017. "Six Ways of Looking at Crip Time." *Disability Studies Quarterly* 37 (3). http://doi.org/10.18061/dsq.v37i3.5824.

Sebok-Syer, S. S., Chahine, S., Watling, C. J., Goldszmidt, M., Cristancho, S., and Lingard, L., 2018. "Considering the Interdependence of Clinical Performance: Implications for Assessment and Entrustment." *Medical Education* 52 (9): 970–980. http://doi.org/10.1111/medu.13588.

Sins Invalid. 2019. *Skin, Tooth, and Bone.* Rev. ed. Berkeley: Sins Invalid.

Stanback, E. B. 2015. "The Borderlands of Articulation." *Pedagogy* 15 (3): 421–440. https://doi.org/10.1215/15314200-2917009.

Tobin, T. J., and Behling, K. 2018. *Reach Everyone, Teach Everyone: Universal Design for Learning in Higher Education.* Morgantown: West Virginia University Press.

Waiari, D. A. K., Lim, W. T., Thomson-Baker, A. P., Freestone, M. K., Thompson, S., Manuela, S., Mayeda, D., Purdy, S. P., and Le Grice, J. 2021. "Stoking the Fires for Māori and Pacific Student Success in Psychology." *Higher Education Research and Development* 40 (1): 117–131. https://doi.org/10.1080/07294360.2020.1852186.

Waitoller, F. R., and Thorius, K. A. K. 2016. "Cross-Pollinating Culturally Sustaining Pedagogy and Universal Design for Learning: Toward an Inclusive Pedagogy that Accounts for Dis/Ability." *Harvard Educational Review* 86 (3): 366–389. http://doi.org/10.17763/1943-5045-86.3.366.

Wong, A. 2020. "I'm disabled and need a ventilator to live. Am I expendable during this pandemic?" *Vox*, April 4, 2020. https://www.vox.com/first-person/2020/4/4/21204261/coronavirus-covid-19-disabled-people-disabilities-triage

Wood, T. 2017. "Cripping Time in the College Composition Classroom." *College Composition and Communication* 69 (2): 260–286.

Zola, I. K. 1993. "Self, Identity and the Naming Question: Reflections on the Language of Disability." *Social Science and Medicine* 36 (2): 167–173. https://doi.org/10.1016/0277-9536(93)90208-L.

4

INDIGENOUS PERSPECTIVES ON INCLUSIVE ASSESSMENT

Knowledge, knowing and the relational

Jessamy Gleeson and Gabrielle Fletcher

What does it mean to "assess" a person's learning? The common answer might appear to be quite clear: a student is "taught" some "thing" and is then required to demonstrate that they "understand" what they have been taught. The way this "demonstration of understanding" takes place may be scaffolded: at first, an explanation of knowledge; followed by an application of knowledge, and so it goes. But these concepts – "assess", "knowledge", "understand", and so on – do not fully capture Indigenous Ways of Valuing, Knowing, Being, and Doing (Arbon 2008; Martin and Mirraboopa 2003). There is not always one right way, and the existence of many viewpoints, standpoints, and knowledges can sit uncomfortably within wider institutions. In short, a "major challenge for academics is decision-making around what students need to know, and how to get them 'to know it' and 'accept it'" (Nakata 2017, 3).

As two First Nations academics, this chapter evolved from us coming together to share and narrate our insights and experience across notions of inclusive education and provide a reflection upon focused Indigenous perspectives in assessment contexts. This chapter moves between two sections: the first, provided by co-author Gleeson, considers First Nations learning spaces in the context of Indigenous and non-Indigenous students; and the second, from co-author Fletcher, examines the tensions of assessment within a more specific First Nations context. Drawing upon these apertures, we consider how inclusive assessment may be enacted, and finally offer some thoughts on how these perspectives and understandings may be further developed.

In providing these perspectives, we acknowledge our standpoints in doing so: not only as First Nations women but also as academics that sit at, and at times, within, the "cultural interface" (Nakata 2002, 2006, 2017). The challenge for us – and our students, both Indigenous and non-Indigenous – exists in drawing on Indigenous perspectives in negotiating this "cultural interface". This interface is

DOI: 10.4324/9781003293101-6

one in which we may be free to assess students on what they have learned, but the ways in which we do so are encompassed by wider structures. These structures prescribe the methods and approaches of assessment to ensure a quantified, consistent result: all students gain a comparable and acceptable level of knowledge and skills upon completion of their degree. We acknowledge it is a space where the particularities of what and how we know is embedded in our subjectivities, our locations and, as we will show, the "self" as a site of knowledge contestation and nuanced tension that requires ongoing negotiation. These encounters can be constraining and sites of collision in many ways, but as we argue, they offer powerful transformative opportunities in revealing inclusive assessment approaches that can dimension understanding and practice as the cultural interface is viewed in relational terms. And as such is an enabler for students and teachers alike.

A note on the cultural interface

The cultural interface may be understood in its most broad terms as an intersection of "higher" knowledge where epistemic systems engage and contest in messy convergence. It is also a liberating space of transformation and understanding. Nakata (2006) suggests it is a "… different conceptualisation of the cross-cultural space, not as a clash of opposites and differences but as a layered and very complex entanglement of concepts, theories and sets of meanings of a knowledge system" (272). Further, the "notion of the Cultural Interface as a place of constant tension and negotiation of different interests and systems of Knowledge means that both must be reflected on and interrogated" (Nakata 2002, 5).

Part I: Indigenous Studies within the university

The Indigenous Studies "space" we refer to within this first section encompasses a series of undergraduate Indigenous Studies units currently taught at Deakin University: both core units and preferred electives. Consequently, our student cohort for these units is quite broad in their academic knowledge and consist of undergraduates commencing degrees in primary and early years education, arts and communication, law, occupational therapy, social work, psychology, and anthropology. Students participating in these units may be Indigenous, non-Indigenous local Australian students, or international students.

In designing and applying the assessment tasks for these units, we were faced with several challenges. Each student brought a different understanding of what constituted "assessment" and "knowledge" to their Indigenous Studies unit. As a result, we needed to both challenge and expand these understandings, whilst simultaneously introducing our own perspectives as First Nations teachers.

Next we outline our perspective on assessment and provide a series of key examples regarding how these have been implemented in our Indigenous Studies undergraduate units. Our account is designed to illustrate the varying approaches to how we view assessment to be "inclusive". We also reflect on the wider systemic issues that First Nations scholars are often faced with when designing units, and how universities can move to address these hurdles to ensure a consistent embedding of First Nations knowledges.

Perspectives on assessment

How do we, as First Nations people, assess knowledge? As oral storytellers, the question of how knowledge is passed down whilst being "accurate" is not a new one. Rather, our knowledges have required these "assessments" for thousands of years, in the form of various checks and balances that each system permits. A "story" could have embedded in it layers of learning, and may be accompanied by dance, music, or told as a part of a wider ceremony depending on its purpose. Sveiby and Skuthorpe (2006) provide the example of the crane and the crow: a story of the Nhunggabarra people, in which the crane and the crow are at odds with one another regarding a piece of fish. The subsequent discussion on layered learning provides an illustrative example of how one story may hold many hidden and deeper meanings, and can therefore contain a community's "archives, law book, educational textbooks, country maps, and Bible – in short the whole framework for generating and maintaining the knowledge base of the people" (Sveiby and Skuthorpe 2006, 42).

In our units, we adopt an approach of layered learning: we return to the same questions, topics, and prompts across units and apply a series of "layers" in doing so. In some ways, this echoes mainstream approaches of scaffolded learning: students are equipped with increasingly complex forms of knowledge, and in turn apply these (Cho and Cho 2016). But the process of learning is also reiterative: in discussing the impacts of colonisation, we turn in one unit to the loss of knowledge, in another the effect on Country, and in a third to the ongoing consequences on community health. Accordingly, the assessment tasks for each of these units and topics must build on, and re-use, the knowledge gathered in previous units.

Breaking down student assumptions

In many ways, our approaches to assessment are negations of what is already in place. The structured nature of colonised knowledge spaces impacts on what students *expect* they will learn: its shape, form, and the allotted number of hours required to master it. But when we shift our understandings of what learning and assessment look like, the associated student expectations are also challenged.

A brief example exists in how we employ yarning. As a practice, yarning is a way to share stories: it is a way we communicate that has been employed for thousands of years. It is broadly understood as a discussion that is free-flowing, uninhibited, and takes place in an environment in which all participants feel safe and respected (Sharmil et al. 2021). In a classroom space, yarning exists beyond PowerPoint slides, tutorial question prompts, and allocated discussion times. Instead, the conversation is free-flowing and reciprocal: it is a "process and an exchange, encompassing elements of respect, protocol, and engagement" (Lowitja Institute 2012). To move beyond these familiar structures into a yarning space can leave students feeling untethered. For some, it can be a welcome difference, whilst others find it uniquely disorienting and challenging. The challenge for us is to simultaneously challenge and reassure students: the learning environment may look and feel different, but that does not mean that they are not learning. For some students, yarning may provide a welcome change: previous research has noted that Aboriginal students have found yarning useful for sharing their perspective (Donovan 2015).

The need to contest and expand student expectations manifests as we set about the business of assessment. Instead of being required to seek out peer reviewed sources, students are asked to prioritise the voices of First Nations people. Rather than an objective analysis of a policy or case study, assessment tasks also include discussions on self-reflection and growth. In this sense, the "inclusive" practices of assessment are an expansion: both of student expectations, and of the wider systems of knowledge that surround these expectations.

The final assumption we seek to contest is that of "learning" itself – and by extension, what each student is permitted to know. Within a Western, positivist framework, students are encouraged – and can feel entitled – to seek out *all* knowledge. This is typically reinforced by systems of assessment: students are rewarded for outstanding use of academic sources. However, this sits at odds with how we, as First Nations people, learn. The right to learn and know isn't assumed: just because we exist as part of a community (whether a community of learners, or elsewhere) this does not immediately equate to an *entitlement* to knowledge.

To return to the earlier point of layered learning: each layer of learning is only unlocked when the learner proves they have fully understood the lessons of the previous one. In much the same way, our students may "unlock" different aspects of a topic or concept as they progress through the units. But simultaneously, they may also only ever cycle through the first layer. The remaining layers of knowledge spiral out beneath them: like ducks on a pond, they may move across the surface of the learning, but rarely dive beneath. The deeper water of the pond contains knowledges that are both sacred and restricted: these knowledges cannot be captured by what we teach, and to attempt to do so would be highly disrespectful and inappropriate.

Instead, we teach students that in undertaking Indigenous Studies, they need to understand that they cannot expect to have access to everything. Simply because a student is enrolled in one of our units, this does not equate to immediate and unrestricted access to our knowledges. The lesson of "learning what you cannot learn" is key: it demonstrates to students our autonomy within a wider Western space and emphasises the need to develop a level of cultural responsiveness in undertaking an Indigenous Studies unit. As First Nations staff, the "learning what you cannot learn" lesson also returns us to Nakata's cultural interface – we are still obliged to formally assess what students *do* know. How we do so, and the challenges faced, are outlined below.

Each of the methods of assessment used exist within wider structures: a three-year degree, a 1000-word essay, a 12-week semester, and so on. Consequently, when we set about the process of assessment, we rapidly arrive at the cultural interface between Western structures, and Indigenous Knowledges. For example, despite thousands of years of oral storytelling practices, if we built a series of units that relied *only* on oral presentations, we would quickly find ourselves needing to justify to wider university committees how these assessment tasks captured a student's knowledge.

These structures can still serve a purpose for us, as First Nations staff – they allow us to change the curricula, and change the teaching approaches, so that we can "do our job more effectively" (Nakata 2013, 298). But these improved outcomes are still dependent on the context and specificities of each university and its associated "Whitefella" practices – those methods and structures of assessment we need to work alongside, to assist the professionalisation and systemisation of our practices of teaching (Nakata 2013). In short, the outcomes for teaching Indigenous Knowledges are only as good as the system they are embedded within.

How we achieve these outcomes, and reconcile these Whitefella practices with our own, is a continuing, collaborative process. Working *alongside* and within these practices requires knowledge of the right conditions: who to talk to for support, when to submit changes to assessment, and what words to use within the submission. In much the same way that Country has indicators of seasonal changes, the university curriculum environment has its own. The right person needs to be in the right place at the right time of year. The right words need to be used on the right form. The right committee members need to be told in advance of the submission, and their support needs to be gained. And finally, the right meeting needs to be attended, and approval granted. These practices – forms, committees, and emails – are not a unique challenge for First Nations staff. But how we reconcile and "style" our knowledges to sit within these Whitefella practices is one of the difficulties faced by First Nations teaching staff. Broader understandings within the university of culturally appropriate assessment are a useful start for respecting (and ideally, embedding) Indigenous Knowledges; but beyond this there are hurdles built within the system itself that cannot be overcome without significant collaboration and partnership from others within the same environment.

Part II: Reflections on a moment of relational subversion in assessment

To this point, we have reflected broadly upon two key considerations – structural tensions and student knowledge – in our own problematising and re-negotiations of the cultural interface in terms of assessing students undertaking Indigenous Studies. We now turn our attention to consider more nuanced experiences of such negotiation as First Nations academics assessing First Nations students. We provide a particular experiential example from Macquarie University that makes visible more explicit tensions and entanglements in simultaneously *approaching* and then *being at* the cultural interface. We aim to provide insight and deeper understanding of a moment of what might be described as *relational subversion* occurring during an assessment task that demonstrates the power of transformation afforded by this closer examination of a "narrative case".

The "representation" of Indigenous culture and presence within units that explicitly explore Indigenous content is ideated by the delivery of such content by Indigenous teachers/academics who might be better positioned culturally and philosophically to do so. As First Nations teachers we bring both the science and art of our Indigenous pedagogy that "... could be described as being founded on the broad principals *(sic)* of identity and relatedness, couched in the contextual values of reciprocity, inclusiveness, nurturance and respect" (Biermann and Townsend-Cross 2008, 150). We further bring understanding that "Indigenous knowledge and Indigenous ways of knowing are about the connected concepts of what one *knows* and *how* one comes to know it" (Santoro et al. 2011, 68), and that this knowledge is relational and exists within a web of interconnection. In this section, we explore what happens when the "seasonal conditions of Country" we have referred to in Part I seem aligned, and yet the relational forged something new.

Backdrop and assessment task

The student cohort discussed within this section were in their second semester of the third year of their course and were undertaking a compulsory unit called *"Indigenous Voices and Perspectives"* within a Bachelor of Early Childhood Education degree at Macquarie University. Previously offered, the unit was redesigned on the basis that these students had not been exposed to content or literature pertaining to an Australian Indigenous education context at all: either the historic backdrop or contemporary experience. Previously the unit had drawn the notion of "Indigenous voices" from "established" Indigenous leaders, artists, and writers as both contemporary and historic figures, and students were required to base "case studies" upon the particular Indigenous "identities" they had chosen. These case studies then formed the basis of a written submission that had a 100% assessment loading, itself problematic.

In discussion with colleagues, we agreed to reformulate and re-form the assessments task, reframed broadly as a "Learner's Biography": however, the case studies would seek to mediate the contextual focal point on Indigenous Education in theory/criticality, policy and lived experience as sub-elements of the total assessment loading of the task. Further, the "voices" were reconceptualised to be constitutive of the students themselves as First Nations Peoples within the educational context that they were participating in and would enter into as Early Childhood teachers. The "lived experience" component was reflective, with the teaching and learning rationale drawing out the biographical experience of the cohort as "learners" to dimension their understanding as "teachers" – providing empathic and explicit terrain for "deeper understanding" of that nexus and exchange. The first part of this element required students to post reflections under four distinct headings in an online discussion board:

> What facilitated your learning; What impeded your learning; How might your learning be enhanced; and commenting upon other people's experience.

This was on an ongoing task, with one reflective post required weekly. The second part of the assessment, examined here, was an extension of the Learner's Biography, where students narrated (Indigenous voice) their learning experience in a Knowledge Circle. Students were asked to draw from their weekly postings, including concepts and literature they had been exposed to. They were encouraged to bring "artefacts" that may have represented anchorage or a sense of meaning to their learning experience, to extend their own personal subjectivity and identity, and their particularity of experience. Each student was allocated ten minutes for their "presentations" in the Knowledge Circle, and the assessment was marked against a rubric that we had developed with key assessment criteria being:

> Connection to Literature and concepts; Engagement; Presentation style and Fielding questions.

Performance of task

The assessment session began with students volunteering the ordering of their presentation in the Knowledge Circle. As each student spoke, it became increasingly evident that their reflective narratives and the concept of the Learning Biography itself as a broader task relating to education were transformed with each recitation. There was a clear and ongoing departure from the "marking criteria", despite students' previous briefing and circulation of all relevant information. What emerged were narratives clearly embedded within personal historiographies, with references to family, community, the Stolen Generations, and policies and practices of ongoing colonisation. Resultantly, the space was transformed to a shared arena of personal and cultural decompressing, and for some students, an exposure of ongoing wounding.

Students focused on their experiences of "being" Indigenous, and their *story*, rather than the experience of being "learners" as a compartmentalised aspect of self, and clearly this demarcation of particularities of "multiple identities" was indivisible with the experience of being *constructed* as "Indigenous" and the cultural aspects and responsibilities of their identities and Indigenous stand-points.

From an assessment perspective, the rubric became a problematic tool. We found attempting to fit each historiography into neatly delineated criteria either did not apply, or there was such significant departure that it was impossible to mark according to the measures and criteria before us, that *we* had devised.

Students began to extend their storied responses and texture these around the growing thematic articulations and collapsing of the strictures of the assessment. And whilst we struggled with the measures of assessment we had carefully developed, we found ourselves equally immersed within a cultural collective focused on the importance of the student's vocality and sensitivity to the emotional difficulty of this "closed but public" discourse.

Over the 90 minutes allocated for the "assessment", it was evident that the culture of the space, and its spatiality had changed significantly. And yet it was an organic, unconscious shift that seemed guided by needs beyond the students and staff present and the learning context. This "Knowledge Circle" became a cultural location and an explicitly Indigenous social context. A locality where all that the students brought and represented not just themselves but their home communities, their histories, and experiences, against an historic backdrop of exclusion and marginalisation – an imagined and real community sharing both similar and different experiences in an inclusive remaking of place that enabled each member to speak, spill, and explore beyond the frame of the dominant knowledge system and its measures.

Reconciling a relational subversion to a Western assessment framework – re-learning ourselves

Most students commented upon the experience afterwards, taking the opportunity to offer insight and translation of what had become a cultural experience beyond the frame of simply an "assessment task". Overwhelming, they reported that it had been "good" and "of value". Interestingly, several older students commented that "it was long overdue", and reported that, as a cohort the sense of "community" had not been given a space to be explored beyond the informality of studying together. One student remarked "It was the good cry we needed to have".

Alongside the student experience, teaching staff also required space to debrief and discuss. In early teacher discussions, some of us felt an initial sense of failure. We felt that every care had been taken with course design and the rigours of Whitefella standards, including explicit attention to ensuring that the unit outline had been peer reviewed; that our Indigenous pedagogical approach supported and valued students in their learning experience; that the assessment was aligned, and that the assessment extended voice and a level of critical rigour for students to contextualise their own commitment to social justice and their pro-active engagement with it. We also noted the constrained evaluative Western index for measuring the assessment – a measure that we had devised.

We began to unpack further to understand more fully what had happened within the setting. What was clear to us was the experience of Indigenous education and the policies and practices that have excluded Indigenous people were clearly settled realities for these students, and the experiences were ineluctable from social and historic context, *and* impossible to separate from the set of relations within which the self comes to know. We also recognised that the assessment *setting* was a transformative enactment of an Indigenous contemporary space, one that was allowing us to draw attention "to the presence of both systems of thought and their history of entanglement and (con)fused practice, all of which conditions the way that contemporary Indigenous lifeworlds can now be understood and brought forward for analysis and innovative engagement and production" and "how Indigenous peoples can defend their interests and construct their arguments in spaces where a wide and complex world of converging knowledge and practice shapes the way lives can be Enacted" (Nakata et al. 2012, 126).

This began to dimension notions of the collective and the manifestation of the relational that this "biographical voicing" moment had revealed and engaged. It was also naturalised and naturalising according to Indigenous values, meaning, and purpose, and although it was recognised that this had been an assessment "task", the difficulty of its emotional terrain and the socio-historic commonality of these students and their multiple subjectivities was much "harder" and more challenging than the "conventional" frame of the marking criteria could possibly capture and measure.

What had emerged was deep learning, value, respect, connectedness, significance, background knowledge, and a diversity of Indigenous perspectives. The richness of this community experience, the storying of each student and the agency and self-determination of their expression and experience could not be rendered in the available assessment tool, and we realised that the assessment tool itself was *not inclusive* and did not form part of an inclusive assessment approach as we had imagined. For us, the tensions *within* this cultural interface were equally about taking account of *approaching* the cultural interface, and the entanglement of what is brought to bear within it from First Nations students – a *whole relational self*. We had asked students in effect to decontextualise that whole relational self to think only of their learner self: a reductive endeavour because that "discreet" component is shaped by myriad complex entanglements that require contextualisation. In this sense, a relational subversion occurred: one that produced new knowledge production and transferability. We were able to reconfigure the assessment tool, taking forward key learnings and grounding for ourselves as First Nations teachers and reflexive practitioners.

Making Indigenous sense – re-negotiations

This experience was a deeply transformative revelation – a complex encounter of entangled knowledge systems for both students and ourselves as First Nations teachers. The visibility of empowered Indigenous identity and its possibility was an enabler to assessment for inclusion, anchored in Indigenous perspective and reciprocity by foregrounding more explicitly the relational and the "whole person" as part of a broader contextual process of learning, teaching, and assessment.

As mentioned earlier, the structural tensions and understandings of knowledge that partialise, depart from or do not acknowledge Indigenous perspectives and standpoints impact upon our encounters of and within the cultural interface.

And we have made clear our own reflexivity to own inclusion in assessing levels of knowledge. But this space is not ours alone. As Nakata (2002, 285) has suggested:

> the intersection of the Western and Indigenous domains ... the place where we live and learn, the place that conditions our lives, the place that shapes our futures and, more to the point, the place where we are active agents in our own lives – where we make our decisions – our lifeworld.

We need to acknowledge "Indigenous individuals, communities and the broader collective differences in responses and in the priority given to different systems of Knowledge and thinking illustrate the dynamism and diversity within the collective" (Nakata 2002, 6). This dynamism and diversity reflect the original heterogeneity of traditional contexts, the varied impacts of colonisation, the diversity of contexts in which First Nations people now live, and the creativity we bring to bridging systems of Knowledge and responding to changing circumstances (Nakata 2002). Further, learning spaces that actively include our Knowledges must accept both these intersections, and the tensions and conditions of "what is possible, but do not directly produce certainty of outcomes" (Nakata 2002, 6). This uncertainty of outcomes in a more "closed" cultural place becomes the locus of tensions of self: in this instance the "us" of First Nations academics who not only must translate, transform, and bridge discursive and ideological theoretic schisms but also navigate complex terrains of practice in relational re-negotiations with our own subjectivities in providing the inclusive, and shaping the delivery of places for agential change and social justice.

Conclusion

This chapter has its focality in the interface of the transformation of assessment to be more inclusive by creating sets of structural conditions that can enable collaboration and diverse standpoints for all. For us as First Nations teachers, we seek to teach and evaluate in ways that are socially explicit and culturally viable, within a theoretic and practical model that can assess according to the value of social justice, Indigenous meaning, relationality, and the whole person.

Reflexively and collaboratively with our non-Indigenous colleagues, we seek to share our insights and perspectives to co-create, explore, and expand the cultural interface as a space of transformation and the new. These examples narrativise the ongoing tensions of the cultural interface – and find ways to liberate an embedded otherness and the ongoing discursive terrain that needs to be continually theorised in finding equitable domains and the enabling points that can resist and register according to the implicit need for emergence and liberation.

Inclusive assessment is an ongoing process, and one that must be *lived* to be enacted upon and alongside. Our accounts in this chapter emphasise the need to "read" the Country of curriculum design, and understand how and where to intercede and change, and then reflexively, change again. We therefore argue for the continued expansion and development of the cultural interface to facilitate opportunities for curriculum refinement and change. Finally, we also note that our experiences outlined here are just two amongst many. We therefore emphasise the need for, and invite, additional accounts and contributions of our peers' insights to provide further standpoints and perspectives in the ongoing and reflexive process of inclusive assessment design.

References

Arbon, V. 2008. *Arlathirnda Ngurkarnda Ityirnda: Being-Knowing-Doing, De-Colonising Indigenous Tertiary Education*. Teneriffe, QLD: Post Press.

Biermann, S., and Townsend-Cross, M. 2008. "Indigenous Pedagogy as a Force for Change." *The Australian Journal of Indigenous Education* 37 (S1): 146–154. http://doi.org/10.1375/S132601110000048X.

Cho, M.-H., and Cho, Y. 2016. "Online Instructors" Use of Scaffolding Strategies to Promote Interactions: A Scale Development Study." *The International Review of Research in Open and Distributed Learning* 17 (6). https://doi.org/10.19173/irrodl.v17i6.2816.

Donovan, M. 2015. "Aboriginal Student Stories, the Missing Voice to Guide us towards Change." *Australian Educational Researcher* 42: 613–625. https://doi.org/10.1007/s13384-015-0182-3.

Lowitja Institute. 2012. "Using Yarning as Research Methodology." Accessed March 12, 2022. https://www.lowitja.org.au/using-yarning-research-methodology.

Martin, K., and Mirraboopa, B. 2003. "Ways of Knowing, Being and Doing: A Theoretical Framework and Methods for Indigenous and Indigenist Research." *Journal of Australian Studies* 27 (76): 203–214. http://doi.org/10.1080/14443050309387838.

Nakata, M. 2002. "Indigenous Knowledge and the Cultural Interface: Underlying Issues at the Intersection of Knowledge and Information Systems." *IFLA Journal* 28 (5–6): 281–291. http://doi.org/10.1177/034003520202800513.

Nakata, M. 2006. "Australian Indigenous Studies: A Question of Discipline." *The Australian Journal of Anthropology* 17 (3). 265–275. https://doi.org/10.1111/j.1835-9310.2006.tb00063.x.

Nakata, M. 2013. "The Rights and Blights of Politics in Indigenous Higher Education." *Anthropological Forum* 23 (3): 289–303. https://doi.org/10.1080/00664677.2013.803457.

Nakata, M. 2017. *Disciplining the Savages — Savaging the Disciplines*. Canberra: Aboriginal Studies Press.

Nakata, M., Nakata, V., Keech, S., and Bolt, R. 2012. "Decolonial Goals and Pedagogies for Indigenous Studies." *Decolonization: Indigeneity, Education and Society* 1 (1): 120–140.

Santoro, N., Reid, J., Crawford, L., and Simpson, L. 2011. "Teaching Indigenous Children: Listening to and Learning from Indigenous Teachers." *Australian Journal of Teacher Education* 36 (10). http://dx.doi.org/10.14221/ajte.2011v36n10.2.

Sharmil, H., Kelly, J., Bowden, M., Galletly, C., Cairney, I., Wilson, C., and Hahn, L. et al. 2021. "Participatory Action Research-Dadirri-Ganma, Using Yarning: Methodology Co-design with Aboriginal Community Members." *International Journal of Equity Health* 20: 160–171. https://doi.org/10.1186/s12939-021-01493-4.

Sveiby, K. E., and Skuthorpe, T. 2006. *Treading Lightly: The Hidden Wisdom of the World's Oldest People*. Sydney: Allen and Unwin.

5

WHAT CAN DECOLONISATION OF CURRICULUM TELL US ABOUT INCLUSIVE ASSESSMENT?

Sarah Lambert, Johanna Funk, and Taskeen Adam

Introduction

One of the strengths of an inclusive approach to education is that all students benefit. It's not just about accommodating and improving education for students with diverse abilities and cultures. Inclusive education that models respectful and productive relationships between students with diverse knowledges, cultures, histories, and identities also shows majority or privileged students the strength and contribution made by those with different backgrounds.

From the perspective of cultural inclusion, inclusive assessment as a sub-set of inclusive education can aim to: provide justice for Indigenous, international and students from minority cultural backgrounds; and cultivate in all students an understanding of the need for cultural justice and the value of multiple cultural knowledge perspectives. Inclusive assessment – particularly if part of inclusive curriculum – has the potential to provide all students with greater graduate outcomes than assessment that draws on only the Western cannon of ideas. The idea is that all students should graduate with multiple kinds of knowledges and leave better prepared to negotiate different worldviews and cultures in their lives.

However, this vision for inclusive education and assessment has not yet generally arrived in practice. Higher Education tends to consider students who are not from White, English-speaking middle-class backgrounds as "disadvantaged", less-capable students who lack the "cultural capital" needed to navigate university terminology and processes. Students from Indigenous, international, or migrant backgrounds are often considered doubly disadvantaged for having to study in a second or third language and for being first in family to go to university.

Our work has been informed by theories of social justice and decolonisation which reject these narratives of underperformance for the way they focus on

DOI: 10.4324/9781003293101-7

what a student lacks (i.e., "proper English") instead of the abilities they possess such as learning across multiple languages and cultures. Focussing on lacks rather than embracing diverse motivations for study is known as "deficit discourse" and higher education is awash with it (Burke 2012). The problem of deficit discourse is that it leads us to want to mould students who are not like us to be more like us. Our assessments and their grading criteria often ask students to think like us, speak like us, and write like us (where the majority of "us" in Western higher education are White) and be rewarded with good marks and university success.

Students may accept, reject, or mediate the need to assimilate to succeed. One mediating response is the contemporary cultural practice of "code-switching". Code-switching is where students who speak different forms of English such as Black English, Aboriginal English, or African-American Vernacular English to learn to switch between their local English and the English required of them at university and beyond. A similar process happens when it comes to writing in English too. Code-switching requires additional cognitive effort but it does allow students to move between two similar but distinctly separate worlds. Rather than making an effort to incorporate the actual English of millions of students into Western education, the sub-text of our learning outcomes is clear: we do not recognise your own English as legitimate, work harder to change.

In addition to our previous understanding of higher education as exclusionary to working-class students' values and language (O'Shea 2016), current approaches to students from different cultural-linguistic backgrounds can be seen as contemporary expressions of racist White assimilationist or White Supremacist policies (Baker-Bell 2020). But what are the alternatives? Social justice and decolonial approaches are an alternative that we explore for assessment for inclusion in the next section before introducing a *Culturally Inclusive Assessment* model developed from a range of empirical and theoretical sources.

Rethinking assessment as social justice and decolonisation

Social justice principles such as *recognitive* and *representational justice* (Fraser et al. 2004) provide a more inclusive narrative and way to relate to students from different socio-cultural backgrounds. Social justice principles focus on recognition of and respect for students' strengths, abilities and cultural knowledges – sometimes known as a "strengths-based approach".

In the context of higher education curriculum and assessment, we can think of *recognitive justice* as ensuring students can see diversity in the examples and resources provided to scaffold learning and assessment. *Representative justice* is about ensuring students can hear and take on board diverse points of view and knowledges in what is taught and assessed. It assumes there is knowledge and expertise in every language and culture, and seeks to avoid dominance of one over the other.

Social justice principles can help us identify and address under-representation and misrepresentation in curriculum, knowledge, and assessment. Under-representation is where socio-cultural diversity of authors and ideas are absent.

Misrecognition is where students' cultural differences are represented in negative or stereotyped ways (Burke 2012).

Decolonial theories address "sexual, political, epistemic, economic, spiritual, linguistic and racial forms of domination and exploitation" that developed during periods of White colonial rule (Grosfoguel 2007, 217), and that are still present even after political emancipation. For example, the need to decolonise higher education in South African is as pressing now as ever, even though technically the rule of "apartheid" has been over for many years. In Australia, the "White Australia" policy is long gone but its insistence on White ways of knowing casts a long shadow on higher education even today.

With regard to assessment practices, decoloniality sheds light on the geopolitics of knowledge production which questions who determines what counts as knowledge. Knowledges produced in North America and Europe tend to be considered more authoritative than knowledge produced elsewhere. This is known as "epistemic hegemony" and it relates to how endogenous and indigenous knowledges have also been pushed to "the barbarian margins of society" (Ndlovu-Gatsheni 2015, 490).

Diversifying what is taught and assessed can help overcome negative stereotypes surrounding those who are seen to be different – particularly Indigenous people, people of different religious beliefs and people of colour as well as women in certain roles and fields. It is important to reduce the marginalisation and trauma that students feel when confronted with education and assessment systems which reinforce racist assumptions and stereotypes about them and their abilities that they already suffer from society on a day-to-day basis. It is important to note that not all differences are visible. So, in the current context of higher education, recognitive and *representational justice* is also a priority to increase the inclusion and success of LGBTQI+ students and those with invisible disabilities whose are present in increasing numbers, even if they are not seen.

Indigenous theorising of education for and with Indigenous students is a particular example of decolonisation of education that also underpins our work. Framing education as a "both ways" model (Yunupingu 1989) between Indigenous Australians and communities – also now known as "two-ways" (Harris 1990) – provides opportunities to enrich and reframe Indigenous and Western learning as complementary. In doing so, the strengths of Indigenous communities and traditional knowledge is acknowledged, helping to overcome deficit discourses and misrepresentation which are still unfortunately all too common.

Framing learning as "two-way" also helps to overcome the tensions between global and local knowledges. The interviewees in Lambert and Fadel's (2022) study debated the extent that particular topics needed more culturally diverse authors, citations, readings, knowledges and ideas. Some wanted a more "Australian" textbook, others preferred a more "global" approach to learning materials and assessment examples. The developing consensus was that both the local and global knowledge and examples were critical to include, and that colonial narratives should not be normalised or centred.

While two-way learning has developed to describe learning between Indigenous/local and settler/Western cultures, its ethos can be used to frame the bridging between a range of cultural knowledges and contexts. For example, in Australian Universities with Asian campuses, "two-way" learning can also be valuable to foster an approach of learning from each other. This might be expressed by allowing students to negotiate assessment topics, examples, and literature relevance across both Western and Asian knowledge bases.

Building on theorisations by Jansen (2017), Adam similarly found that a decolonised education can involve "situating one's culture at the centre of one's learning while still drawing on other cultures" (Adam 2020a, 200), or it can be taken even further to be "learning about all cultures and their entanglements" (ibid). Indigenous and Eastern scholars (Bates et al. 2009; Bhabha 2004) have critiqued the idea of "traditional knowledge" as some kind of pure cultural knowledge that was static pre-colonisation. In the contemporary world, ideas are fluid - our knowledges are tangled together with ideas moving from Indigenous to coloniser, settler to Indigenous, east to west and west to east. From the knowledge-as-entanglement point of view, no one region is the sole authority. The role of the educator can be as a facilitator of two-ways learning that encourages students to recognise the benefit of their own cultural knowledges, and new/additional cultural knowledges.

To avoid further marginalising minority students, we need to ensure that we don't reject their cultural beliefs and "other ways of being, thinking and rationalising" (Gonzalez 2011, 7) in the way we grade and provide feedback on their assessments. Nor do we need to accept them wholly without question. We can model critical questioning across multiple knowledges by drawing on different cultural ideas and frameworks to discuss and analyse topics in our lectures and tutorial discussions and even to challenge the ideas put forth by the educator. At the post-graduate level, we can support our students to critique and weave new knowledge from multiple cultural knowledge sources. We can also respect multi-cultural students' differing identities and motivations for study (see Stephens et al. 2012 relating to communal vs individualistic reasons for studying) by designing assignments that give students the choice to do a project or research in partnership with their community. We can also frame any discussions about the rationale and benefits of our assignments in terms of both helping individuals get jobs as well as a broader benefit to the community.

We can also learn to take an inclusive stance on the kinds of global Englishes our students speak, and to mark their written and spoken assessments on the strength of their ideas and ability to demonstrate the learning outcomes, and not for how much their syntax and descriptive language habits match our own (for more on Habits of White Language (HOWL), see Inoue 2021). Institutions on a path to decolonisation could also reflect on whether it is time to allow students to submit assignments in Indigenous and other official languages, such as the case in some institutions in South Africa (Mbamalu 2018).

In Adam's (2020a) study students interviewed reflected on how colonial and apartheid legacies have affected their educational experiences and identities through inferior quality of education, forced languages, forgotten histories and incongruent values, cultural norms and practices. Assessment is implicated in each of these issues. Students' views ranged from: wanting to learn and be assessed on local knowledges in their local languages (Africanisation); wanting to centre their learning and assessments on their own cultural history topics relevant to their daily lives (Afro-centrism); and wanting to learn and be assessed about all cultures and their entanglements equally (knowledge as entanglement).

Adams also spoke to MOOC designers who strove towards decolonising their MOOCs. She found they used three approaches: *justice-as-content* where reading lists and curriculum was diverse and decolonised; *justice-as-process* where co-creation and a plurality of thought were actively sought in the design of the course and its content; and *justice-as-pedagogy* where students were encouraged to critically engage, reflect on, and even challenge what was being taught (Adam 2020b; Freire 1970). These approaches could be taken up by educators in many colonial/settler contexts and they underpin the *Culturally Inclusive Assessment* model that we describe with further examples in the next section of this chapter.

Culturally Inclusive Assessment model

We have identified some common themes across our decolonisation work which we have drawn together to develop a *Culturally Inclusive Assessment* model. The themes map across the *justice-as-content*, *justice-as-process* and *justice-as-pedagogy* dimensions (after Adam 2020b), as shown in Table 5.1. The following section discusses each dimension in detail and provides additional examples.

Within the *justice-as-content* dimension, a content diversification approach is taken replacing Western case studies and other examples used in assessment with

TABLE 5.1 Culturally Inclusive Assessment model

Dimension	*Common themes*
***Justice-as-content*:** decolonising what is taught.	Removing deficit discourse from learning materials, texts, discussions, assessment examples and feedback. Correcting under-representation or misrepresentation.
***Justice-as-process*:** decolonising education processes; a plurality of thought is designed into the course curriculum, assessment, and content	Two-way learning; relational processes; personal positioning and critical consciousness; student co-creation of decolonised learning materials as an assessment task.
***Justice-as-pedagogy*:** students are encouraged to critically engage, reflect on, and even challenge what is being taught; assessments or whole subjects designed to teach the ideas of socio-cultural justice, decolonisation or cultural competence.	Modelling and scaffolding critical thinking and reading skills to challenge deficit discourses and power difference; learning how to apply socio-cultural justice, diversification and decolonisation to new experiences and contexts.

Source: Adapted from Adam (2020b).

local/Indigenous/Asian examples or those more relevant to students' context. While this is not without some risk of romanticisation of the local (Jansen 2017), it allows for marginalised knowledges to be reclaimed.

The *justice-as-content* dimension also emphasises overcoming deficit language which describes students as "underperforming" or lacking knowledge or "cultural capital". Deficit language is commonplace and hard to shift. Therefore, it may need to be the focus of some assessment items, which students "read" as more important than lectures and other activities. Related literature suggests that assessment is needed to support unlearning of deficit, sexist, racist and colonial ideas and assumptions of the world and the field the student expects to graduate into (Cross 2003; Mize and Glover 2021). One approach is the use of a structured "deconstruction assessment" (Sjoberg and McDermott 2016) where early phase medical students undertake a class discussion and a reflective assignment addressing a set of anonymous questions about race and health issues. The assignment reveals and addresses a wide range of misrepresentations and assumptions which would be undesirable to carry through to their medical practice.

From this we can see that there is some overlap in the model's dimensions – it would be hard to design an assessment for unlearning racist and colonial ideas (*justice-as-pedagogy*) without first addressing deficit language (*justice-as-content*).

While staff in Lambert and Fadel's (2022) study said they used lectures or tutorials to counter outdated and sometimes racist language and ideas found in textbooks, they also acknowledged that students relied on these same textbooks to write their assignments, which then might carry outdated ideas and deficit discourses with them. To ensure alignment between what is said and read it would be necessary to regularly review and revise lists of essential readings recommended to students to complete their assignments (*justice-as-content*). An idea to take this further would be to offer students a simple process such as a web-form to allow them to provide feedback comments on outdated or racist sections of texts and to suggest new texts from a wider cultural perspective (*justice-as-process*).

Another approach used to respond to colonialist knowledge in an outdated textbook was to invite students to update it (*justice-as-process*). An assessment option was provided to students to convert their final written assessment into a chapter of a new textbook to be used by future cohorts (Funk 2021). To support the assessment, students were guided in critical reading and two-way learning (*justice-as-pedagogy*), which was also modelled in the discussions (*justice-as-process*). Decolonised thinking in the form of the students' book chapters were provided by students with both Indigenous and settler identities and the class modelled how to position themselves with humility (*justice-as-pedagogy*).

Since the assessment required students to produce an analysis of a cultural event in recent social media, the examples incorporated into the new textbook were both culturally diverse and very current.

The *justice-as-process* dimension recognises that diversifying and decolonising learning and assessment can and must address more than the surface level symptoms of colonialist thinking and euro-centric content in assessment and curriculum content. The *justice-as-process* dimension is personal and relational no matter whether we are teaching on-site or online. There is an emphasis on centring learners and their cultural backgrounds within formative and summative assessment conversations and processes.

For example, the MOOC designers in Adam's study (2020b) and the RPL process in Funk's work (2021)-centred relationships (between learners/participants and communities) within assessment processes so that feedback is located within the context of trusting and open practices. Participants are taught how to "position themselves" by acknowledging their cultural position and power differentials associated with their roles. Trust emerges from the development of a "critical consciousness" which is when one takes a conscious stance to investigate one's positionality in the world in relation to others (Freire 1970).

The *justice-as-process* dimension is underpinned or framed by two-way and complementary learning between multiple knowledge traditions. For example, two-way learning can also be extended to recognition of prior learning (RPL) between institutions and Indigenous communities – a form of decolonising access to higher education credit.

Funk (2021) was involved in the development of RPL processes with students' deep on-Country knowledge and community leadership roles in mind. For those outside Australia, being and doing "on Country" refers to identities, relationships and practices between Indigenous people and their land that shifts from region to region. RPL processes allowed for a contextualised demonstration of cultural knowledge and skills such as exhibiting awareness of power relationships and cultural norms in a work setting. These skills enabled students to gain credit for these learning outcomes in a mandatory first-year cultural studies unit. Prior qualifications and work experience related to the cultural studies subject also counted towards the RPL credit gained. A student working "on-Country" as an Aboriginal liaison officer could, for example, submit work produced in their employ that showcases their ability to work in a "two-ways" capacity. One recent student and Indigenous business owner developed three of his own papers on Indigenous Business perspectives into an open book chapter (Wickey 2022). These RPL records lodged in an institutional electronic portfolio begin to populate institutional digital platforms with examples of more diverse cultural knowledges. Such records can be read by other staff and students and in turn provide more examples of assessment equivalence for students from a range of cultural backgrounds. Wickey (2022) also used these papers as a basis for cultural orientations to new non-Indigenous work colleagues and the "open" nature of the book chapter allows wider uptake within a wide range of educational and other institutions due to the lack of login or payment needed to access the book.

Wickey's commitment to his own development alongside his commitment to sharing Indigenous knowledge with non-Indigenous business leaders and workers remind us that Indigenous and international students are experts at cultural "code-switching", as they've been living in two-worlds for all their lives. It is more the case that Universities have been slow to accept their responsibilities for two-way learning or "bridging the socio-cultural divide" (Devlin 2013; O'Shea 2016) as a process of reconciliation between Western and non-Western, working- and middle-class modes of thinking, being and doing at university.

Funk's work also highlights that the students being taught may already be leaders in their own communities, so it is not helpful for teachers to position themselves as always more knowledgeable than students in student-teacher relationships. Educators can choose to position themselves as leaders in one area, while deferring to students' leadership, authority and experience in other areas. The complementary nature of both educators and students' cultural knowledges can be made explicit in class and assessment conversations, and the benefit to the class of the collective knowledges shared. This development of "critical consciousness" as a process of "mutual humanisation" can take place for both teacher and learner, coloniser and settler – as a two-way approach in situ and online (Freire 1970).

The *justice-as-pedagogy* dimension extends the decolonised processes to the explicit teaching of socio-cultural justice as the focus for whole assessments or even whole subjects. The focus is on teaching critical thinking and reading skills attuned to cultural power differentials. This is often an interdisciplinary exercise. For example, an assessment on Indigenous nursing within a series of assessments or a whole unit on culturally inclusive nursing, teaching, business, or environmental management. If students can learn to critically read cultural situations and exchanges, they will be empowered to apply it to a host of new situations in their life, future studies, and careers.

Opportunities in assessment for inclusion

Although we have provided some ideas and examples in the previous section, different disciplines, year levels and cultural contexts usually require something more tailored. Using the *Culturally Inclusive Assessment* model as a framework, the following questions can be used to diversity and/or decolonise assessment in one's own context through consideration of content, process and pedagogy.

Justice-as-content opportunities

- Whose cultural knowledges are the focus of assessment questions; is there a rationale for this? How might students use more diversified cultural examples or options?
- Whose knowledges and perspectives might be missing from reading lists and assessment resources? To what extent are, for example, women and authors of colour cited in practical examples and theoretical frameworks?
- How frequently do staff review essential and assessment related readings and examples to weed out deficit language which might unintentionally reinforce exclusionary stereotypes? Libraries and/or teaching and Learning

centres can contribute to this. Institutional Inclusive language guides may be available. If key readings are historic and use what is now considered inappropriate terminology, students need to know what has changed and why the older reference is still useful.

- Whose knowledge is legitimate to be included and cited by students? How will new authors be evaluated?
- How will deficit discourse be re-storied in the ways that feedback information is provided without speaking on behalf of those from other cultural backgrounds?
- What digital resources of cultural leadership can students be referred to, to allow leaders of colour to be represented in assessments?

Justice-as-process opportunities

- How can assessments be designed to allow students to situate their culture at the centre of their learning, while still recognising and appreciating other cultures?
- How can students be supported to develop skills in learning about all cultures and their entanglements within particular fields of study?
- How might students' high impact contributions to their socio-cultural communities be recognised as knowledge in pre-admission assessments of students' capability?
- How can a recognition of prior learning approach be brought into classroom conversations to recognise students' existing cultural knowledge within examples and assessment conversations?
- How can two-way learning and dialogue be modelled rather than one-way "inputs" provided in feedback and assessment?

Justice-as-pedagogy opportunities

- How can assessments that foster "unlearning" be introduced in early classes to explicitly address students' pre-existing assumptions and language of difference as a foundational learning activity for the discipline?
- In upper-level classes, how can students be engaged in a process of addressing under- and misrepresentation in curriculum materials by assessing the research and development of newly decolonised learning materials?
- How and when can students be scaffolded to critically read new material, including materials they source as part of assessment work, to avoid reinforcing stereotypes or misrepresentations in the field?
- What kinds of assessment items could be modified to include reflections or measures of students' development of critical consciousness from the beginning of their learning journey?
- When should questions be added to course feedback surveys asking students how assessments could be more inclusive?

While the main aim of this chapter has been to focus on diversifying and decolonising learning and assessment, it is important to recognise that the broader educational landscape is founded on many colonial logics. Drawing on Bali (2018, 305), "[a]ttempts at inclusion can only be authentic and meaningful when we make the content, process, and outcome of education more egalitarian, open, and inclusive". Decolonising assessment practices will be more effective when coupled with decolonising content and curriculum, embracing critical pedagogy and praxis, diversifying staff, encouraging interdisciplinary and cross-disciplinary collaboration, questioning academic processes that determine what counts as knowledge and what doesn't, and questioning power structures within our institutions. These diverse angles on knowledge practices can offer justice as content, process, and pedagogy at the level of the institution, which can better lead to more just and inclusive assessment.

References

Adam, T. 2020a. *Addressing Injustices through MOOCs: A Study among Peri-Urban, Marginalised, South African Youth*. University of Cambridge. https://doi.org/10.17863/CAM.56608.

Adam, T. 2020b. "Between Social Justice and Decolonisation: Exploring South African MOOC Designers' Conceptualisations and Approaches to Addressing Injustices." *Journal of Interactive Media in Education* 2020 (1). https://doi.org/10.5334/jime.557.

Baker-Bell, A. 2020. *Linguistic Justice: Black Language, Literacy, Identity, and Pedagogy*. New York: Taylor and Francis. https://doi.org/10.4324/9781315147383.

Bali, M. 2018. "The 'Unbearable' Exclusion of the Digital." In *Disrupting the Digital Humanities*, edited by Dorothy Kim and Jesse Stommel, 295–319. Brooklyn: Punctumbooks. https://doi.org/10.21983/P3.0230.1.00.

Bates, P., Chiba, M., Kube, S., and Nakashima, D., eds. 2009. *Learning and Knowing in Indigenous Societies Today*. Paris: UNESCO Publishing.

Bhabha, H. K. 2004. *The Location of Culture*. 2nd ed. London: Routledge. https://doi.org/10.4324/9780203820551.

Burke, P. J. 2012. *The Right to Higher Education: Beyond Widening Participation*. London and New York: Routledge.

Cross, B. E. 2003. "Learning or Unlearning Racism: Transferring Teacher Education Curriculum to Classroom Practices." *Theory into Practice* 42 (3): 203–209. https://doi.org/10.1207/s15430421tip4203_6.

Devlin, M. 2013. "Bridging Socio-Cultural Incongruity: Conceptualising the Success of Students from Low Socio-Economic Status Backgrounds in Australian Higher Education." *Studies in Higher Education* 38 (6): 939–949. https://doi.org/10.1080/03075079.2011.613991.

Fraser, N., Dahl, H. M., Stoltz, P., and Willig, R. 2004. "Recognition, Redistribution and Representation in Capitalist Global Society: An Interview with Nancy Fraser." *Acta Sociologica* 46 (4): 374–382. https://doi.org/10.1177%2F0001699304048671.

Freire, P. 1970. *Pedagogy of the Oppressed*. London and New York: Penguin Books.

Funk, J. 2021. "Caring in Practice, Caring for Knowledge." *Journal of Interactive Media in Education* 2021 (1): 1–14. https://doi.org/10.5334/jime.648.

Gonzalez, J. M. 2011. "Suspending the Desire for Recognition: Coloniality of Being, the Dialectics of Death, and Chicana/o Literature." UC Berkeley.

Grosfoguel, R. 2007. "The Epistemic Decolonial Turn." *Cultural Studies* 21 (2–3): 211–223. https://doi.org/10.1080/09502380601162514.

Harris, S. 1990. *Two-Way Aboriginal Schooling: Education and Cultural Survival/Stephen Harris*. Canberra: Aboriginal Studies Press.

Inoue, A. B. 2021. "Habits of White Language (HOWL)." Asao B. Inoue's Infrequent Words. 2021. https://asaobinoue.blogspot.com/2021/07/blogbook-habits-of-white-language-howl.html.

Jansen, J. 2017. *As by Fire: The End of the South African University*. Cape Town: Tafelberg.

Lambert, S. R., and Fadel, H. 2022. "Open Textbooks and Social Justice: A National Scoping Study." Perth, Australia. https://www.ncsehe.edu.au/publications/open-textbooks-social-justice/.

Mbamalu, S. 2018. "Nompumelelo Kapa, First Academic to Write Thesis in IsiXhosa in 102 Years." This Is Africa. 2018. https://thisisafrica.me/african-identities/nompumelelo-kapa-isixhosa-phd-thesis-fort-hare/.

Mize, M., and Glover, C. 2021. "Supporting Black, Indigenous, and Students of Color in Learning Environments Transformed by COVID-19." *International Journal of Multicultural Education* 23 (1): 162–173. https://doi.org/10.18251/ijme.v23i1.2559.

Ndlovu-Gatsheni, S. J. 2015. "Decoloniality as the Future of Africa." *History Compass* 13 (10): 485–496. https://doi.org/10.1111/hic3.12264.

O'Shea, S. 2016. "Avoiding the Manufacture of 'Sameness': First-in-Family Students, Cultural Capital and the Higher Education Environment." *Higher Education* 72 (1): 59–78. https://doi.org/10.1007/s10734-015-9938-y.

Sjoberg, D., and McDermott, D. 2016. "The Deconstruction Exercise: An Assessment Tool for Enhancing Critical Thinking in Cultural Safety Education." *International Journal of Critical Indigenous Studies* 9 (1): 28–48. https://doi.org/10.5204/ijcis.v9i1.143.

Stephens, N. M. et al. 2012. "Unseen Disadvantage: How American Universities' Focus on Independence Undermines the Academic Performance of First-Generation College Students." *Journal of Personality and Social Psychology* 102 (6): 1178–1197. http://doi.org/10.1037/a0027143.

Wickey, T. 2022. "Indigenous Business Perspectives." In *Cultural Knowledges and Work Integrated Learning*, edited by Johanna Funk. Darwin: Charles Darwin University. https://cduebooks.pressbooks.pub/cuc107/chapter/6-indigenous-business-perspectives/.

Yunupingu, M. 1989. "Language and Power: The Yolngu Rise to Power at Yirrkala School." *Ngoonjook* 2: 1–6. https://search.informit.org/doi/10.3316/informit.151805372855431.

6

INCLUSIVE ASSESSMENT, EXCLUSIVE ACADEMY

Juuso Henrik Nieminen

Assessment as a partition for abledness

Higher education, as a societal institution, has travelled a long way from its elitist roots. If a higher education degree was once a sign of intelligence and social class, nowadays it is a modern commodity: a necessity for entry into the job market in the knowledge society. The mass higher education model has led to diversification of the student population as people from marginalised backgrounds have gained increased access to academia. This "massification" has provided important opportunities for marginalised students to reinvent their identity by attending higher education and thus enhance their quality of life (Moriña 2017). Yet, it has been noted how disabled students often participate in higher education as "the Others"; as the ones who are *inside* but recognised to be *different* (Dolmage 2017). Inaccessible learning environment design plays a key role in how disabled students come to understand themselves as *unfit* rather than as fully accepted members of academia (Nieminen and Pesonen 2022).

The role of assessment has only rather recently been emphasised in the processes of belonging, inclusion, and social justice. This is surprising given the substantial role that assessment plays in student learning. The predominant way to address diversity in assessment in higher education is to provide individual accommodations (or "adjustments", depending on one's context, e.g., extra time for tests or separate testing rooms). Often, the reasons for accessing such accommodations include psychological and medical conditions such as disabilities, illnesses, mental health issues, and so forth. The accommodation system prevails globally and is currently mandated in legislation in various countries. Yet, the accommodation model is unable to address the deeper issues of exclusion as related to assessment. In fact, the accommodation model relies on a conceptualisation of disability and diversity as something that obscures assessment and should

DOI: 10.4324/9781003293101-8

thus be mitigated. Assessment constitutes a partition that divides students into normal/abnormal, able/disabled, and "ideal students"/"equity group students" (Nieminen 2020, 2021, 2022). To challenge this view, research has advocated for inclusive assessment design that would *by design* reduce the need for accommodations through accessible assessment practices (Hanafin et al. 2007; Tai, Ajjawi, and Umarova 2021). Unfortunately, not much has changed: the accommodation model remains the norm for both research and practice.

This chapter widens our understanding of assessment for inclusion amidst the broader political landscapes of higher education. Drawing on my earlier work (Nieminen 2022), I examine the rationale of assessment as a way of bringing assessment from the margins of inclusion work into its very centre. Focusing on disabled students, I discuss the role of inclusive assessment in enhancing inclusion during this era of growing inequity and segregation. I ask: How far can we go to promote inclusion through assessment design? Who are the people who benefit from "inclusive assessment"? Answering these questions is crucial: assessment is often a key reason for disabled students to feel like they do not belong in academic communities (Hanafin et al. 2007; Nieminen and Pesonen 2022). In this chapter, then, I introduce three conceptualisations for inclusive assessment. I argue that two of them have been unsuccessful in their quest to promote inclusion. Finally, I discuss how the third conceptualisation could be implemented in practice in the form of authentic assessment for social justice.

Inclusive assessment: What's in a name?

Inclusive assessment has been understood in multiple ways in earlier research. This is understandable: after all, "inclusion" and "assessment" are both complex, social concepts. Here, I introduce three ways of conceptualising inclusive assessment, drawing on different epistemological underpinning of both "inclusion" and "assessment".

The accommodation model and the false sense of inclusion

The most common way of *dealing with diversity* in assessment is the accommodation model. Individual accommodations (e.g., extra time in tests and separate testing rooms) are administered for students with a medical and/or psychological diagnosis or a similar, often medicalised reason for support. The accommodation model can be identified in most higher education institutes, emphasising their role as the "norm" when it comes to inclusive assessment policies. Often, this model relies on a specific understanding of assessment as a process of valid and reliable measurement. Disabilities (and similar "conditions" such as mental health issues and illnesses, often presented as yes/no boxes to be ticked in accommodation applications) are then seen to threaten the validity of assessment by obscuring the results. For example, if a student with dyslexia is not granted accommodations in a mathematics test, the test might not be measuring "mathematical skills" anymore but other non-related constructs such as perhaps "reading comprehension skills". By offering enough support (but not too much) on the disability-specific hindrances (but not for anything else), it is possible to provide a fair access to assessment for disabled students (see e.g., Holmes and Silvestri 2019; Lovett and Lewandowski 2020).

This approach to "inclusive assessment" reflects the *medical model of disability* which understands disabilities mainly as personal deficits that need to be cured, fixed, and accommodated. This model sees disabilities as something to be mitigated in assessment, rather than something that enriches it (Nieminen 2021). As the support mechanisms of higher education rely on the medical model, disabled students might be further marginalised and excluded in academic communities (Nieminen and Pesonen 2022).

Within such a medical model, assessment accommodations are likened to medical treatment. Just as a certain illness is cured with certain medicine, a certain disability type (e.g., dyscalculia) should be paired with an adequate type of assessment accommodations (e.g., a possibility for a calculator). Assessment accommodations should, then, be based on objective psycho-cognitive knowledge. Accommodation literature is dominated by psychometrics, leaving the approaches of ethics, care, and social justice in the margins of the literature. For example, advocacy roles are commonly portrayed as risks in assessment:

> Assuming an advocacy role can lead practitioners to make recommendations that are not based on demonstrated need but are instead based on preferences or supports that might actually provide undue advantage or simply make life easier for students.
>
> *(Holmes and Silvestri 2019, 8)*

Overreliance on the accommodation model, ultimately, frames inclusion as a procedural matter, as "inclusive assessment" is seen to ensure students' equal participation in testing. Seen through this lens, inclusion has been successfully provided when the test results of students have been improved. However, portraying inclusive assessment mainly as a way of ensuring students' right to attend tests creates a false sense of inclusion: the accommodation model provides access to testing while neglecting deeper issues of exclusion and equal participation. Furthermore, the psycho-cognitive approach has been unable to address how assessment itself marginalises disabled students. Assessment accommodations have been shown to stigmatise disabled students and frame them as "unfit" and "abnormal" (Hanafin et al. 2007; Nieminen 2020). There is thus a need for alternative approaches beyond psychometric epistemologies.

Accessible assessment design for all students

Another way of conceptualising inclusive assessment is through "accessible assessment". This view is far more rare both in research and in practice (Tai, Ajjawi, and Umarova 2021). To negate the marginalising nature of the accommodation model, inclusive assessment design is based on *accessible assessment design* that is designed to suit the diversity of students (see Ketterlin Geller, Johnstone, and Thurlow 2015 for "Universal Design for Assessment" and Chapter 12 in this book). Such design locates the inaccessible and exclusionary elements of assessment design *before* assessment is conducted. This conceptualisation of disability then follows *the social model* that acknowledges the social, cultural, and historical underpinnings of disabledness. Assessment *disables* students: inclusion is provided by *designing out* the inaccessible, marginalising aspects of assessment.

In practice, inclusively designed assessment has been connected with the overall principles of "student-centred assessment", such as transparent learning criteria, diverse assessment practices (e.g., self- and peer-assessment) and student-centred, engaging feedback practices (e.g., Hanafin et al. 2007; Tai, Ajjawi, and Umarova 2021). Inclusive assessment, as understood through the social design epistemology, then aims to reduce the need for accommodations through assessment design.

The profound issue with such inclusive assessment design is that it has largely not found its way into practice (Tai, Ajjawi, and Umarova 2021). Overall, challenging the testing-driven assessment cultures has been notoriously tricky in higher education (Medland 2016). Riddell and Weedon (2006) argued that what stands in the way of inclusive assessment is the meritocratic ideology that underlies assessment in higher education. Testing and grades are the key elements in ranking the best students and best universities. As testing maintains the social legitimacy of higher education in this process of selection, disabled students are seen to challenge not only assessment but the very idea of academic standards (Riddell and Weedon 2006). In the increasingly "measured university" driven by grades, rankings, and indicators (Manathunga et al. 2017), assessment remains stubbornly test-driven despite the overwhelming amount of evidence of student-centred assessment practices (see, e.g., Medland 2016).

Furthermore, as I have fully argued elsewhere (Nieminen 2022), inclusive assessment design initiatives run the risk of "pedagogisation", that is, mainly understanding the deep, societal issues of exclusion as simply a matter of pedagogy and design. A true reimagination of higher education as an inclusive space requires transformation not only at the level of assessment design but also at the broader societal and political levels.

Inclusive assessment for all? Towards critical approaches

To avoid the risk of suggesting procedural solutions to profound forms of exclusion, "inclusive assessment" must be understood as a deeply *political* issue. This idea is built on the following premises. First, the inclusion of disabled people at various tiers of society is always a political quest, tied to prevailing national and institutional policies. Second, it is argued that higher education has a moral imperative to play a pivotal role in such inclusion work, namely, that disabled people have the human right to partake in higher education (Uditsky and Hughson 2012). Third, assessment is recognised as a key factor in students' learning and studying in terms of the full spectrum of "learning" as a cognitive, social, affective, cultural, historical, and political phenomenon. Inclusive assessment is, then, understood as a moral and ethical practice that plays a role in promoting societal inclusion in higher education and beyond.

I argue that earlier attempts to promote "inclusive assessment" have addressed this moral imperative through a limited approach. Both the approaches of the accommodation model and inclusive assessment design have operated *within* the boundaries of higher education, assuming that equal access to higher education has already been achieved. So, can inclusive assessment fulfil the promise of inclusion for the large numbers of disabled people who never reach higher education?

Here, the concept of ableism helps to reframe the question of "inclusion" in political terms. Dolmage (2017) discusses the concept of academic ableism to show how higher education environments – with their physical, social, and cultural features, amongst others – are designed for the "ideal, able student". Ableist practices provide information about bodies and minds, steering people to understand themselves against the ideals of normality, ability, and productivity. Here, assessment plays a key role as it provides students with knowledge about the development of their abilities throughout their studies. Assessment portrays students as certain kinds of students: as weak or talented, slow or fast, normal or abnormal (Nieminen 2020). Test-driven assessment reflects the valued modern citizen who is cognitively able and productively takes part in the market economy. Disabled people challenge this view (Riddell and Weedon 2006), and indeed, disabled people have been historically excluded from academic settings as unsuitable for the knowledge economies that higher education prepares people for.

So, who are the students who get to enjoy "inclusive assessment" in higher education? Let me offer the example of Finnish universities. Finland is largely considered as an inclusive country from the viewpoint of access to higher education. For example, attending higher education is free for students in the EU/EEA area. Has the system been able to include disabled people? While Finland does not collect systematic data on the issue, recent self-reported health surveys conducted at all Finnish higher education institutions have indicated that disabled students are a small minority in universities (Korkeamäki and Vuorento 2021; Kunttu, Pesonen, and Saari 2016). In part, this reflects the minority status of disabled people in the society at large. In Kunttu, Pesonen, and Saari's survey, "a learning difficulty or other illness or disability" was reported by 10.6% of the students in universities of applied sciences, and by 6.5% of the students in academic universities. Dyslexia was reported as the most common disability (5.0%) and attention deficit disorder as the next most common one (0.9%). Korkeamäki and Vuorento (2021) noted that learning disabilities were reported by 4.8% of female and 3.8% of male university students. These numbers imply that Finnish academia remains a space with limited diversity from the viewpoint of disabilities and neurodiversity.

What about people with intellectual disabilities? In Finland, people with intellectual disabilities remain largely excluded from society. According to the disability organisation Väylä (2022), of the 3000 people with intellectual disabilities, only 16% are integrated into the society through work, and only 2% have a full-time job. It is reported that many people with intellectual disabilities work for free as they are not told their rights for salary. According to Väylä, the average pay for people with intellectual disabilities is 7 euros per day on average, from which a lunch fee (€4.90) is often deducted. In fact, Väylä was founded to ensure that "in the future, every person with intellectual disabilities receives an appropriate salary for their work" (Väylä 2022, my translation). These shameful statistics remind us of the inability of Finland to include people with intellectual disabilities in society – and definitely not in universities.

How could "inclusive assessment" challenge ableism on a broader societal level? One possible answer can be found in Finnish legislation for universities. Finnish universities have a three-fold mission of 1) independent academic research, 2) research-based education, and 3) the promotion of socially impactful research (Universities Act 2009). However, academic funding models consistently prioritise the first two missions, while the third has remained non-implemented and without support (Heinonen and Raevaara 2012). Behold, the measured university! Inclusive assessment, understood through an anti-ableist stance, brings all these three missions together.

Authentic assessment for inclusion and social justice

One solution to combine these three purposes of higher education is research-based (purpose 1) authentic assessment (purpose 2) that aims to foster inclusion for communities within and beyond higher education (purpose 3). In many ways, this idea is not novel, as critical research has advocated transformative teaching practices. However, similar approaches remain in the margins of assessment (e.g., McArthur 2022; Nieminen 2022).

"Authentic assessment" offers an interesting starting point for such work. In higher education, authentic assessment has referred to assessment and feedback tasks that "mirror the capability of the students to use their knowledge beyond their academic environment" (Sokhanvar, Salehi, and Sokhanvar 2021, 2). Authentic assessment is often defined in relation to "traditional" assessment. For example, Sokhanvar, Salehi, and Sokhanvar (2021) list performances, projects, exhibitions, portfolios, case studies, reflective journals, interviews, and group work as forms of authentic assessment. Such conceptualisations offer a suitable starting point for "assessment for inclusion" but are not enough to capture its complexity. To fulfil its promise of inclusion, authentic assessment needs to connect not only with the context of work but society at large (McArthur 2022). I draw on Dawson and Bearman (2020) who discussed *future-authentic* assessment that "faithfully represents not just the current realities of the discipline in practice, but the likely future realities of that discipline" (292). Authentic assessment for inclusion does not only aim to guess and replicate authentic futures, but aims to *redefine* them. This is achieved through an activist stance that draws explicitly on an advocacy role that earlier assessment research warned against (e.g., Holmes and Silvestri 2019).

Through such a stance, assessment is harnessed as a vehicle for creating more inclusive futures in higher education.

How could such an idea be put into practise? One concrete example is the study by Thompson (2009) who introduced community action projects as a form of authentic assessment in statistics education. Students took part in authentic projects in which they provided statistical analyses for the needs of blind adolescents and adults for independent living, and to create multi-sensory education environments for disabled students. This study is an inspiring example as the students worked in close collaboration with the communities and with the *end users* of the statistical tools in particular. Other examples of authentic assessment projects might be collaborations with disability organisations and other relevant stakeholders whose voice is rarely heard when developing inclusive higher education. Moreover, such projects might include activism and campaigns for more inclusive teaching and assessment policies in higher education. In social sciences, students might help to organise a system-wide professional development program for staff on diversity and disabilities. These are of course just a few examples. Below, I outline some guidelines for authentic assessment for inclusion.

Authentic assessment criteria and feedback

While designing authentic assessment for inclusion, one must challenge the traditional understanding of academic standards and assessment criteria. Predetermined assessment criteria and learning objectives often leave little room for diversity to flourish. While assessment criteria are often framed through the metaphor of transparency, Bearman and Ajjawi's (2021) proposal of a metaphor of *invitation* is a more powerful way to consider how the quality of students' work could be determined in assessment for inclusion. No one person, such as the teacher, can determine the assessment criteria for such assessment: instead, all stakeholders (e.g., teachers, students, teaching assistants, representatives from organisations and industry) are invited to a "productive space" to negotiate quality criteria (Bearman and Ajjawi 2021). This way, the criteria represent the real needs and voices of people in and out of academia.

Such productive spaces disrupt the ableist assumption that academics should decide what counts as successful activism and inclusion work. It might be left up to the "end users" of inclusion-related assessment projects to determine whether assessment has truly led to desirable changes. As such, authentic assessment criteria do not aim to lower academic standards but indeed to raise the bar higher. When assessment is evaluated in terms of the social good it provides (McArthur 2022), students are asked to truly connect with the world rather than to produce work only for their teachers.

Reimagined approaches to assessment criteria ultimately lead into assessment design that celebrates diversity and personalised forms of achievement (see Jorre de St Jorre, Boud, and Johnson 2021). As Jorre de St Jorre and colleagues note, evaluative judgement plays a key role here, as it ties together co-constructed assessment criteria and the personalised presentations of skills that demonstrate such criteria. Authentic feedback is needed to communicate both criteria and judgements about students' work. Dawson, Carless, and Lee (2021) introduced the idea of authentic feedback in various disciplines. In authentic assessment for inclusion, feedback processes are not restricted to classrooms but might concern multiple authentic stakeholders such as the "end users" themselves.

Authentic assessment accommodations

Authentic assessment accommodations are a crucial part of "assessment for inclusion". The usual menu of assessment accommodations – extra time in exams, separate testing rooms – is indeed rather *inauthentic*: few of us face these practices after graduation. As accommodations are redesigned from the viewpoint of authenticity, they represent the authentic contexts in professional work situations and beyond. If carefully facilitated, authentic assessment projects might develop students' assessment literacies as they learn to reflect and communicate on their access needs in assessment. In tandem, teachers' assessment literacies are developed as they co-design accommodations together with students. Both parties might indeed develop their assessment and feedback literacies specifically from the viewpoint of diversity.

The teacher perspective

In practice, the success of such authentic assessment depends on whether teachers have agency over their assessment practices. In many ways, teacher agency, expertise, and support are all at the heart of inclusive assessment: assessment is contextual and situational, it cannot always be standardised through rules, regulations, and rubrics. Importantly, inclusive assessment should also be inclusive for teachers. We, teachers, are also diverse! For example, marking a pile of essays is an inaccessible practice for many of us. Authentic assessment projects might offer novel approaches to including disabled teachers as full members of academic communities too.

Undoing barriers: The question of grades

"Assessment for inclusion" not only promotes inclusion and social justice but also actively undoes the barriers to such goals (Nieminen 2022). Assessment and grading policies often focus on social selection and competition – these ideals run contrary to inclusion. Changing grading is essential given its major role in maintaining the legitimacy of meritocratic ideologies in higher education (Riddell and Weedon 2006). Indeed, grading is a key mechanism that grounds higher education in individualistic ideologies. One starting point might then be systemic, institution-wide "ungrading" or a similar process of rendering individual grades meaningless for students. Jorre de St Jorre, Boud, and Johnson (2021) offered other interesting future trajectories by discussing assessment that, instead of grading, allows for multiple portrayals of achievement for different audiences. As they argue, such approaches to certification in higher education might benefit all stakeholders, as assessment might then provide more meaningful evidence of achievement rather than simply a number (see also Chapter 13).

Closing words: Bringing assessment to the centre of inclusion work

In this chapter, I have outlined how inclusive assessment literature has moved from technical (the accommodation model) to social (accessible assessment design) conceptualisation of the inclusivity in assessment. I have argued that in order to be successful, inclusivity in assessment needs to be rethought through a critical and political stance. Inclusive assessment must disrupt rather than complement the prevalent and often ableist discourses of measurement, individualisation, and competition in assessment. Without critical approaches, inclusive assessment runs the risk of being yet another mechanical, pedagogical response to the deeper political issues concerning the exclusion of disabled people (see Nieminen and Pesonen 2021).

The politically oriented idea of inclusive assessment humbly reminds us that assessment cannot do everything: we will not end societal exclusion through assessment design. However, assessment could do a lot more than it is currently doing for inclusion. Thus far the initiatives to enhance the inclusivity of assessment have remained within the boundaries of the classroom. I have proposed some future trajectories for inclusive assessment to reach communities beyond higher education. This idea links with multiple current strands of assessment research, such as authentic assessment, group assessment and project assessment. There is a lot to build on.

Assessment is often presented as its own object that can be developed separately from other entities such as teaching, pedagogy, and inclusion work. Yet, in the measured university (Manathunga et al. 2017) assessment is *everywhere*: it is intertwined in all activities in academia. Many have argued that academia has started to lose its meaning on the altar of measurement, metrics, and competition. Inclusive assessment presents a way to bring together the three purposes of the university to refocus academia towards what is truly meaningful. It turns assessment – a current mechanism for individualisation and social selection – into a vehicle of collectivity. Inclusive assessment highlights the moral and ethical imperative of higher education to provide social good (Uditsky and Hughson 2012). It is time to bring assessment to the very centre of inclusion work.

References

Bearman, M., and Ajjawi, R. 2021. "Can a Rubric Do More than Be Transparent? Invitation as a New Metaphor for Assessment Criteria." *Studies in Higher Education* 46 (2): 359–368. https://doi.org/10.1080/03075079.2019.1637842.

Dawson, P., and Bearman, M. 2020. "Concluding Comments: Reimagining University Assessment in a Digital World." In *Re-Imagining University Assessment in a Digital World*, edited by Margaret Bearman, Phillip Dawson, Rola Ajjawi, Joanna Tai, and David Boud, 291–296. Cham: Springer.

Dawson, P., Carless, D., and Lee, P. P. W. 2021. "Authentic Feedback: Supporting Learners to Engage in Disciplinary Feedback Practices." *Assessment and Evaluation in Higher Education* 46 (2): 286–296. https://doi.org/10.1080/02602938.2020.1769022.

Dolmage, J. T. 2017. *Academic Ableism: Disability and Higher Education*. University of Michigan Press. http://doi.org/10.3998/mpub.9708722.

Hanafin, J., Shevlin, M., Kenny, M., and Neela, E. M. 2007. "Including Young People with Disabilities: Assessment Challenges in Higher Education." *Higher Education* 54 (3): 435–448. http://doi.org/10.1007/s10734-006-9005-9.

Heinonen, A., and Raevaara, T. 2012. "Yliopistojen Kolmas Tehtävä jää Vaille Toteutusta ja Tukea." [*The Third Mission of Universities Is Left without Implementation and Support.*] *Tieteessä Tapahtuu* 30 (5): 3–8. https://journal.fi/tt/article/view/6875/5527.

Holmes, A., and Silvestri, R. 2019. "Extra Time or Unused Time? What Data from a College Testing Center Tells Us about 50% Extra Time as an Accommodation for Students with Learning Disabilities." *Psychological Injury and Law* 12 (1): 7–16. https://doi.org/10.1007/s12207-019-09339-9.

Jorre de St Jorre, T., Boud, D., and Johnson, E. D. 2021. "Assessment for Distinctiveness: Recognising Diversity of Accomplishments." *Studies in Higher Education* 46 (7): 1371–1382. https://doi.org/10.1080/03075079.2019.1689385.

Ketterlin Geller, L. R., Johnstone, C. J., and Thurlow, M. L. 2015. "Universal Design of Assessment." In *Universal Design in Higher Education: From Principles to Practice*, edited by Sheryl E. Burgstahler, 163–176. Cambridge, Massachusetts: Harvard Education Press.

Korkeamäki, J., and Vuorento, M. 2021. *Students with Self-Reported Health Problems and Disabilities in Higher Education. Eurostudent VII Article Series*. Publication of the Ministry of Education and Culture, Finland: 16. https://urn.fi/URN:ISBN:978-952-263-841-0.

Kunttu, K., Pesonen, T., and Saari, J. 2016. "Student Health Survey 2016: A National Survey among Finnish University Students." *Finnish Student Health Service*. https://1285112865.rsc.cdn77.org/app/uploads/2020/03/KOTT_2016_ENG.pdf.

Lovett, B. J., and Lewandowski, L. J. 2020. "Private Room Testing Accommodations for Students with ADHD." *The ADHD Report* 28 (8): 1–5. https://doi.org/10.1521/adhd.2020.28.8.1.

Manathunga, C., Selkrig, M., Sadler, K., and Keamy, K. 2017. "Rendering the Paradoxes and Pleasures of Academic Life: Using Images, Poetry and Drama to Speak Back to the Measured University." *Higher Education Research and Development* 36 (3): 526–540. https://doi.org/10.1080/07294360.2017.1289157.

McArthur, J. 2022. "Rethinking Authentic Assessment: Work, Well-Being, and Society." *Higher Education*: 1–17. https://doi.org/10.1007/s10734-022-00822-y.

Medland, E. 2016. "Assessment in Higher Education: Drivers, Barriers and Directions for Change in the UK." *Assessment & Evaluation in Higher Education* 41 (1): 81–96. https://doi.org/10.1080/02602938.2014.982072.

Moriña, A. 2017. ""We Aren't Heroes, We're Survivors": Higher Education as an Opportunity for Students with Disabilities to Reinvent an Identity." *Journal of Further and Higher Education* 41 (2): 215–226. https://doi.org/10.1080/0309877X.2015.1070402.

Nieminen, J. H. 2020. "Student Conceptions of Assessment Accommodations in University Mathematics: An Analysis of Power." *Nordic Studies in Mathematics Education* 25 (3–4): 27–49. http://ncm.gu.se/wp-content/uploads/1605/83/25_34_027050_nieminen.pdf.

Nieminen, J. H. 2021. "Governing the "Disabled Assessee": A Critical Reframing of Assessment Accommodations as Sociocultural Practices." *Disability and Society*. https://doi.org/10.1080/09687599.2021.1874304.

Nieminen, J. H. 2022. "Assessment for Inclusion: Rethinking Inclusive Assessment in Higher Education." *Teaching in Higher Education*. https://doi.org/10.1080/13562517.2021.2021395.

Nieminen, J. H., and Pesonen, H. V. 2022. "Politicising Inclusive Learning Environments: How to Foster Belonging and Challenge Ableism?" *Higher Education Research and Development* 41 (6): 2020–2033. https://doi.org/10.1080/07294360.2021.1945547.

Riddell, S., and Weedon, E. 2006. "What Counts as a Reasonable Adjustment? Dyslexic Students and the Concept of Fair Assessment." *International Studies in Sociology of Education* 16 (1): 57–73. https://doi.org/10.1080/19620210600804301.

Sokhanvar, Z., Salehi, K., and Sokhanvar, F. 2021. "Advantages of Authentic Assessment for Improving the Learning Experience and Employability Skills of Higher Education Students: A Systematic Literature Review." *Studies in Educational Evaluation* 70, 101030. https://doi.org/10.1016/j.stueduc.2021.101030.

Tai, J., Ajjawi, R., and Umarova, A. 2021. "How Do Students Experience Inclusive Assessment? A Critical Review of Contemporary Literature." *International Journal of Inclusive Education*. https://doi.org/10.1080/13603116.2021.2011441.

Thompson, C. J. 2009. "Educational Statistics Authentic Learning CAPSULES: Community Action Projects for Students Utilizing Leadership and E-Based Statistics." *Journal of Statistics Education* 17 (1). https://doi.org/10.1080/10691898.2009.11889508.

Uditsky, B., and Hughson, E. 2012. "Inclusive Postsecondary Education—An Evidence-Based Moral Imperative." *Journal of Policy and Practice in Intellectual Disabilities* 9 (4): 298–302. http://doi.org/10.1111/jppi.12005.

Universities Act (558/2009). Ministry of Education and Culture. https://www.finlex.fi/fi/laki/kaannokset/2009/en20090558.pdf.

Väylä. 2022. Vaikuttaminen [*Influence*]. Accessed 2 February 2022. https://vaylary.fi/page/9/vaikuttaminen.

7

ONTOLOGICAL ASSESSMENT DECISIONS IN TEACHING AND LEARNING

Ben Whitburn and Matthew Krehl Edward Thomas

Orientation

Concerned with the design and implementation of assessment for inclusion, in this conceptual chapter we discuss sustainable orientations towards equitable ways of working by adopting a theory that embraces the ontological turn. What we mean by this is that we want to use theory to think with (Jackson and Mazzei 2011) which concentrates on the "nature of being and the basic categories of existence" (St. Pierre, Jackson, and Mazzei 2016, 99) as an ethical project. This contrasts with what assessment tends to emphasise; a constructivist approach to evidencing understanding and knowing against preconceived learning outcomes (Sadler and Reimann 2017). Our reason for taking this conceptual pathway will become clearer as this chapter unfolds; though to briefly introduce it here, a push for evidence-informed practices in education tends to obfuscate context and circumstance, ignoring complex structural and social impacts on student achievement. As Spina observes, "arguments in favour of standardised testing and evidence-informed decision making are frequently framed around the need for evidence as a means of increasing achievement and equity" (Spina 2018, 335). However, as she and others (e.g., McArthur 2016) have forcefully argued, approaches to equity in education that start with evidence-based "best practices", and that espouse equity in so doing, tend to be framed by a determination to set a level playing field, whereby difference among student groups is minimised. Consequently, social justice in education through these practices remains elusive.

In this chapter, then, we build a case for centring ontology in assessment for inclusion and social justice by paying attention to the implications of diversity in educational design. The discussion takes place in two interrelated movements. In the first, we explore ways inclusive education has been differentially framed in the tertiary sector across 40 years, and correspondingly, how educational design

DOI: 10.4324/9781003293101-9

can present temporal barriers to diverse students. Accounting for institutional assessment decisions to be highly contingent (Dawson et al. 2013) and the experiences of students in higher education to be highly varied in terms of temporal engagement (Bennett and Burke 2017; Whitburn and Thomas 2021). In the second movement, we explore the ontological turn. Here we advance a framework for orientating towards ontology to reframe assessment for social justice and inclusion in higher education (McArthur 2016). We draw on an evidence-making intervention (EMI) framework adapted from Rhodes and Lancaster (2019) to advance an approach to assessment design and implementation from an ontological position, discussing how this can be more equitable for students in ways that difference is treated differently.

Inclusive times

We live in a fascinating period of educational and social history, in which matters of equity underpin policies and practices in higher education. Indeed, widening participation in higher education has been a prominent policy strategy in Australia since the late 1980s for students whose profile and/or living conditions are not reflective of the mainstream (Bennett and Burke 2017). This has not been straightforward, with divergent priorities taken over this period. For instance, whereas once heightening participation for student diversity in higher education was initially taken to mean ensuring that institutions are more representative of their populations, at present this concept has been expanded: broader inclusion in higher education is prioritised for its contribution to a more functional economy (Adam 2003). Rights-based arguments have also been prevalent internationally, although these centre on a liberal humanist universal norm to which to aspire, and in so doing, they have tended to favour inclusion for discrete categories of identity, such as people with disabilities, cultural diversities, and sexualities (Whitburn and Thomas 2021).

Indeed, whichever mast we nail our colours to, the underlying premise behind contemporary inclusive education discourse across the sectors is that all individuals can take part on the basis that they are equal stakeholders in the marketplaces which dominate our lives (Simons and Masschelein 2015). Though as scholars of inclusive education have pointed out (Dolmage 2017; Whitburn and Thomas 2021), interventions targeting specific student identities do little to address entrenched barriers to inclusion in education. Here we want to take the notions of equity and social justice further, to consider how they shape teaching practices in higher education, and more specifically how they influence what Dawson et al. (2013) refer to as assessment decisions. That is, how conditions in the higher education sector lead to making particular decisions about the role and purpose of assessment in educational design. Indeed, these concerns pertain both to the "what" and "how" of assessment – both in the ways assessments are designed and implemented, and "the role of assessment in nurturing the forms of learning that will promote greater social justice within society as a whole"

(McArthur 2016, 968), which together form the root of the present discussion across both movements of the chapter.

Supplying fair opportunities to local and global communities through inclusive teaching and learning features highly on university strategic mission statements internationally. However, rigid practice standards, academic integrity, and the development of individual students' core skills to increase employability are often given centre stage, leading McArthur (2016) to consider that institutional concerns for procedural fairness overtake aspirations for increasing and responding to student diversity. Regulatory compliance is at the fore when compelling students to disclose disabilities to institutions, as a way to ensure that they can then expect reasonable adjustments to be made to their programs of learning, rather than to consider the inclusiveness and accessibility of courses writ large (Bunbury 2020). We suggest that educators would do well to consider what is reasonable, and inclusive, about adjustments, and further, how, and why assessment decisions are made that foster learning conditions through which adjustments are necessitated for designated student groups. In noting that extensions to time are a core means by which universities adjust programs of assessment for particular students (Dolmage 2017), rather than engage with them to demonstrate learning development (McArthur 2016), we acknowledge that assessment in higher education is inescapably temporal.

Consider how time mediates learning design in higher education. Courses of higher education are designed according to pre-conceived temporal milestones, cast against national benchmarks of duration, be they 3-year undergraduate courses or 2-year Masters programs. Years are typically divided into semesters, splitting the year into teaching periods framed within pockets of time. Each bi- or trifurcated measure is replete with regularly established pauses that students must utilise to catch up should they fall foul of the predetermined pace of learning progression; or perhaps if they can, to push forward in time, gaining the elusive edge over their fellow students in a race against the clock to demonstrate fledgling competency. Summative tasks in such programs are simultaneously mediated by time, for "educational attainment targets and assessment apply the invariable norm as measure" (Adam 2003, 63). Students are expected to turn in assessment tasks on specific dates corresponding with their contractual agreements as stipulated in course outlines (McArthur 2016), or else produce knowledge on cue under timed examination conditions (Gilovich, Kerr, and Medvec 1993). Adjustments to such temporal expectations can be made, but only to those who have verifiable reasons to make such interruptions, and only if those adaptations are considered reasonable (Bunbury 2020).

For committed students and engaged educators alike, these conditions to study and receive judgement on submitted evidence of learning (Dawson et al. 2013) may seem entirely feasible, and unassailable. Yet, these approaches to assessment favour a normative, top-down approach to working with difference, in which disruptions to the temporal order of teaching and learning are sanctioned on the basis that they are documented as reasonable adjustments. Put differently, students' propensities for learning are associated with assumptions of being able to comply with timed deadlines. Time pressures are moreover a principal reason that underrepresented students exclude themselves from higher education (Bennett and Burke 2017), giving little heed to the ways that normative frameworks of hegemonic time affect student engagement. There are two points of significance worthy of consideration, related to matters of assessment procedures in higher education. Firstly, as they are easier and quicker to control than the ways students engage with relevant and professional knowledge, procedural concerns are given primacy in assessment over ontological ones (Bennett and Burke 2017; McArthur 2016). As McArthur (2016) notes, a "focus on procedure in assessment thus leads students away from the most important aspect of what they should be doing – critical engagement with complex knowledge" (972). Secondly, these ways of working with assessment and the design of education programs more broadly are predicated on linear, neoliberal-driven notions of learning progression (Lingard and Thompson 2017), which emphasise individualised skill development in support of economies. Theorists have surmised that we live in a period of sped up and individualised psychology, and that higher education has consequently never been as hyper-accelerated as in the present (Vostal 2014), wherein temporal compressions, such as shortened teaching periods containing tight assessment deadlines have become de rigueur. As we have foreshadowed, while many can thrive in fast-paced and self-driven environments of learning, left behind are those students who are unable to conform to linear, normative progression, and institutions of higher education risk marginalising these students further (Bennett and Burke 2017; Whitburn and Thomas 2021). In the next movement of this chapter, we turn to ontology, and consider its productive possibilities for assessment, and making evidence of learning.

Turning to ontology

To recap, what we have argued for is to recognise how higher education institutions invoke assessment in their course designs to privilege particular ways of being and engaging with knowledge; ways that evoke universalist ideals that everybody can be equally included in a classroom and that balancing fairness in assessment by way of procedural means to attempt achieving a level playing field stifles critical engagement with knowledge for students. This approach neglects to account for diversity, and how time – "the way it is lived, experienced and (re)constructed through our location, positionality and experience – is gendered, classed and racialised and tied to unequal power relations and socio-cultural differences" (Bennett and Burke 2017, 2). To that end, the extent to which assessment can be meaningfully understood as a hallmark of inclusive practice is contingent, in our view, on how it can go beyond epistemological limitations – ways of knowing or not knowing – to incorporate ontological awareness: the ways that knowledge affects co-existence.

As we briefly presaged at the start, the ontological turn in social science inquiry is concerned with the nature of being (St. Pierre, Jackson, and Mazzei 2016).

It primarily shifts focus away from knowledge as fixed, infallible, and separate to bodies, and thereby to be learned, held, and applied incontrovertibly, to an alternative point of departure that instead emphasises matter and meaning-making. We draw here from the new materialism (St. Pierre, Jackson, and Mazzei 2016), which is an orientation to social science inquiry that emphasises ontology to challenge categorical assumptions, including that which is material such as objects, texts, and buildings and that which is non-material such as mood, time, and intention. To consider inclusion through assessment in higher education gives us scope to draw students' attention towards the interconnections between things that affect their experiences while engaging in the processes of meaning-making about and for their chosen course of study. It supplies conditions for contexts of learning in which students are made aware that educational programs and assessment procedures are constructed (McArthur 2016), and that the knowledge that is produced through learning is co-created, contingent on other variables, temporary and forever changeable.

The co-creation of knowledge is of particular significance to an ontological orientation to assessment in higher education. Similarly compelled to engage ontology in approaches to assessment, Bourke (2017) observes that unnatural divisions take shape through assessment practices in higher education: ones that prevent teachers from forming legitimate partnerships with students, and that also functions to detach students from their learning. As she writes, "students take less responsibility for their own assessment because they have learned to rely on assessments that tell them that they had learned, and by how much" (Bourke 2017, 829), or perhaps, how little. Bourke (2017) advocates instead for self-assessment approaches, which, in co-production with teachers and peers, allow students to identify questions for investigation, and grow professionally through their inquiries. Significant to ensuring this approach led to strong outcomes for students, teaching staff were themselves made to justify the decisions they made about the types of assessment tasks set, and their purpose in supporting professional development. Assessment in use, then, is always changeable, being contingent on the profile of learners and teachers in context, and they have their utility in showing student learning aligned to these contexts.

Designing assessment: An evidence-making intervention framework

Institutions of higher education increasingly rely on authentic forms of assessment to judge student learning, identified as such by the implied connection of tasks to real-world applications. While evidence for their fitness to purpose remains illusory (Hathcoat et al. 2016), the benefits of authentic assessment to shoring up academic integrity are in doubt, not least because authenticity can differ starkly for different stakeholders (Ellis et al. 2019). A corresponding issue is that despite there being little understanding about how teachers in higher education purposefully engage in assessment design and implementation practices, social constructivist conceptualisations dominate the field (Sadler and Reimann 2017). On the surface, engaging students in the active development of their knowledge in conjunction with others, as per social constructivist theories of learning espoused by Bruner and Vygotsky, seems appropriate for ensuring education is an initiative-taking pursuit. Yet, we would caution that social constructivism trades in psychological individualism, assuming pre-existing agency, rationality, and developmental normativity, and its continued dominance in the field of education is antithetical to an inclusive design (Whitburn and Corcoran 2019). To expand on these and the above points, we draw on an EMI framework as a way of attending to questions of ontological relevance in assessment design and implementation.

Originally developed and applied in the health field and implementation sciences, Rhodes and Lancaster (2019) outline an ontology-driven framework, which emphasises the "processes and practices through which 'evidence', 'intervention' and 'context' come to be" (1); foregrounding matters that, to us, make inclusive assessment possible for the ways that the approach orientates to difference. A distinction is made between evidence-based interventions (EBIs) and EMIs, primarily in laying the groundwork for questioning what evidence is, what it does, and how it contributes to sense-making. EBIs developed in education as a crossover from evidence-based medicine, creating notions of best practice that are centred on evidence to inform ongoing improvement to aspects of learning including course design, teaching practices, and assessment. While EBIs are sensitive to contextual specificity in populations and complex adaptive systems, they draw very closely on epistemological (randomised controlled trials, meta-analyses) evidence, and it is Rhodes and Lancaster's contention that EBIs do not account sufficiently for material practices in the constitution of evidence as fluid, emergent practice. EMIs, on the other hand, start with practice; they concentrate on "what interventions *become* through their implementations; how they are worked-with into *different things* with *multiple effects*; and crucially, how they are *made-to-matter* locally" (Rhodes and Lancaster 2019, 2). An EMI framework has been used across broad contexts, for example, to interrogate how evidence informs programs of school-wide behaviour (Corcoran and Thomas 2021), as well as media accounts of temporal implications in public sentiment about COVID-19 vaccinations (Harrison, Lancaster, and Rhodes 2021). Based on the ways this work centres ontological concerns at the core of their subject matter, we are similarly drawn to consider its contribution to assessment decisions in higher education, for supplying a sustainable approach to centring ontological concerns in the design and implementation of assessment.

Before offering an example of how to apply an EMI framework to the design of assessment for inclusion, we situate it alongside policies and principles of learning design in higher education. Evidence is a core concern of the EMI framework, for how it is associated with assessment and learning design. Yet, assessment is a form of learning intervention – a process by which students demonstrate understanding (Dawson et al. 2013). While evidence about appropriate approaches to the design and implementation of assessment is unsurprisingly varied (Sadler and Reimann 2017), rigorous institutional criteria articulate assessment as the form by which students develop cumulative evidence of their learning. Focusing squarely on outcomes, the evidence here quantifies levels of achievement against standardised learning progression expectations. Similarly, evidence is used to inform the ongoing development of the course and assessment design. We wish to emphatically state that it is not itself a problem that evidence is held in such high regard for its capacity to demonstrate knowledge attainment and improvement. However, and aligned with the EMI framework, "[b]eing evidence-based is largely a function of *method*, a question of *epistemology*, of how we judge an appropriate, and optimum, way of knowing an intervention and its effects" (Rhodes and Lancaster 2019, 2). We contend this ought to be accounted for more explicitly when making assessment decisions so that institutions of higher education can provide more inclusive ways of engaging evidence of a students' learning.

In directing the application of their EMI framework to public health research, Rhodes and Lancaster (2019) offer a series of tenets for researchers and practitioners concerned with pursuing different approaches to explicating how evidence is made, and how it is used, and how it is made to matter. Drawing on the principles of new materialism and adapting these EMI-oriented tenets for application to assessment decisions, design and implementation in higher education, our approach proposes:

- Material-discursive practices inform learning outcomes and assessment, and a multiplicity of practices generates multiple realities.
- Multiple human and non-human agents create assessment events.
- Evidencing learning should develop diverse ways of intervening in matters of concern.

Let us now discuss each of these tenets in turn, for how they set the groundwork for an ontological orientation to assessment, drawing on an example applicable to each to invite others to pursue a similar orientation in their assessment decisions.

Material-discursive practices inform learning outcomes and assessment, and a multiplicity of practices generates multiple realities

The intention is to problematise rigid binaries, which were and continue to be recklessly dispensed to situate divisions between things such as learner/teacher, ability/disability, adjusted and non-adjusted programs of study. Instead, in recognition that such categories are contingent on context and emergent through practice, an inclusive curriculum and associated programs of assessments can obviate the necessity for reasonable adjustments when multiplicity is given consideration (Bunbury 2020). Emphasis on the processual nature of learning, and an ontological orientation favours assessment tasks that highlight the co-existence of students' knowledge-creating processes in heterogenous connections with one another. Learning outcomes are thereby formed to not assume static indicators of knowledge or skill acquisition, but on the realities (evidence) created through relational interconnection. In an example of such an approach to learning design in inclusive education for preservice teachers (Whitburn and Corcoran 2019), students are set summative assessment tasks in which they are asked to articulate their conceptualisations of heterogeneous learning environments, while decentring focus away from diagnostic categories in favour of inclusive pedagogical approaches and accessibility considerations. In so doing, they are assigned assessment partners and asked to reflect on their interactions with one another in the development of their knowledge. What is assessed, then, is how students come to recognise the ways that an ontological orientation affects their understanding about diversity, and how they will use this approach to knowledge making in their practices as school-based educators.

Multiple human and non-human agents create assessment events

All matter is agentic, and inclusion in education is temporal, emergent, and multiple, rather than representing a fixed or aspirational state (Whitburn and Thomas 2021). Emphasis is given to affect: bodies and things mutually affect and can be affected, through constitutive actions or events. This has implications for assessment design and implementation, requiring a focus on the specific interactions that occur within such events. EMIs foreground the constitutive forces of material (e.g., technology) and non-material (e.g., study motivation), human (students, teachers) and non-human (institutional assessment policy) agents at work, whose interactions are fluid, transversal and temporary. Returning to the example cited above (Whitburn and Corcoran 2019), students have their attention drawn to the human and non-human interactions they experience in undertaking paired work and are assessed on their capacity to apply analysis to the implications of these on the knowledge they learned. These include how they named their strengths and those of their assigned partner, how they centred equity in working together, and as well how digital tools and knowledge traditions influenced their assessment responses. The focus is on the continuous making and remaking of students' ways of being within relationships. Importantly, reasonable adjustments are not considered a bolt-on or extra procedural considerations but are anticipated and accounted for in assessment design, in recognition that all students will have divergent strengths, accessibility capabilities and temporal capacities to engage in their studies, and that these will shape their learning achievements.

Evidencing learning should develop diverse ways of intervening in matters of concern

To abstract knowledge from its ontological and political context is to make an intervention that promotes outcomes limited to pre-set criteria. Shifting from matters of fact to matters of concern (Latour 2004) is to emphasise context, and focuses on evidencing and intervening as ontological and political undertakings (Corcoran and Thomas 2021). Returning once more to our example of assessment design (Whitburn and Corcoran 2019), students are supplied with assessment tasks that show their learning by explaining how matters of concern affect them, and how they can in turn affect inclusive possibilities for learners. One political matter of particular concern to education jurisdictions internationally has been individualised planning for students with disabilities – a process that is a key policy driver for inclusive education in our context in Victoria (Department of Education and Training 2021). The paired assessment task focuses on students' contexts of teaching and the implications of individualised planning on their roles, centring on individualisation as a key concern for its ability to affect inclusion or exclusion. Students are invited to articulate how they are affected by this and related policies, and how inclusive curriculum design and pedagogy become their matters of concern.

Conclusion

This chapter has sought to centre ontological awareness in assessment decisions as the means to develop inclusiveness. Drawing on evidence using an EMI framework it engages with relational and temporal concepts to orientate towards assessment for inclusion, providing examples of how these principles have been used to develop assessment tasks in the scholarship of inclusive education. By designing assessment activities that attentively engage students in assessing their ongoing development, that encourage them to identify and work within the parameters of their strengths and those of their peers, and applying these skills to the context of the profession in which they are studying, educators can move focus away from quantifying knowledge and shifting conceptual focus towards assessment for inclusion. We optimistically predict wider acceptance of ontological orientations in the field, for escaping the clutches of constructivism and giving educators the necessary theoretical resources to think with that promote affirmative ways of engaging difference.

References

Adam, B. 2003. "Reflexive Modernization Temporalized." *Theory, Culture and Society* 20 (2): 59–78. https://doi.org/10.1177/0263276403020002004.

Bennett, A., and Burke, P. J. 2017. "Re/Conceptualising Time and Temporality: An Exploration of Time in Higher Education." *Discourse: Studies in the Cultural Politics of Education* 39 (6): 913–925. https://doi.org/10.1080/01596306.2017.1312285.

Bourke, R. 2017. "Self-Assessment to Incite Learning in Higher Education: Developing Ontological Awareness." *Assessment and Evaluation in Higher Education* 43 (5): 827–839. https://doi.org/10.1080/02602938.2017.1411881.

Bunbury, S. 2020. "Disability in Higher Education – Do Reasonable Adjustments Contribute to an Inclusive Curriculum?" *International Journal of Inclusive Education* 24 (9): 964–979. https://doi.org/10.1080/13603116.2018.1503347.

Corcoran, T., and Thomas, M. K. E. 2021. "School-Wide Positive Behaviour Support as Evidence-Making Interventions." *Research in Education* 11 (1): 108–125. https://doi.org/10.1177/00345237211034884.

Dawson, P., Bearman, M., Boud, D. J., Hall, M., Molloy, E. K., and Bennett, S. 2013. "Assessment Might Dictate the Curriculum, but What Dictates Assessment?" *Teaching and Learning Inquiry* 1 (1): 107–111.

Department of Education and Training. 2021. "Individual Education Plans (IEPs) Policy." Last modified 22 November 2021. https://www2.education.vic.gov.au/pal/individual-education-plans-ieps/policy.

Dolmage, J. T. 2017. "Disability on Campus, on Film: Framing the Failures of Higher Education." In *Academic Ableism: Disability and Higher Education*, edited by Jay T. Dolmage, 153–184. Ann Arbor: University of Michigan Press. https://www.jstor.org/stable/j.ctvr33d50.

Ellis, C., van Haeringen, K., Harper, R., Bretag, T., Zucker, I., McBride, S., Rozenberg, P., Newton, P., and Saddiqui, S. 2019. "Does Authentic Assessment Assure Academic Integrity? Evidence from Contract Cheating Data." *Higher Education Research and Development* 39 (3): 454–469. https://doi.org/10.1080/07294360.2019.1680956.

Gilovich, T., Kerr, M., and Medvec, V. H. 1993. "Effect of Temporal Perspective on Subjective Confidence." *Journal of Personality and Social Psychology* 64 (4): 552–560. http://doi.org/10.1037/0022-3514.64.4.552.

Harrison, M., Lancaster, K., and Rhodes, T. 2021. ""A Matter of Time": Evidence-Making Temporalities of Vaccine Development in the COVID-19 Media Landscape." *Time and Society* 31 (1): 132–154. https://doi.org/10.1177/0961463x211032201.

Hathcoat, J. D., Penn, J. D., Barnes, L. L. B., and Comer, J. C. 2016. "A Second Dystopia in Education: Validity Issues in Authentic Assessment Practices." *Research in Higher Education* 57 (7): 892–912. https://doi.org/10.1007/s11162-016-9407-1.

Jackson, A. Y., and Mazzei, L. 2011. *Thinking with Theory in Qualitative Research: Viewing Data across Multiple Perspectives*. London: Taylor and Francis.

Latour, B. 2004. "Why Has Critique Run Out of Steam? From Matters of Fact to Matters of Concern." *Critical Inquiry* 30 (2): 225–248. https://doi.org/10.1086/421123.

Lingard, B., and Thompson, G. 2017. "Doing Time in the Sociology of Education." *British Journal of Sociology of Education* 38 (1): 1–12. https://doi.org/10.1080/01425692.2016.1260854.

McArthur, J. 2016. "Assessment for Social Justice: The Role of Assessment in Achieving Social Justice." *Assessment and Evaluation in Higher Education* 41 (7): 967–981. https://doi.org/10.1080/02602938.2015.1053429.

Rhodes, T., and Lancaster, K. 2019. "Evidence-Making Interventions in Health: A Conceptual Framing." *Social Science and Medicine* 238: 1–12. https://doi.org/10.1016/j.socscimed.2019.112488.

Sadler, I., and Reimann, N. 2017. "Variation in the Development of Teachers' Understandings of Assessment and Their Assessment Practices in Higher Education." *Higher Education Research and Development* 37 (1): 131–144. https://doi.org/10.1080/07294360.2017.1344199.

Simons, M., and Masschelein, J. 2015. "Inclusive Education for Exclusive Pupils: A Critical Analysis of the Government of the Exceptional." In *Foucault and the Government of Disability*, edited by Shelley Tremain, 208–228. Ann Arbor, MI: University of Michigan Press. https://doi.org/10.3998/mpub.8265343.

Spina, N. 2018. ""Once upon a Time": Examining Ability Grouping and Differentiation Practices in Cultures of Evidence-Based Decision-Making." *Cambridge Journal of Education* 49 (3): 329–348. https://doi.org/10.1080/0305764x.2018.1533525.

St. Pierre, E. A., Jackson, A. Y., and Mazzei, L. A. 2016. "New Empiricisms and New Materialisms." *Cultural Studies ↔ Critical Methodologies* 16 (2): 99–110. https://doi.org/10.1177/1532708616638694.

Vostal, F. 2014. "Academic Life in the Fast Lane: The Experience of Time and Speed in British Academia." *Time and Society* 24 (1): 71–95. https://doi.org/10.1177/0961463x13517537.

Whitburn, B., and Corcoran, T. 2019. "Ontologies of Inclusion and Teacher Education." In *Global Perspectives on Inclusive Teacher Education*, edited by Bethany M. Rice, 1–15. Hershley, PA: IGI Global.

Whitburn, B., and Thomas, M. K. E. 2021. "A Right to Be Included: The Best and Worst of Times for Learners with Disabilities." *Scandinavian Journal of Disability Research* 23(1): 104–113. https://doi.org/10.16993/sjdr.772.

SECTION II

Meso contexts of assessment for inclusion: Institutional and community perspectives

8

INCLUSIVE ASSESSMENT

Recognising difference through communities of praxis

Penny Jane Burke

Assessment is a relation of power in higher education. It is not only about the criteria, the methods, or the grading systems; it is also about how we make sense of potential, capability, and belonging as assessors and assessed. It is about how experiences of assessment become part of our subjective relationship to higher education, knowledge, and knowing. Because assessment is entrenched in the many institutionalised judgements we encounter as knowers and learners – even when this is an experience of exclusion from higher education – it is embodied in our sense of self. Those involved in assessment processes are also subjected to the technologies of assessment in higher education; for example, through performance review processes, peer review practices, and through our power and participation in the assessment of students. Thus, developing a strong, critical reflexivity about how we experience this and enact it might help us to re/form our assessment practices especially when we are explicitly and formally engaged in making judgements of others. This chapter illuminates how unequal power relations and taken-for-granted values and practices shape assessment, which makes inclusivity an ongoing challenge. I introduce the concept of "Communities of Praxis" as a framework to engage with these challenges and work collaboratively towards developing possibilities for assessment for inclusion.

Experiences and practices of assessment take place in time and space. The discourses of meritocracy, aptitude, and capability are longstanding features of assessment in higher education, and are central to national level assessment systems, such as the Australian Tertiary Admissions Rank (ATAR) and the American Scholastic Aptitude Test (SAT). Such systems are built on notions of standardisation, objectivity, and the commitment to equality of opportunity, but the decontextualised frameworks underpinning these systems are unable to grapple with the inequities of educational systems. Indeed, what merit means and how it is judged across time and space has been extensively researched and

DOI: 10.4324/9781003293101-11

shown to be fluid, dynamic, and tied to unequal relations of power. Karabel's (2006) meticulous study of "the hidden history of admission and exclusion" is an outstanding examination of the exclusionary power of meritocracy embedded in national systems such as the SAT. He traces in fine detail how the "definition of 'merit' changed fundamentally several times" over twentieth-century America (Karabel 2006, 4). Yet, what is often absent are explicit discussions about the relationship between assessment and the historical struggles over the right to higher education, who is seen to belong, and how merit, aptitude, and capability are discursively produced. These discourses powerfully shape – and limit – our pedagogical imaginations about what kinds of assessment frameworks and practices are possible.

Some conceptual tools for reimagining assessment

Drawing from Barbara Adam (1998), I use the concept of timescapes to extend the notion of the landscape of higher education and to foreground how time and space are critical and related dimensions of inequality in higher education. The discourses, practices, and relations by which time and space are unequally structured, managed, and negotiated become more visible through the lens of timescapes. This is crucial as temporal inequalities play out in and through everyday experiences and practices but are often reduced to notions of effective "time management" skills (Bennett and Burke 2018). Time management tends to ignore that students negotiate assessment from a range of different and unequal positions in relation to time and space. This might include having to negotiate the demands of paid and unpaid labour while studying, having no quiet space to study or having a long commute to university via unreliable or unsafe transportation. Despite this, the articulation of experiences of time tends to be limited by discourses of individualism and management, constructed as mechanistic and technocratic, whereby simply providing staff and students with the training to develop the skills to effectively manage their time is identified as a central focus of equity and inclusion. This reinforces deficit discourses of the problem, which are often perceived as simply fixed by better time management skills. Related to this is the problematic idea of "teaching smarter", which implies spending less time supporting students who are constructed as "needy". This severely limits pedagogical opportunities to fully engage students with assessment processes, and to demystify academic literacy practices and expectations, reproducing inequities and exclusion (Lillis 2001). Rather, a remedial approach to study skills is problematically bolted on, leaving little time and space for students from under-represented backgrounds to decode the unfamiliar academic practices that underpin specific assessment frameworks within a field of study and are crucial to inclusion.

In the body of my work (Burke 2002, 2012), and through the development of the Centre of Excellence for Equity in Higher Education (CEEHE) (Burke 2020), I have foregrounded *praxis* as key to building what I call transformative equity, which is underpinned by social justice theories/practices. Praxis brings theory and practice together in ongoing conversation, creating new relationalities to time and space that prioritise reflection-action and action-reflection (Burke 2002, 2012) drawing on Freire's significant work (Freire 1970). This differs significantly from hegemonic deficit models of equity which focus primarily on the remediation of the supposed deficiencies of students associated with equity policies. A praxis-based framework enables the collective interrogation of taken-for-granted values, assumptions, and perspectives (Lather 1991) that are embedded in institutionalised histories of exclusion to generate new forms of research-informed practice and practice-informed research (Burke 2020).

Praxis-based approaches enable the disruption of deficit models that reproduce impoverished notions of inclusion and diversity that locate the problem of equity in the supposed deficiencies of the individual. I have argued in my work (e.g., Burke 2012) that such deficit models lean heavily into problematic and decontextualised forms of student support based on remediation rather than to tackle the complex dynamics of power and knowledge in the formation of studenthood; the recognition of capability that is central to a sense of belonging in higher education and for which assessment plays a major role (Burke et al. 2015). It is through praxis-oriented approaches that we can grapple with these complexities and move away from simplistic deficit models of equity to more transformative social justice ones.

So, what do I mean by an impoverished view of inclusion? My body of research has demonstrated that "inclusion" often operates as a form of symbolic violence; a way of regulating difference and constructing difference as Other (Said 1993) and as a problem to be fixed (Burke 2015). That is, inclusion becomes an institutional mechanism to "transform" students seen as Other or different to fit into the dominant values, practices, and ways of being in order that they are recognisable as capable university students within specific disciplines and/or fields of study.

Assessment is a technology (I use technology here in a Foucauldian sense, see Foucault 1977) that reinforces such forms of symbolic violence; a technology that excludes those who are misrecognised as incapable of meeting the criteria, which is designed to aid assessors to rank, grade, judge, categorise, hierarchise, and/or measure the assessed (Burke 2002, 90–91). The assessment criteria are presented as neutral and transparent tools for the assessor to make fair judgements, rather than as embedded in the shared values, assumptions, and perspectives of the *community of practice* in which the assessment has been designed and conducted.

Assessment generated in communities of practice

Communities of practice (CoP) (Lave and Wenger 1991) are significant spaces in which our academic, discipline-based, and professional knowledge is legitimated and developed. However, inclusion in the community of practice emphasises that which is shared rather than grappling with ontological differences and epistemological contestations that generate exclusions, Othering and not belonging (Burke 2020). In the context of contemporary higher education timescapes, including the intensified pace of work, knowledge-production and assessment experienced by both staff and students, there is little time/space to interrogate our taken-for-granted assumptions, values, and perspectives through forms of *ethical reflexivity.* I offer the concept "ethical reflexivity" to signal an ongoing commitment to examining one's situatedness in complex relations of power and to critically consider the values, assumptions, and perspectives that shape key higher education discourses and practices, including assessment. This involves a deep and sustained ethical orientation to generating inclusive assessment.

Although communities of practice are important sites in which academic, disciplinary, and professional knowledge is shared, formed, and developed, the implicit sense of knowing of the collective body often undermines the capacity to exercise ethical reflexivity about how these ontological and epistemological framings might be experienced as exclusive to other bodies (of knowledge and people). An example is that we often attempt to "decolonise the curriculum" without attention to the Western- and White-centric epistemologies that frame a discipline. Or we often aim to create inclusive practices whilst requiring students from diverse communities to conform to the implicit (and explicit) values embedded institutionally without careful attention to the different values at play that relate to the diverse experiences and communities that student identities are situated in.

Assessment is embedded in the communities of practice (e.g., Maths, Psychology, Sociology, Science, Arts, etc.) in which our mutual knowledge provides important epistemic foundations and developments, providing significant and meaningful spaces of shared understanding, belonging, and identity. This mutual knowledge can afford important opportunities towards developing forms of inclusive assessment. However, communities of practice also produce significant forms of exclusion and misrecognition often realised through explicit assessment practices, undermining students' sense of capability, success, identity, and belonging (Burke et al. 2015). The tendency to (mis)represent assessment as neutral, fair, and value-free leads to the reproduction of inequalities through the erasure of the implicit knowledge, values, and perspectives that frame it. There is thus a circularity of the legitimation of the knowledge, values, and perspectives of those who are included in the community of practice and who are in a position to determine the assessment framework in the first place.

These exclusionary assessment practices are entangled in relations of inequality in ways that are often invisible, particularly in the absence of close analysis and ethical reflexivity. Social justice theories provide important analytical and reflexive tools to bring to light the exclusionary dimensions of assessment practice otherwise unseen. Furthermore, moving away from theory and practice and towards "praxis" (Burke 2002; Freire 1970; Lather 1991) enables new dialogical spaces of critical reflection/action to support the development of social justice oriented forms of "inclusive assessment" (Burke et al. 2015).

A case study: *Art for a Few*

The research project *Art for a Few* (Burke and McManus 2009) provides a compelling case to bring such exclusionary processes to light. As part of this research, we observed 70 selection interviews across five UK higher education institutions, which consisted of the pre-interview assessment of the art portfolio, the interview itself and the post-interview assessment. These technologies of assessment, ranking and judgement, taking place within particular communities of practice, were revealed to reproduce gendered, classed and racialised exclusions. This was most evident in our observation of the selection interview process of Nina (pseudonym), a young Black British woman from a poor inner-city area who was applying for a BA in Fashion. Nina met the academic assessment criteria, and her art portfolio was ranked as good. However, when she replied to the standard interview question about major artistic influences, she cited hip-hop and explained that she would like to design sports tops. Her interview was cut short and she was rejected immediately. Shortly after, a young middle-class, White British male, cited a range of contemporary artists as his influences and he was offered a place, despite having significantly poorer qualifications than Nina, including having failed his General Certificate in Secondary Education in Art. In their post-interview discussion, the assessment panel formally justified their decision in reference to Nina's portfolio, which they claimed later to be ranked as "below average". They also referred to Nina's "immaturity" due to her desire to stay home while at university and negatively judged her attire as unfashionable.

Nina is misrecognised as lacking fashion flair; despite wearing similar clothing to the White female candidates offered places, Nina was judged as deficient in her embodied performance of self. Through the technologies of assessment of the selection interview, which included what were seen as transparent, fair, and standardised questions, Nina was judged as immature because she did not want to move away from home to study at university. The White male candidate embodied the values and practices embedded in the assessment questions; he expressed that leaving home is key to the university experience, he dressed and spoke in a way that signalled talent, and he referenced contemporary artists and designers, all of which was viewed as signifying his potential and creativity. This case study demonstrates how the shared values, practices, and knowledge within a community of practice (in this case Fashion) can unwittingly work to reproduce classed, gendered, and racialised inequalities, misrecognitions, and exclusions in ways that appear to the assessment panel as fair, objective, and transparent.

Following publication of *Art for a Few* (Burke and McManus 2009), we disseminated the report widely holding workshops with those teaching arts across higher education institutions. This led one program team, responsible for one of the most selective fine arts programs in England, to dig deep into their assumptions and taken-for-granted practices. Engaging with the research, they looked closely at their admissions, pedagogical and assessment practices, and a new perspective emerged that deeply concerned them. They realised they had no representation from the immediate schools, colleges, and communities in their local area and the student profile was homogenous – mainly White, middle-class students from across more affluent areas in England. The programme team started to work closely with the Widening Participation Unit, local schools and colleges, and developed regular program team meetings to collectively reform the ways they thought about what counted as potential, talent, and capability. Working with the analysis provided by *Art for a Few*, they interrogated their values, perspectives, and assessment practices. Through this, they developed inclusive capacity to accommodate diverse artistic expressions that better represented the university's under-represented local communities.

Sustaining this commitment to transformation of the program over time, their student profile has dramatically shifted to a highly diverse student profile with strong representation from the institution's immediate local communities. The curriculum developed organically as new artistic expressions emerging from their now diverse student communities were recognised, valued, and represented. The programme team effectively developed what I call a *community of praxis* in which they exercised ethical reflexivity through social justice perspectives bringing new forms of practice to play and thus transforming the program.

Towards communities of praxis

Considering the benefits of working with, through and against the communities of practice in which our assessment practices are differently situated, I argue for the value of building and sustaining *communities of praxis*. In order to generate time and space for creative, collaborative, and innovative development of inclusive assessment, we need to draw from our points of connection, supporting our sense of belonging and purpose. However, in order to extend this sense of belonging in ways that challenge harmful forms of institutionalised misrecognition, we need to attend to the politics of difference, perhaps discovering that difference becomes a pedagogical resource for re-imagining inclusive assessment. In resituating assessment through the lens of difference, and through building communities of praxis, we might generate counter-hegemonic timescapes to create meaningful forms of inclusion.

Creating counter-hegemonic timescapes through communities of praxis enables us to collectively grapple with the ways that inclusion can so easily slip into being a mechanism of regulation, misrecognition and the exclusion of difference, coercing students to fit into or conform to the hegemonic ways of being, knowing, and doing (Archer 2003). Inclusion therefore demands the recognition of difference through ethical reflexivity (Burke 2015), rather than the regulation and exclusion of difference, or the pernicious willingness to transform those seen to be different into the preferred ways of being as framed by a community of practice. This is undoubtedly challenging and requires deep work within our communities of praxis, examining the taken-for-granted ontological and epistemological foundations that underpin assessment frameworks. I suggest that we draw from Paulo Freire's concept of the circle of knowledge to do this deep, reflexive, praxis-oriented work. This circle of knowledge brings together knowledge emerging from across difference, including the knowledge of the assessor but also knowledge within community contexts, to transform the limitations of how knowledge is legitimated. Such approaches strive to open time and space for the cyclical and reciprocal reformation of knowledge and knowing in the commitment to inclusion and diversity. This is a process of bringing together disciplinary knowledge with the heterogeneous knowledge of those groups, communities, and societies that have often been denied representation in higher education curricula. This is demonstrated clearly in the example provided above of the Fine Art team's sustained commitment to bringing together in new ways marginalised bodies of art with hegemonic bodies of art, in a project of transformative equity.

Engaging a multi-dimensional social justice framework for inclusive assessment

Nancy Fraser (2008) argues that social justice requires attention to, and the holding together of, redistribution, recognition, and representation, with a focus on enabling parity of participation. Understanding these three dimensions of social justice as interwoven is crucial for reconceptualising "inclusion" in higher education timescapes and assessment practices, challenging hegemonic discourses (Burke, Crozier, and Misiaszek 2017).

In keeping with Fraser's position, inclusive assessment requires holding together the multi-dimensions of justice, even when these create tensions, dilemmas, and challenges. Following Fraser (1997, 2003, 2008), it is crucial to shift attention away from deficit discourses with its problematic focus on the remediation of what individual students are seen to lack. Instead, we need to re/situate our communities of praxis through practices of curiosity and unknowing (Lather 2007) as part of grappling with difference and multi-dimensional injustices. Through this sustained and collaborative grappling, and by drawing on the theoretical tools provided through social justice frameworks, we might open counter-hegemonic timescapes for thinking and doing inclusion with and through difference. This requires *sustained* and *reflexive* processes; not one-off programmatic design and delivery. This means that the community of praxis think through and develop practices that address the inter-connected dimensions of distribution, recognition, and representation.

Inclusion is more complex than overcoming barriers through access to financial and material resources, as important as these resources are. This one-dimensional approach to inclusion is flawed because it is unable to grapple with the more insidious dimensions of misrecognition and misrepresentation. Processes of misrecognition are about the institutionally legitimatised values and judgements that are imposed on the misrecognised person in ways that effectively exclude them from inclusion (Burke 2012). In order to have parity of participation, a student must have access to the resources and high-quality pedagogical opportunities that enable access to esoteric practices and institutionally legitimised epistemologies. The students must also though be *recognised* and have *access to representation* as a fully valued member of the community (Burke, Crozier, and Misiaszek 2017) which means the inclusion of their experiences, knowledge, and ways of knowing.

This requires valuing different ways of knowing and being and addressing the historical inequalities that have shaped processes of institutional legitimacy. It is also important to capture the affective, emotional, subjective, and lived experiences of misrecognition and misrepresentation, that are felt in and through the body as forms of symbolic violence and injury on the self (Burke 2012; McNay 2008, 150). This often leads to feelings of shame and fear (Ahmed 2004; Burke 2017) and is not a matter of lack of confidence but of sustained experiences of symbolic violence over time.

Success in higher education depends on navigating assessment practices that operate to recognise a student as "successful" or not. The student must decode (often esoteric) forms of academic practice that are granted legitimacy through the community of practice in which the assessment is located. Students from socially privileged contexts often have access to a range of resources that enable them to decode how to demonstrate academic capability through assessment practices. The successful student must first understand how to write, speak, construct an argument, hypothesis, and read (and so forth) in ways that is recognised as institutionally legitimate forms of practice within a particular community of practice.

These academic practices are highly contextual, requiring students to develop complex skills of decoding expectations and conventions across the different communities of practice in which they are studying. Academic practices (e.g., constructing an argument, debating, formulating a problem, presenting with clarity and coherence, bring critical, etc.) tend to be misrepresented as neutral, decontextualised sets of technical skills and literacy that can be straightforwardly assessed (Lillis 2001) and that students from disadvantaged social contexts simply lack. That these academic practices are historically embedded in classed, racialised, and gendered ways of doing is erased from view thus perpetuating exclusive forms of what is named "inclusion".

Final reflections

I have argued that resituating assessment through the lens of difference, and through building communities of praxis, we might generate new timescapes to consider what assessment-for-inclusion means in the context of our fields and how we might affect social justice transformation. I suggest this requires orientations towards social justice praxis; the bringing together of theoretical insights on the working of knowledge, power, and inequality with commitments to transformative forms of practice. I have also suggested that moving towards communities of praxis might open counter-hegemonic timescapes to grapple with the ways that assessment can unwittingly become a mechanism of regulation, misrecognition, and the exclusion of difference. Inclusion is often a mechanism in which students are coerced to fit into or conform to the hegemonic ways of being, knowing and doing or to risk exclusion. My position is that striving towards inclusive assessment demands the recognition of difference, rather than its regulation and exclusion, presenting us with significant challenges and possibilities to spark our pedagogical imaginations.

I recognise that this requires more than the development of communities of praxis – it demands transformation institutionally, epistemologically, and ontologically – and that is deeply challenging. However, I suggest that forming communities of praxis is a good starting point – to generate timescapes for us to work differently together and through this collective praxis to challenge the competitive, individualistic, performative, and instrumentalist discourses, practice, and structures at play.

So what shape might an actual community of praxis take? An example is the Excellence in Teaching for Equity in Higher Education (ETEHE) program. This program was developed to redress the misframing of equity as a remedial project located outside of the core work of education and to create critical timescapes and conceptual resources to engage participants in the complexity of making sense of and generating inclusive practices across a range of disciplinary fields. ETEHE opens up reflexive spaces of ethical praxis, deepening participants' engagement with equity as researchers-practitioners. In generating collaborative communities of praxis, institutional, community-based, and personal transformation is facilitated through processes of peer exchange to co-produce meaning and practice. ETEHE redistributes resources (research funding, mentorship, space, and time) for a number of project teams to develop a research project with a strong emphasis on creating social justice-oriented forms of impact. Each project team works closely together on their research with the support of a senior academic mentor, with research funding granted. As part of the ETEHE framework, each project team also joins a transdisciplinary community of praxis, which brings ETEHE participants together to focus time and energy on the challenges and dilemmas emerging from their specific and collective projects. The meetings of the community of praxis are sustained over time, to develop peer mentoring spaces and rich opportunities for critical exchange, interrogation of assumptions and identification of the possibilities for transformative practice. The space facilitates dialogue across disciplinary, epistemological, and ontological differences and time to consider the contested meanings of equity and the implications of these for practice. Although this has provoked difficult discussions and problematic issues, the space and time of the community of praxis has allowed for participants to work through these differences together. One of the difficult dimensions of this approach is to accept that there are simple answers and that working with and through difference in transdisciplinary and collaborative communities of praxis requires that we "stay with the trouble" (Haraway 2016) of developing inclusive assessment in collaborative timescapes.

Staying with the trouble cultivates an orientation towards ongoing questioning through curiosity and a form of unknowing (Lather 2007). In the spirit of generating possibilities for dialogue within communities of praxis beyond this chapter, I end my reflections by offering some questions for further consideration:

- How might we create the time and space to interrogate the values and assumptions about the purpose(s) of HE and the right to higher education in relation to assessment structures, practices, and inclusion?
- How might we more clearly articulate – and question – how we understand potential, capability, and success? Who judges, how and with what implications?
- What might it mean to work *with* rather than *against* difference? How does this translate to assessment practices?
- What are the opportunities to build on our communities of practice to recreate these as *communities of praxis*? In what ways and contexts could these be of value?
- How might we cultivate *counter-hegemonic timescapes* and collectively challenge the hegemonic timescapes of contemporary higher education? What are the possibilities? What are the challenges?

By bringing ETEHE participants together within communities of praxis, their research praxis enabled them to address such questions through their projects and with their mentors together in the workshops. This opened new timescapes for ethical reflexivity to reimagine inclusivity not through the lens of deficit and/or remediation but through the collective interrogation of whose knowledges, values, and experiences are included and excluded through assessment frameworks.

References

Adam, B. 1998. *Timescapes of Modernity*. London: Routledge.

Ahmed, S. 2004. *The Cultural Politics of Emotion*. New York, NY: Routledge.

Archer, L. 2003. *Race, Masculinity and Schooling: Muslim Boys and Education*. Berkshire, MA: Open University Press.

Bennett, A., and Burke, P. J. 2018. "Re/conceptualising Time and Temporality: An Exploration of Time in Higher Education." *Discourse: Studies in the Cultural Politics of Education* 39 (6): 913–925. https://doi.org/10.1080/01596306.2017.1312285.

Burke, P. J. 2002. *Accessing Education Effectively Widening Participation*. Stoke-on-Trent: Trentham Books.

Burke, P. J. 2012. *The Right to Higher Education: Beyond Widening Participation*. London: Routledge.

Burke, P. J. 2015. "Re/imagining Higher Education Pedagogies: Gender, Emotion and Difference." *Teaching in Higher Education* 20 (4): 388–401. https://doi.org/10.1080/13562517.2015.1020782.

Burke, P. J. 2017. "Difference in Higher Education Pedagogies. Gender, Emotion and Shame." *Gender and Education* 29 (4): 430–444. https://doi.org/10.1080/09540253.2017.1308471.

Burke, P. J. 2020. "Contradiction and Collaboration in Equity and Widening Participation: In Conversation with Geoff Whitty." In *Knowledge, Policy and Practice in Education and the Struggle for Social Justice*, edited by Andrew Brown, and Emma Wisby, 233–254. London: UCL Press.

Burke, P. J., Bennett, A., Burgess, C., Gray, K., and Southgate, E. 2015. *Capability, Belonging and Equity in Higher Education*. Callaghan: University of Newcastle. https://nova.newcastle.edu.au/vital/access/services/Download/uon:32939/ATTACHMENT02?view=true.

Burke, P. J., Crozier, G., and Misiaszek, L. I. 2017. *Changing Pedagogical Spaces in Higher Education: Diversity, Inequalities and Misrecognition*. London and New York: Routledge.

Burke, P. J., and McManus, J. 2009. "Art for a Few: Exclusions and Misrecognitions in Higher Education Admissions Practices." *Discourse: Studies in the Cultural Politics of Education* 32 (5): 699–712. https://doi.org/10.1080/01596306.2011.620753.

Foucault, M. 1977. *Discipline and Punish: The Birth of the Prison*. New York, NY: Random House.

Fraser, N. 1997. *Justice Interruptus: Critical Reflections on the 'Postsocialist' Condition*. London and New York: Routledge.

Fraser, N. 2003. "Social Justice in the Age of Identity Politics: Redistribution, Recognition and Participation." In *Redistribution or Recognition? A Political- Philosophical Exchange*, edited by Nancy Fraser and Alex Honneth, 7–109. London and New York: Verso.

Fraser, N. 2008. *Scales of Justice: Reimagining Political Space in a Globalizing World*. Cambridge and Malden, MA: Polity Press.

Freire, P. 1970. *Pedagogy of the Oppressed*. New York, NY: Continuum.

Haraway, D. 2016. *Staying with the Trouble: Making Kin in the Chthulucene*. Durham: Duke University Press.

Karabel, J. 2006. *The Chosen: The Hidden History of Admission and Exclusion at Harvard, Yale and Princeton*. Boston and NY: Mariner Books.

Lather, P. 1991. *Getting Smart. Feminist Research and Pedagogy with/in the Post-Modern*. New York and London: Routledge.

Lather, P. 2007. *Getting Lost. Feminist Efforts toward a Double(d) Science*. Albany, NY: State University of New York Press.

Lave, J., and Wenger, E. 1991 *Situated Learning: Legitimate Peripheral Participation*. Cambridge: Cambridge University Press.

Lillis, T. 2001. *Student Writing: Access, Regulation, Desire*. London: Routledge.

McNay, L. 2008. *Against Recognition*. Cambridge: Polity.

Said, E. 1993. *Culture and Imperialism*. London: Chatto and Windus.

9

INCLUSIVE ASSESSMENT AND AUSTRALIAN HIGHER EDUCATION POLICY

Matt Brett and Andrew Harvey

Introduction

Equity is a concept that is interwoven with concepts of underrepresentation, fairness, diversity, and inequality, defined, and measured by groups that are more likely to participate (or are included) in higher education, and groups that are less likely to participate (thereby facing exclusion). The ways in which inclusion and exclusion are understood and defined in Australian society vary over time. This book's focus on *assessment for inclusion* can be considered a contemporary and specific manifestation of concern for equity and fairness that spans the history of Australian higher education from its genesis.

To understand the possibilities of assessment for inclusion in Australian higher education it is important to understand the dominant paradigm for inclusion and exclusion, and how this is sustained through policy and practice. The chapter undertakes a policy analysis of "*assessment for inclusion*" drawing upon the social and legal frameworks of the policy analysis toolkit (Althaus, Bridgman, and Davis 2018) to understand how assessment for inclusion is framed, aligned, implemented, and evaluated within higher education policy.

Australia introduced an equity policy framework in the 1990s that prioritised access to higher education for designated equity groups, a framework that remains intact 30 years later (Harvey, Burnheim, and Brett 2016). A major feature of the equity framework is an equity performance indicator that captures and reports data on designated equity group access, participation, success, and retention (Martin 2016a).

The framework and complementary subsequent policies such as creation of the demand-driven system have been remarkably successful in expanding access (Zacharias 2017). Notwithstanding successes in increasing participation, there are nevertheless enduring challenges with the equity framework. Equitable

DOI: 10.4324/9781003293101-12

access to undergraduate study does not flow through to access to postgraduate study (Grant-Smith, Irmer, and Mayes 2020). There is variance in equity group access, participation, success, retention, and completion across universities (Pitman et al. 2020). Some disciplines are more inclusive than others, demonstrating higher rates of equity group participation than others. Some disciplines formalise the exclusion of students with specific characteristics through publishing inherent requirements (Boucher 2021). Student success and retention is persistently lower for designated equity groups (Department of Education Skills and Employment (DESE) 2022). Finally, graduate outcomes vary substantially across student groups (Harvey, Cakitaki, and Brett 2018), with some sub-groups recording relatively low employment rates upon graduation (Harvey, Szalkowicz, and Luckman 2020).

These data confirm a paradox of equity and inclusion in higher education. Equity group participation rates steadily increase, suggesting a trend towards inclusion, but coincide with sustained disparities in success, retention, and completion indicative of entrenched exclusion. These disparities are most pronounced for students with disabilities and Indigenous students (DESE 2022), through disparities indicative of exclusion at different points of the student lifecycle. For example, despite relatively low success and retention rates, the Graduate Outcomes Survey reveals that Indigenous graduates earn more than all graduates irrespective of course level (Grant-Smith, Irmer, and Mayes 2020). By contrast, students with a disability record the lowest graduate employment outcomes of any equity group. While graduate outcomes are affected by several influences outside the university's scope (Harvey, Cakitaki, and Brett 2018), specific government policies and funding clearly affect the participation, success, and outcomes of student equity groups. These policies enable focused examination of the relationships between equity, inclusion, and assessment.

Assessment practices themselves are likely to be central to the equity paradox of rising access alongside continuing inequities in success, retention, and outcomes. International evidence suggests that differences in grades among students of different ethnicities and backgrounds cannot be explained by prior academic achievement. The attainment gap between Black, Asian and Minority Ethnic (BAME) students and White students in the United Kingdom (UK), for example, is longstanding, unexplained by prior achievement, and variable across fields of education (AdvanceHE 2017; Cramer 2021). Similar findings in the United States and elsewhere suggest that some assessment practices are exclusionary and lead to variable outcomes across a range of different student groups. Increasing the inclusivity of assessment is thus central to the broader project of increasing student equity in higher education.

This chapter examines contemporary Commonwealth policies relating to higher education for references to equity, inclusion, and assessment. We identify policies where these terms are represented, acknowledging that these terms are contested but avoid aligning with particular definitions beyond those utilised within policy. Our policy analysis includes higher education standards, higher education financing, university enabling legislation, and institutional assessment policies. This chapter also considers the role of non-higher education specific policies influencing inclusive assessment, particularly disability discrimination legislation. We conclude with opportunities for strengthening higher education policies to advance inclusive assessment.

Commonwealth higher education policy

Higher education standards

To deliver higher education courses in Australia, institutions must be registered with the Tertiary Education Quality and Standards Agency (TEQSA). TEQSA has the primary function of regulating higher education against the *Higher Education Standards Framework (Threshold Standards) 2011*.

There is no requirement to be inclusive or adopt inclusive assessment in the Threshold Standards. There are, however, requirements to accommodate "diversity and equity", contextualised by reference to identified underrepresented groups, and specific reference to admission, participation, and completion of Indigenous students. Whilst diversity and equity are distinct and non-interchangeable terms, the manner in which the Threshold Standards juxtaposes these terms highlights that equity and inclusion are part of a broader overlapping lexicon.

The framing of equity and inclusion within the Threshold Standards highlights the significance of the equity paradigm, whilst simultaneously failing to engage with assessment as a fundamental property of the higher education system. Another Threshold Standard is that learning outcomes are specified and assessed with validity. There is no reference within the "learning outcomes and assessment" standard nor related guidance notes (TEQSA 2017a) as to how assessment might be structured to be equitable or inclusive, nor how it might interact with equity and diversity standards.

Access is generally prioritised within Commonwealth policy, with little attention to learning experiences of designated equity groups. One might see each standard as a holistic set of equivalent requirements, but some standards exert more influence than others. For example, efforts to decolonise the curriculum have been evident for decades (see Anderson et al. 1998), but only now do we see evidence of success in integrating Indigenous knowledges in the curriculum (Harvey and Russell-Mundine 2019). This integration of Indigenous knowledge in the curriculum can be understood as a means of bringing distinct equity and assessment focused standards into coherence. Generating coherence between equity and assessment standards is challenging because diversity and equity considerations are, as evidenced by use in TEQSA registration processes, non-core, and have limited influence over learning outcomes and assessment standards. These core standards have proven resistant to change, and their primacy is validated and reinforced through regulation and registration processes.

Universities are assessed for compliance with the Threshold Standards through cyclical registration processes. Application guides and evidentiary requirements for re-registration make no reference to diversity and equity standards (TEQSA 2017b). Course accreditation proposals are a core evidentiary requirement for re-registration, and this directly relates to learning outcomes and assessment standards, but again with no specific reference to inclusion. The registration process positions diversity and equity standards as non-core and there are few if any consequences arising from systemic exclusion of students from designated equity groups.

Higher education financing

Registration with TEQSA makes Australian universities eligible for public subsidies mediated by the *Higher Education Support Act (HESA) 2003* (Cth). HESA objectives embed a focus on equity of access. A small proportion of HESA subsidies are distributed for "Grants to promote equality of opportunity in higher education". There are several grant programs that distribute funds based on enrolments by designated equity groups. This approach entrenches a focus on access rather than experience or success.

One word that is not found within HESA is "inclusion". We do observe, however, that legislative instruments established under HESA have progressively introduced the language of inclusion. For example, Indigenous funding is currently contingent on requirements that include inclusion of Indigenous knowledge in the curricula (*Indigenous Student Assistance Grants 2017* Cth s13.c.). Earlier iterations of grants made under HESA to support Indigenous students made funding conditional on strategies to support access, participation, retention, and success (*Other Grant Guidelines Education 2012* Cth). Grants made under HESA for disability have also emphasised the importance of inclusive teaching and learning practices (*Amendment No. 3 to the Other Grants Guidelines 2006* Cth 1.55.5.1). The amounts of money allocated for inclusion-related purposes via Indigenous and disability grants represent a small proportion of system financing, which limits their potential impact on the broader system (Brett 2018).

Victorian government higher education policy

Space constraints prohibit a detailed account of equity, inclusion, and assessment in higher education policy across each Australian state, but attention here is placed on the State of Victoria. Each university operating in Victoria is the product of legislation of the Victorian parliament. Diverse legislative histories and inconsistencies were standardised across Victoria in 2009. A distinctive narrative for each institution was prepared as a short preamble for each Act. The preamble was followed by standardised text around the purposes, functions, and processes of governance in each institution. Equity and social justice are referenced in the standard text across each Act, as are commitments to Aboriginal and/or Torres Strait Islander people.

The preambles of Victorian public university Acts reveal distinct narratives for each institution's mission, history, and orientation. The preambles highlight specific institutional priorities on comprehensiveness, technology, technological education, specific communities, international orientation, equity, social justice, progressiveness, serving disadvantaged learners, and inclusion.

Paralleling observations made about Commonwealth policy, equity and inclusion sits at the margins of a dominant paradigm. University Acts adopt standardised text of university purpose and membership of governing bodies. Whilst there is interest in matters of diversity in the composition of University Councils (Kang, Cheng, and Gray 2007), including Indigenous representation (Weerasinghe 2021), Victorian university Acts are silent on matters of diversity.

A defining characteristic of Australian universities is that they are set up as self-governing and self-accrediting institutions (Orr 2012). This enables them to make policy within policy frameworks set and monitored by council. These policies cannot ignore Commonwealth policy requirements nor localised interests of State governments. Nonetheless, there remains significant latitude for university policies to be framed in line with institution-specific preferences. We next examine how equity and inclusion features in publicly accessible policies of Victorian universities, with specific reference to assessment.

Victorian university assessment policies

Assessment policies for eight Victorian universities were examined for references to equity and inclusion (Table 9.1). Each institution is referred to by the distinctive orientation evident in the preamble of its Act of establishment. The specific title of the policy mediating assessment is described, along with policies mediating legally mandated reasonable adjustments. References to Indigenous students and students with disability within the relevant assessment policy are described. Text from assessment policies is presented to highlight how equity and inclusion-related concepts are phrased within assessment policies.

The majority of universities appear to be devising assessment policies with reference to each other rather than the founding, regulation or financing legislation. This approach arguably contributes to policy misalignment across the Victorian sector. Six of eight institutions do not include reference to Indigenous students in assessment policies, despite it being a feature of their mission and Threshold Standards. Conversely, six of eight institutions include reference to students with disability in assessment policy, even though this does not feature within their mission or Threshold Standards. These discrepancies highlight that policy drivers beyond higher education exert influence over universities, particularly the *Disability Discrimination Act* (1992 Cth).

Our policy analysis of the dominant funding, legislative, and policy architecture suggests that Commonwealth and State level equity and inclusion related commitments are peripheral as policy requirements, and linked to weak accountability measures. Similar claims can be made about equity and inclusion requirements of institutional assessment polices. No clauses were identified in Victorian university assessment or adjustment policies that would evaluate the efficacy of

TABLE 9.1 Equity and inclusion references in assessment policies of select Victorian universities

Victorian university	*Assessment policy title*	*Adjustment policy title*	*Indigenous reference in assessment policy*	*Disability reference in assessment policy*	*Inclusion-related policy statement within assessment policy*
Comprehensive orientation	Assessment and results policy		No	Yes	Assessment must be fair, equitable, inclusive, objective, and auditable and accessible by, and meet the needs of a diverse student population
Disadvantaged learner orientation	Assessment policy		No	No	Assessment is designed to be fair and equitable and is designed to ensure that students have an opportunity to demonstrate their achievement of learning outcomes… adjustments to assessment tasks are available to students experiencing significant disadvantage.
International orientation	Assessment and academic integrity policy		No	Yes	Assessment is designed to be fair and equitable and is designed to ensure that students have an opportunity to demonstrate their achievement of learning outcomes.
Local orientation	Assessment for learning policy	Assessment for learning – adjustments to assessment procedure	No	No	Assessment is fair and equitable … Assessment variations/adjustments and processes for allowing and recording any variations/adjustments to the stated conditions of assessment, submission and grading rules are in line with the University Student Equity and Social Inclusion Policy
Progressive orientation	Assessment (higher education courses) procedure		Yes	Yes	To ensure that all students have a consistent and fair opportunity to demonstrate their achievement of learning outcomes, alternative assessment arrangements may be provided for students with a disability or health condition.
Regional orientation	Higher education assessment policy	Disability learning access plan procedure	No	Yes	Tasks are fair and can be undertaken by a range of students with diverse background and/or additional learning needs to minimise unfair discrimination and protected attributes
Technical orientation	Assessment and assessment flexibility policy		No	Yes	Flexible, equitable, and inclusive assessment with a commitment to caring for students whose circumstances require assessment flexibility.
Technology orientation	Assessment and results policy		Yes	Yes	Ensure that assessment practices are transparent, consistent, and fair

Source: Victorian university policy library websites as of 6 March 2022.

a reasonable adjustment. Assessment policies include clauses to align and assure assessment with learning outcomes, but in no case was this explicitly connected to an evaluation of equity and inclusion policy values. One policy referred to making "reasonable and evidence-based adjustments" but this too failed to specify any explicit mechanism of how this should be implemented or evaluated. The language of "adjustment" is consistent with the *Disability Discrimination Act* Cth and *Equal Opportunity Act* (2010) Vic which embed requirements to make reasonable adjustments for students with disabilities. Whilst other attributes and characteristics are the subject of protections under Commonwealth and Victorian anti-discrimination legislation, reasonable adjustments are uniquely available to students with disabilities. This gives impetus to explore implementation and accountability in disability discrimination legislation.

Disability and higher education policy

The *Disability Discrimination Act* makes it unlawful to develop or accredit curricula that exclude a person with disability or subjects them to any other detriment. Curricula in this context include assessment. Assessment for inclusion, is thus embedded as a policy requirement. Discrimination on the basis of disability in Australian higher education may be unlawful but is commonly reported by students with disabilities as a feature of their experience. The 2018 Survey of Disability Aging and Carers (Australian Bureau of Statistics 2021) estimates that 14% of higher education students with a disability have experienced discrimination.

The Survey of Disability, Aging, and Carers does not allow us to identify whether assessment is a feature of the discrimination experienced by students with disabilities. The substantive point is that generalised requirements that make discrimination unlawful do not prevent discrimination.

The recourse available to students through the Disability Discrimination Act is complaint, with complaints that fail to be resolved through conciliation potentially considered by the Federal Court (Australian Human Rights Commission 2021). In 2018, there were a handful of complaints heard by the Federal Court (Australian Legal Information Institute 2021) relating to discrimination in education. None of these related to higher education. This may be the outcome of successful institutional complaint management systems. However, we suggest that it is at least in part a systemic flaw in how accountability is framed for inclusion-related policy objectives.

The general absence of case law on higher education and disability makes it hard to make specific claims about the extent to which legal requirements for inclusive assessment are upheld. We do, however, have empirical evidence on how universities are complying with other requirements of the Disability Discrimination Act that might be extrapolated to assessment.

Website accessibility is a legal requirement under the Disability Discrimination Act and policy commitment of universities. There is evidence of a high rate of inaccessibility associated with Australian university websites. A 2015 study reviewed accessibility requirements in three specific webpages of universities, including a selection of Australian universities (Alahmadi and Drew 2017). Thousands of accessibility errors were identified in every university website, the most common of which were the absence of alt tags for images and absence of nested headers.

These web accessibility assessments suggest that universities actual operations do not reflect institutional policy, requirements of the higher education standards framework, and legal requirements for delivering an inclusive curriculum. It is likely that weak accountability for inclusion is evident in other facets of higher education, including assessment design, implementation, and evaluation. We next consider what might be done differently to normalise more inclusive assessment practices.

Towards more inclusive Australian higher education assessment policy

A straightforward proposition in transitioning towards more inclusive Australian higher education assessment policy is that existing policy requirements be upheld. Threshold Standards for diversity and equity, for example, should be actively considered by TEQSA. It is plausible that a system wide focus on inclusive assessment could be catalysed if a university (or universities) were to have conditions placed on its registration for not meeting diversity and equity standards evidenced by lower rates of access, success, and/or completion for one or more designated equity groups.

The reporting frameworks for equity groups have maintained their core structures since being introduced three decades ago. Emphasis on group access, participation and success should be augmented with a more nuanced understanding of how inclusion and diversity play out within the student experience. Other elements of exclusion are likely to be invisible. In the UK, a Black, Asian and Minority Ethnic (BAME) attainment gap is evident, in which BAME students receive lower grades than other students, even after controlling for entrance grades and other factors such as wealth (Akinbosede 2019). Little similar analysis has been conducted in Australia. There is a vast United States (US) research and policy agenda around campus climate (e.g., University of Southern California 2017). More granular analysis of assessment and grading is possible in the United Kingdom (e.g., Universities UK 2019) and could be extended to Australia. Such data, if collected and monitored, might confirm the extent of exclusionary and discriminatory practices in assessment.

A framework for assessment of student learning outcomes to measure university performance has been proposed (Martin 2016b). This framework embeds consideration of assessments against standards for learning outcomes aligned to clusters of graduate learning outcomes commonly utilised by Australian universities. The framework integrates graduate attribute traits of equity and social justice, and Indigenous cultural understanding (Martin 2016b, 89). State

Governments can exert influence over equity, inclusion, and assessment through embedding Martin's assessment performance indicator framework in reporting requirements to State parliaments.

There are opportunities for higher education financing to exert a stronger influence on inclusive assessment. Equity grants made under HESA currently include reporting requirements that dilute their impact. PhillipsKPA (2012) found the cost of reporting for each $1,000 of funding was higher for equity grants compared to core operating grants, as high as 49 times higher for disability grants. PhillipsKPA conclude that reporting on equity activities should be consolidated with a focus on accountability. We suggest there is an opportunity to purposefully link funding for equity and inclusion with teaching and assessment policy that embed stronger accountability requirements.

Finally, there are opportunities to build a strong evidence base and culture of evaluation for reasonable adjustments. A recent review of the Disability Standards for Education (DESE 2021) was concerned with optimising access to reasonable adjustments. The review recommended a more proactive approach to making reasonable adjustments available, reducing the need for complaints. The review recognised issues of alignment across various State and Commonwealth policy frameworks.

Conclusion

We have highlighted in this chapter the misalignment of policies relating to equity, inclusion and assessment across Commonwealth, State, and institutional policies. Across each level there are shortcomings in how policy requirements are implemented and/or upheld. We suggest there is potential for greater understanding of practices influencing inclusion and exclusion, including better transparency and monitoring of grading practices and assessment outcomes within and across institutions. Moving from a reliance on individual complaints towards stronger institutional accountability is also critical, as is better regulation and enforcement of existing codes and legislation. The explicit inclusion of equity accountabilities within institutional re-registration and related requirements would also elevate the priority of inclusion. Finally, there remains a need for better education of institutional staff, from academics, support staff, and web designers through to senior managers, on the legislative requirements and moral imperatives of inclusion. This educative approach is central to recent research into disability in higher education (Pitman 2022). Much current research and practice considers specific types of assessment, technology, and activities, and their potential inclusiveness for students with a disability. However, attention is also required to understand why inclusiveness, including in assessment, appears to remain a relatively low priority for institutions and the sector at large, notwithstanding existing legislative and policy requirements. While individual assessment practices and innovations provide cause for some optimism, institutions also need to focus on the elevation of inclusion as an urgent policy priority.

References

AdvanceHE. 2017. *Equality in Higher Education: Statistical Report 2017.* https://www advance-he.ac.uk/knowledge-hub/equality-higher-education-statistical-report-2017.

Akinbosede, D. 2019. "The BAME Attainment Gap Is Not the Fault of BAME Students." *Times Higher Education*, 5 December 2019. https://www.timeshighereducation.com/opinion/bame-attainment-gap-not-fault-bame-students.

Alahmadi, T., and Drew, S. 2017. "An Evaluation of the Accessibility of Top-Ranking University Websites: Accessibility Rates from 2005 to 2015." *Journal of Open, Flexible, and Distance Learning* 21 (1): 7–24.

Althaus, C., Bridgman, P., and Davis, G. 2018. *The Australian Policy Handbook: A Practical Guide to the Policy-Making Process.* Rev. ed. Abingdon: Allen and Unwin.

Amendment No. 3 to the Other Grants Guidelines. 2006. Commonwealth of Australia. https://www.legislation.gov.au/Details/F2007L01158

Anderson, L., Singh, M., Stehbens, C., and Ryerson, L. 1998. *Equity Issues: Every University's Concern, Whose Business?: An Exploration of Universities' Inclusion of Indigenous Peoples' Rights and Interests.* Evaluations and Investigations Programme. Higher Education Division. Department of Employment, Education, Training and Youth Affairs.

Australian Bureau of Statistics. 2021. *TableBuilder, Disability, Ageing and Carers, 2018.*

Australian Human Rights Commission. 2021. *Conciliation – How It Works.* https://humanrights.gov.au/complaints/complaint-guides/conciliation-how-it-works.

Australian Legal Information Institute. 2021. *Federal Court of Australia Decisions.* http://classic.austlii.edu.au/au/cases/cth/FCA/.

Boucher, S. 2021. "Inherent Requirements and Social Work Education: Issues of Access and Equity." In *Research Anthology on Mental Health Stigma, Education, and Treatment*, edited by Information Resources Management Association 681–697. Hershey, PA, US: IGI Global.

Brett, M. 2018. *Equity Performance and Accountability.* National Centre for Student Equity in Higher Education and La Trobe University. https://www.ncsehe.edu.au/publications/equity-performance-accountability.

Cramer, L. 2021. "Equity, Diversity and Inclusion: Alternative Strategies for Closing the Award Gap between White and Minority Ethnic Students." *eLife*, 4 August 2021. https://doi.org/10.7554/eLife.58971.

Department of Education Skills and Employment. 2021. *Final Report of the 2020. Review of the Disability Standards for Education 2005.* https://www.dese.gov.au/disability-standards-education-2005/resources/final-report-2020-review-disability-standards-education-2005.

Department of Education Skills and Employment. 2022. *Higher Education Statistics – 2020 Section 16 Equity Performance Data.* https://www.dese.gov.au/higher-education-statistics/resources/2020-section-16-equity-performance-data.

Disability Discrimination Act. 1992. Commonwealth of Australia. https://www.legislation.gov.au/Details/C2022C00087.

Equal Opportunity Act. 2010. Victorian Legislation. https://www.legislation.vic.gov.au/in-force/acts/equal-opportunity-act-2010/029.

Grant-Smith, D., Irmer, B., and Mayes, R. 2020. *Equity in Postgraduate Education in Australia: Widening Participation or Widening the Gap?* Perth: National Centre for Student Equity in Higher Education, Curtin University. https://www.ncsehe.edu.au/wp-content/uploads/2020/09/GrantSmith_2020_FINAL_Web.pdf.

Harvey, A., Burnheim, C., and Brett, M. 2016. *Student Equity in Australian Higher Education: Twenty-Five Years of a Fair Chance for All.* Singapore: Springer.

Harvey, A., Cakitaki, B., and Brett, M. 2018. *Principles for Equity in Higher Education Performance Funding*. Report for the National Centre for Student Equity in Higher Education Research. Melbourne: Centre for Higher Education Equity and Diversity Research, La Trobe University. https://www.ncsehe.edu.au/wp-content/uploads/2020/04/La-Trobe-University-Performance-Funding-REPORT-28-April-2020.pdf.

Harvey, A., and Russell-Mundine, G. 2019. "Decolonising the Curriculum: Using Graduate Qualities to Embed Indigenous Knowledges at the Academic Cultural Interface." *Teaching in Higher Education* 24 (6), 789–808. http://doi.org/10.1080/13562517.2018.1508131.

Harvey, A., Szalkowicz, G., and Luckman, M. 2020. *Improving Employment and Education Outcomes for Somali Australians*. Melbourne: Centre for Higher Education Equity and Diversity Research, La Trobe University.

Higher Education Standards Framework. 2011. TEQSA. https://www.teqsa.gov.au/higher-education-standards-framework-2011.

Higher Education Support Act. 2003. Australian Government. https://www.legislation.gov.au/Details/C2022C00005.

Indigenous Student Assistance Grants Guidelines. 2017. Commonwealth of Australia. https://www.legislation.gov.au/Details/F2017L00036.

Kang, H., Cheng, M., and Gray, S. J. 2007. "Corporate Governance and Board Composition: Diversity and Independence of Australian Boards." *Corporate Governance: An International Review* 15 (2): 194–207. http://doi.org/10.1111/j.1467-8683.2007.00554.x.

Martin, L. 2016a. "Framing the Framework: The Origins of a Fair Chance for All." In *Student Equity in Australian Higher Education: Twenty-Five Years of a Fair Chance for All*, edited by Andrew Harvey, Catherine Burnheim, and Matthew Brett, 21–37. Singapore: Springer.

Martin, L. M. 2016b. "Using Assessment of Student Learning Outcomes to Measure University Performance: Towards a Viable Model." Ph.D., University of Melbourne.

Orr, J. L. 2012. "Australian Corporate Universities and the Corporations Act." *International Journal of Law and Education* 17 (2): 123–148.

Other Grants Guidelines (Education). 2012. Commonwealth of Australia. https://www.legislation.gov.au/Details/F2013C00350.

PhillipsKPA. 2012. *Review of Reporting Requirements for Universities. Final Report*. Melbourne: LH Martin Institute. https://www.phillipskpa.com.au/dreamcms/app/webroot/files/files/PhillipsKPA%20Review%20of%20University%20Reporting%20Requirements.pdf.

Pitman, T. 2022. *Supporting Persons with Disabilities to Succeed in Higher Education: Final Report*. Perth: National Centre for Student Equity in Higher Education, Curtin University.

Pitman, T., Edwards, D., Zhang, L. C., Koshy, P., and McMillan, J. 2020. "Constructing a Ranking of Higher Education Institutions Based on Equity: Is It Possible or Desirable?" *Higher Education* 80 (4): 605–624. http://doi.org/10.1007/s10734-019-00487-0.

Tertiary Education Quality and Standards Agency. 2017a. *Guidance Note: Course Design (including Learning Outcomes and Assessment) Version 1.3*. https://www.teqsa.gov.au/latest-news/publications/guidance-note-course-design-including-learning-outcomes-and-assessment.

Tertiary Education Quality and Standards Agency. 2017b. *Application Guide for Registered Higher Education Providers – Renewal of Registration for Existing Providers. Version 2.7*. https://www.teqsa.gov.au/sites/default/files/application-guide-for-re-registration-v2.7.pdf?v=1535500067.

Universities UK. 2019. "Black, Asian and Minority Ethnic Student Attainment at UK Universities: Closing the Gap." Last modified 9 September 2021. https://www.universitiesuk.ac.uk/what-we-do/policy-and-research/publications/black-asian-and-minority-ethnic-student.

University of Southern California. 2017. *Campus Climate Literature Review and Report.* https://academicsenate.usc.edu/files/2017/12/CampusClimateReport_FINAL121117.pdf.

Weerasinghe, L. A. A. P. 2021. "Cultural Diversity and Indigenous Participation on Australian Corporate Boards." Ph.D., Queensland University of Technology.

Zacharias, N. 2017. *The Australian Student Equity Programme and Institutional Change: Paradigm Shift or Business as Usual.* https://www.ncsehe.edu.au/wp-content/uploads/2017/06/Nadine-ZachariasThe-Australian-Student-Equity-Program.pdf.

10

INCLUSION, CHEATING, AND ACADEMIC INTEGRITY

Validity as a goal and a mediating concept

Phillip Dawson

When designing assessment, educators think about a range of competing concerns, including how they will deal with cheating (Bearman et al. 2017). Some of the dominant assessment practices currently in use are deployed because there is a belief that they will in some way prevent or detect cheating. Examinations are trusted in part due to their perceived anti-cheating properties (Carless 2009). In an online context, remote proctoring software is used primarily to secure exams against cheating (Dawson 2021). Outside the context of exams, educators deploy other strategies such as using short turnaround times on tasks to limit opportunities for cheating (Wallace and Newton 2014). Each of these choices attempts to privilege the detection or prevention of cheating, knowingly or unknowingly harming inclusion in the process.

Much of the exclusion that happens in assessment, happens out of a desire to prevent or detect cheating. In this chapter, I will argue that to be more inclusive we need to re-think cheating, anti-cheating approaches, and inclusion in terms of how they influence validity.

There are two main tensions at play in traditional conversations about cheating: academic integrity and assessment security (Dawson 2021). Academic integrity is a positive mission to develop and promote particular capabilities and values in students (Fishman 2014) so that they can and do complete their work honestly, and that they value doing so. The International Centre for Academic Integrity espouses six fundamental values of academic integrity: honesty, trust, fairness, respect, responsibility, and courage (Fishman 2014). Students pledging to adhere to an honour code (McCabe, Treviño, and Butterfield 1999), and education programs that develop student capabilities and understandings of ethical scholarship are examples of academic integrity approaches to addressing cheating. In contrast, assessment security takes more of an adversarial approach, focused on detecting and deterring cheating (Dawson 2021). Examples of assessment security include text-matching tools, proctoring/invigilation of exams, and

DOI: 10.4324/9781003293101-13

surveillance of students while they complete online tasks. Debate in this space can become polarised and dichotomous at its extremes, but in practice most institutions deploy some combination of the two approaches. If you attempt to educate students about referencing and ethical scholarship, while also checking that they have not submitted the same assignment as a peer, you are adopting a mix of academic integrity and assessment security approaches.

This chapter focuses specifically on assessment security approaches, as most of the harms to inclusion that have occurred in addressing cheating have been due to these attempts to police and surveil students. Academic integrity does not punish you for needing to use the bathroom, having an atypical gaze pattern or living in insecure housing, but assessment security might. To further focus the chapter, it is largely interested in assessment of learning rather than assessment for learning; as I have argued elsewhere, assessment security does not matter as much (or sometimes, at all) in assessment for learning, and we should focus on positive academic integrity instead in those assessments (Dawson 2021). The chapter proposes that validity can act as a mediating concept that inserts inclusion as a necessary part of any conversation about cheating.

Tensions between cheating, inclusion, and assessment security

Inclusion has not traditionally been a focus for assessment security beyond the provision of targeted adjustments for specific students. For example, exams are predominantly used for assessment security, and substantial resources are devoted to providing a range of adjustments for students who need supports during exams. But this bolt-on or band-aid approach to addressing the deficiencies caused by assessment security is not an in-depth engagement with inclusion. It involves holding the approaches used in assessment security as constant as possible while making the most minimal adjustments required for individual students who have been identified as needing them; there are other students who are excluded by assessment security who do not fit within (or choose not to disclose they are within) the identified categories deemed as needing support.

In contrast, concerns about cheating are often raised as one of the reasons why more inclusive assessment practices cannot be adopted in some contexts. For example, many students with caring responsibilities may find it difficult to attend a synchronous exam – face-to-face or online – and a more inclusive approach may be to offer an open-ended take-home task that assesses the same outcomes. However, such a shift can be hard to implement when the spectre of cheating is raised. Traditional exams are viewed as more trustworthy (Carless 2009), partly due to perceptions that in take-home tasks students will be more likely to cheat, or that cheating will be more difficult to detect – even though the data may not always support these perceptions (Harper, Bretag, and Rundle 2021). The perceived anti-cheating benefits of traditional assessment approaches create great inertia, slowing any shift towards more inclusive practices.

There is a third, meaner connection between cheating and inclusion: the arguments raised in committee meetings and occasionally in the literature (e.g., Madriaga et al. 2011) that the provision of adjustments to students is tantamount to cheating. That these adjustments provide such an unfair advantage to a subset of students that they will be able to be lazy and outperform their peers. This is a flawed argument, as the process of providing adjustments is carefully regulated to ensure they enable the student to be assessed fairly, providing only the minimal assistance required for them to participate fully.

Assessment security is to blame at least in part for the need for bolt-on adjustments, inertia that is slowing a shift towards inclusive practices, and a reluctance to offer adjustments. The desire to address cheating seems to trump a desire to be inclusive in assessment. These are unfortunately old, engrained effects. More recently, with the rapid shift to online assessment during the COVID-19 pandemic, tensions between inclusion and assessment security have boiled over due to the use of new assessment security technologies. Critical pedagogy scholars such as Logan (2020) and Swauger (2020) question the fundamentals of our systems of assessment that are seen to require such technologies. They level strong criticism at remote proctoring in particular, for example, Logan (2020) states that:

> students must endure the racist, ableist technology peddled by companies like Proctorio, ProctorU, and ExamSoft, which frames students' bodies as abnormal. Have dark skin? The racist technology cannot see you. Wear glasses? The ablest technology sees you, but it doesn't believe you are you because it can't detect your eyes.

In this view, remote proctoring is akin to "cop shit" (Moro 2020): "any pedagogical technique or technology that presumes an adversarial relationship between students and teachers". Given this definition, assessment security and cop shit are arguably synonymous terms, the former carrying a more sanitised or euphemistic tone, and the latter a sense of activism and disgust. But whatever term you ascribe to it, there are inclusion consequences for the rapidly developing set of assessment security/cop shit technologies.

While there is a significant body of work critiquing assessment security as a problem for inclusion, the inclusion problems of cheating itself have been discussed much less. Modern cheating has become commercialised, with multi-billion dollar publicly traded companies offering cheating services to paying customers (Lancaster and Cotarlan 2021). There are financial barriers to cheating, with wealthier students able to purchase better quality bespoke assignments from contract cheating services. Less well-off students might turn to assignment swapping services (Rogerson 2014), which expose them to a much greater risk of getting caught when someone else submits their assignment. There are language barriers to cheating, with students who have more capability in the language of instruction being better able to engage in sham paraphrasing. And there are technological barriers to cheating, with those students who have better technological expertise having access to a range of additional cheating approaches (Dawson 2021). So, in addition to creating problems for inclusion, cheating is not inclusive. Cheating is not a level playing field, and it disproportionately preys on the disadvantaged and offers premium services to the advantaged.

The wrongness of cheating

That cheating is wrong is often taken for granted. Entire papers are written about cheating that never justify why cheating is a problem. If we just accept that cheating is wrong without any further discussion it makes it easy to accept all manner of wrongs that are done in the name of assessment security. When the wrongness of cheating is discussed, there are two main default arguments: that cheating provides an unfair advantage, and that cheating hurts learning (Bouville 2009).

The view that cheating is wrong because it is unfair has been critiqued by Bouville (2009, 1) as requiring a view of education as a "race of all against all". In such a view, if one student cheats they are placed in an advantaged position over their peers. This sort of competitive view of assessment suggests an implicit norm referencing perspective, whereby students are judged against each other. In a norm-referenced assessment context, one student cheating and performing better than they should hurts the grades of their peers, as individual student grades are adjusted based on how well the student body performs. However, modern views of criterion-referenced or standards-based assessment are incompatible with this view of assessment as a zero-sum game. Standards-based assessment rejects the idea that students should be judged against each other, and instead seeks to judge student performance against predetermined standards. In a well-functioning system where student achievement is evaluated against standards, the assessor's ability to judge any student's performance is not affected by other students cheating.

The view that cheating is wrong because it hurts learning holds promise, as cheating robs students of the time on meaningful tasks they would otherwise spend. The assessment for learning tradition contends that a primary purpose of assessment is to support student learning (Carless 2017) – and if students do not complete the task themselves without taking shortcuts, then they miss out on meaningful learning opportunities. Bouville (2009) identifies three conditions necessary for this justification of the wrongness of cheating to be acceptable. Firstly, the assessment must be a worthwhile learning activity. Not all assessments fulfil this criterion. Motz et al. (2021) found that during the COVID-19 pandemic, some students experienced many more hastily-designed online assignments that appeared to harm rather than help their academic performance – Motz et al. (2021) classified those tasks as "busywork". Secondly, for cheating to be wrong due to its effects on learning, it should actually hinder learning. This is not universally the case; Bouville gives the example of unauthorised peer collaboration as something that might help rather than hurt learning. There is a fine line between, for example, the positive practices of feedback seeking and peer learning, and the forbidden practices of cheating. Heavy-handed anti-cheating messages to students' risk hindering effective independent learning strategies. Thirdly, for cheating's wrongness to be based in the harms it does to learning, other activities that hurt learning need to be punished just as much as cheating. This would include punishing students for not completing tasks, as non-completion poses at least the same threat to learning that cheating does, or even going as far as punishing students for having hobbies or jobs which could distract from their studies (Bouville 2009). Punishing students for activities in general that harm their learning like hobbies or jobs is not just ridiculous, but more importantly it goes against student academic freedom to learn how they want to learn (Macfarlane 2016). Based on these three criteria, harms to learning do not appear to be solid ground on which to stake the wrongness of cheating.

Sidestepping the ethical wrongness of cheating, Cizek and Wollack (2017) argue that cheating should be viewed as a threat to validity:

> There may be disagreement about the ethical dimensions of cheating, but it is uncontestable that cheating represents a threat to the valid interpretation of a test score. When cheating takes place – whether in the form of copying from another test taker, collusion, prior access to secure test materials, inappropriate manipulation of answer documents, or any other form – the resulting test scores are not likely to be an accurate measurement of an examinee's true level of knowledge, skill, or ability. In short, a concern about cheating can be viewed as a psychometric concern about the validity or 'interpretive accuracy' of test scores.
>
> *(Cizek and Wollack 2017, 8)*

Here, cheating is wrong not based on an ethical argument but a pragmatic argument about the problems it creates for assessment in terms of validity. Cizek and Wollack (2017) come at validity and cheating from a psychometric perspective, which conjures up images of testing and statistics. But validity is a core concern for any assessment: assessment for learning, assessment of learning, high-stakes assessment, low-stakes assessment, self-assessment, and peer assessment. At its most basic level, validity is a concern that an act of assessment assesses what it is supposed to assess – that claims made about a student from what they have done reflect what they are capable of. Assessment validity is ultimately what allows institutions to fulfil their contract with society to graduate students who are capable of what is written on their testamurs. Assessment validity is how a maths educator knows that students who pass mathematics 1 are ready to study mathematics 2, and that students who fail mathematics 1 are not. Assessment validity is why I feel confident that a newly-qualified teacher can teach my children. I acknowledge that there are problems with validity in higher education, including the extent to which claims made about performance in one context are meaningful in predicting performance in another (Tummons 2020). But regardless of how imperfect assessment validity in higher education already is, cheating makes assessor judgements less valid, and it is this threat to validity that I find resonates most with a concern for the impacts of (anti-)cheating on inclusion.

The impact of cheating, inclusion, and assessment security on validity

Validity is both an aim in itself, and a powerful mediating concept in conversations about cheating, inclusion and assessment security. If cheating is wrong primarily or partly because of its impacts on validity, then this should inform arguments about assessment security and inclusion. Anti-cheating approaches often bring with them harms to inclusion. Assessment security should be concerned that the trade-offs made to address cheating validity threats are, on balance, worth it. If our attempts to stop cheating create more substantial threats to validity than what cheating itself creates, then they are unjustifiable from a cheating-as-validity-threat perspective – they are nothing more than cop shit.

There are many competing interpretations of validity. The core conversation about validity has been occupied by measurement researchers from education and psychology who are interested in testing (e.g., American Educational Research Association, American Psychological Association, and National Council on Measurement in Education, 2014). That community has moved from an understanding of validity as being an endpoint – the idea of a "valid" test – to validity being about processes and evidence in support of inferences, and from a focus on testing to including all acts of assessment (Iliescu and Greiff 2021).

Assessment security consists of two core components that can support validity: authentication and control of circumstances (Dawson 2021). Authentication supports validity through attempting to ensure that the student did the assessed task themselves. When an invigilator checks a student identification card at the start of an exam, they are helping the assessor make a more valid judgement as it is more likely the judgement will be about the assessed student rather than some other third party. Control of circumstances supports validity by limiting the supports that are available to students during a task so that they are in line with what the assessment designer intended. When a task is set as closed-book, perhaps because it assesses lower-level learning outcomes that can be easily looked up in a book, assessment security approaches that stop students from having access to the book improve the validity of the assessor's judgements about what the student is capable of. This is not an argument in favour of closed-book exams; just that if the closed-book restriction is in place, there is a validity threat to not enforcing it. Closed-book can be seen as imposing its own problems for validity if it fails to represent the authentic professional practice of the discipline; elsewhere I have challenged assessment designers to think in terms of "authentic restrictions" vs "inauthentic restrictions" (Dawson 2021).

One significant problem with assessment security is that little is known about the effectiveness of various approaches in terms of addressing cheating (and consequentially supporting validity). For example, there is a common assumption that exams are more secure than take-home assignments, in part because of the authentication that is used. However, when Harper, Bretag, and Rundle (2021) asked Australian academics and students in a survey about their experiences, the results were surprising. Students self-reported much higher rates of "third party cheating" (e.g., contract cheating and exam impersonation) in exams than in take-home assignments, but staff reported this was only rarely detected in exams. Staff reported detecting third party cheating much more in take-home assignments, even though students reported it was less prevalent than in exams. This suggests the third-party cheating problem is bigger and more poorly detected in exams than assignments. There are also conspicuous gaps in the literature around the effectiveness of some assessment security technologies. For example, there are many papers showing that students perform worse in remote proctored exams than unproctored exams. These papers usually conclude that this means proctoring is an effective measure against cheating (e.g., Akaaboune et al. 2022; Alessio et al. 2017; Davis, Rand, and Seay 2016; Dendir and Maxwell 2020; Reisenwitz 2020; Stapleton and Blanchard 2021) – despite the other potential explanations for such a result. But there are, to my knowledge, zero studies where the effectiveness of remote proctoring at detecting cheating is tested by someone trying to cheat. For years I have tried to conduct such a study but I am unable to get a proctoring company to agree to let me do one, and I have received legal advice that it would be unwise to do this sort of research without their permission. Taken together, the research that exists and the research that does not exist suggests that assumptions about the anti-cheating (and therefore validity) benefits of assessment security approaches might not always be founded in solid, transparent evidence.

Inclusion can similarly be justified through a range of arguments, including validity. Not adequately attending to inclusion is a threat to validity. Logically, the problems for validity created by cheating and exclusion are of the same formulation: if the assessment only produces meaningful information about student capability for some students but not all then it is less valid, regardless of if the reason is cheating or exclusion. Validity is threatened when an assessment requires materials only some students can afford; is conducted under time constraints only some students can meet; or assumes linguistic skills only some students have but that are unrelated to the outcomes being assessed. Exclusion is a validity threat.

Cheating, inclusion, and assessment security therefore each have a role to play with validity. Cheating as a threat to validity, assessment security as either a threat or a support to validity, and inclusion as a support for validity. Inclusion is therefore vital to the evaluation of assessment security approaches. If an assessment security approach hurts validity more through exclusion than it helps through addressing cheating, then it should not be adopted. If it excludes or disproportionately affects one group of students more than another, it creates a validity problem. For example, if in remote proctored exams, students with trait test anxiety are affected more negatively than other students (Woldeab and Brothen 2019), we create a new validity problem trying to fix an old one. The problem is, comparing the validity effects of assessment security and exclusion requires some complex qualitative calculus. There are no easy metrics. And straightforward notions of validity, about the accuracy of a judgement with respect to some standard, are only the beginning of this complexity.

While this chapter has largely focused on traditional notions of validity, similar arguments can be made with respect to broader understandings of validity. Consequential validity is an extension of validity to include effects beyond the immediate act of assessment (Sambell, McDowell, and Brown 1997). For example, when students sit a multiple choice exam focused on lower-level knowledge they may choose to cram right before the test rather than space their study out, choosing an effective short-term strategy, with consequential validity effects in the form of poorer longer-term learning. Assessment security has a variety of consequential validity effects. These include exclusionary effects, which can be viewed as both validity threats in the traditional sense as discussed previously, as well as consequential validity threats. For example, when a remote proctored exam is set without allowance for a bathroom break, it risks impairing traditional validity (examinees may perform worse due to no bathroom break, which misrepresents their capabilities). But it also presents risks to consequential validity (e.g., discomfort, pain, exclusion, and ultimately barriers in place for certain categories of people into particular professions). Consequential validity has been criticised as conflating too many ideas underneath the banner of validity (Mehrens 1997). But regardless of whether other harms to inclusion done by assessment security fall inside the concept of validity or outside it, they remain important counterbalances to any validity gains made by assessment security.

Validity holds significant promise as a mediating concept that can insert inclusion as a necessary component in any conversation about cheating, academic integrity or assessment security. Cheating is wrong, and measures need to be taken to both detect it and deter it; our need to only graduate students who can do what we say they can do requires us to. But those anti-cheating measures need to be weighed against their unintended consequences. The razor to be applied to any changes in the name of assessment security is this: at an absolute minimum, assessment security needs to help validity more than it hurts it. A similar standard should be applied to existing, dominant practices as well; if they entrench exclusion, they may be as much of a threat to validity as cheating is.

References

Akaaboune, O., Blix, L. H., Carrington, L., and Henderson, C. 2022. "Accountability in Distance Learning: The Effect of Remote Proctoring on Performance in Online Accounting Courses." *Journal of Emerging Technologies in Accounting* 19 (1): 121–131. https://doi.org/doi:10.2308/JETA-2020-040.

Alessio, H. M., Malay, N., Maurer, K., Bailer, A. J., and Rubin, B. 2017. "Examining the Effect of Proctoring on Online Test Scores." *Online Learning* 21 (1): 146–161. https://doi.org/10.24059/olj.v21i1.885.

American Educational Research Association, American Psychological Association, and National Council on Measurement in Education. 2014. *Standards for Educational and Psychological Testing*. Washington, DC: American Educational Research Association.

Bearman, M., Dawson, P., Bennett, S., Hall, M., Molloy, E., Boud, D., and Joughin, G. 2017. "How University Teachers Design Assessments: A Cross-Disciplinary Study." *Higher Education* 74 (1): 49–64. https://doi.org/10.1007/s10734-016-0027-7.

Bouville, M. 2009. "Why Is Cheating Wrong?" *Studies in Philosophy and Education* 29 (1): 67. https://doi.org/10.1007/s11217-009-9148-0.

Carless, D. 2009. "Trust, Distrust and Their Impact on Assessment Reform." *Assessment and Evaluation in Higher Education* 34 (1): 79–89. https://doi.org/10.1080/02602930801895786.

Carless, D. 2017. "Scaling Up Assessment for Learning: Progress and Prospects." In *Scaling up Assessment for Learning in Higher Education*, edited by David Carless, Susan M. Bridges, Cecilia Ka Yuk Chan, and Rick Glofcheski, 3–17. Singapore: Springer Singapore.

Cizek, G. J., and Wollack, J. A. 2017. "Exploring Cheating on Tests: The Context, the Concern, and the Challenges." In *Handbook of Quantitative Methods for Detecting Cheating on Tests*, edited by Gregory J. Cizek, and James A. Wollack, 3–19. New York: Routledge.

Davis, A. B., Rand, R., and Seay, R. 2016. "Remote Proctoring: The Effect of Proctoring on Grades." *Advances in Accounting Education: Teaching and Curriculum Innovations* 18: 23–50. Bingley: Emerald Group Publishing Limited. https://doi.org/10.1108/S1085-462220160000018002.

Dawson, P. 2021. *Defending Assessment Security in a Digital World: Preventing E-Cheating and Supporting Academic Integrity in Higher Education*. Abingdon, Oxon: Routledge.

Dendir, S., and Maxwell, R. S. 2020. "Cheating in Online Courses: Evidence from Online Proctoring." *Computers in Human Behavior Reports* 2: 100033. https://doi.org/10.1016/j.chbr.2020.100033.

Fishman, T. 2014. *The Fundamental Values of Academic Integrity*. Rev. ed. International Center for Academic Integrity: Clemson University.

Harper, R., Bretag, T., and Rundle, K. 2021. "Detecting Contract Cheating: Examining the Role of Assessment Type." *Higher Education Research & Development* 40 (2): 263–278. https://doi.org/10.1080/07294360.2020.1724899.

Iliescu, D., and Greiff, S. 2021. "On Consequential Validity." *European Journal of Psychological Assessment* 37 (3): 163–166. https://doi.org/10.1027/1015-5759/a000664.

Lancaster, T., and Cotarlan, C. 2021. "Contract Cheating by STEM Students through a File Sharing Website: A Covid-19 Pandemic Perspective." *International Journal for Educational Integrity* 17 (1): 3. https://doi.org/10.1007/s40979-021-00070-0.

Logan, C. 2020. "Refusal, Partnership, and Countering Educational Technology's Harms. Hybrid Pedagogy." Accessed 19 November 2021. https://hybridpedagogy.org/refusal-partnership-countering-harms/.

Macfarlane, B. 2016. *Freedom to Learn: The Threat to Student Academic Freedom and Why It Needs to Be Reclaimed*. London and New York: Routledge.

Madriaga, M., Hanson, K., Kay, H., and Walker, A. 2011. "Marking-Out Normalcy and Disability in Higher Education." *British Journal of Sociology of Education* 32 (6): 901–920. https://doi.org/10.1080/01425692.2011.596380.

McCabe, D. L., Treviño, L. K., and Butterfield, K. D. 1999. "Academic Integrity in Honor Code and Non-Honor Code Environments." *The Journal of Higher Education* 70 (2): 211–234. https://doi.org/10.1080/00221546.1999.11780762.

Mehrens, W. A. 1997. "The Consequences of Consequential Validity." *Educational Measurement: Issues and Practice* 16 (2): 16–18. https://doi.org/10.1111/j.1745-3992.1997.tb00588.x.

Moro, J. 2020. "Against Cop Shit." Accessed 19 November 2021. https://jeffreymoro.com/blog/2020-02-13-against-cop-shit/.

Motz, B. A., Quick, J. D., Wernert, J. A., and Miles, T. A. 2021. "A Pandemic of Busywork: Increased Online Coursework Following the Transition to Remote Instruction Is Associated with Reduced Academic Achievement." *Online Learning* 25 (1): 70–85. https://doi.org/10.24059/olj.v25i1.2475.

Reisenwitz, T. H. 2020. "Examining the Necessity of Proctoring Online Exams." *Journal of Higher Education Theory and Practice* 20 (1): 118–124.

Rogerson, A. M. 2014. "Detecting the Work of Essay Mills and File Swapping Sites: Some Clues They Leave behind." In *the 6th International Integrity & Plagiarism Conference*. Newcastle-on-Tyne. https://ro.uow.edu.au/cgi/viewcontent.cgi?article=1441&context=gsbpapers.

Sambell, K., McDowell, L., and Brown, S. 1997. "'But Is It Fair?'": An Exploratory Study of Student Perceptions of the Consequential Validity of Assessment." *Studies in Educational Evaluation* 23 (4): 349–371. https://doi.org/10.1016/S0191-491X(97)86215-3.

Stapleton, P., and Blanchard, J. 2021. "Remote Proctoring: Expanding Reliability and Trust." In *the 52nd ACM Technical Symposium on Computer Science Education, Virtual Event*. USA. https://doi.org/10.1145/3408877.3439671.

Swauger, S. 2020. "Our Bodies Encoded: Algorithmic Test Proctoring in Higher Education." https://hybridpedagogy.org/our-bodies-encoded-algorithmic-test-proctoring-in-higher-education/.

Tummons, J. 2020. "Education as a Mode of Existence: A Latourian Inquiry into Assessment Validity in Higher Education." *Educational Philosophy and Theory* 52 (1): 45–54. https://doi.org/10.1080/00131857.2019.1586530.

Wallace, M. J., and Newton, P. M. 2014. "Turnaround Time and Market Capacity in Contract Cheating." *Educational Studies* 40 (2): 233–236. https://doi.org/10.1080/03055698.2014.889597.

Woldeab, D., and Brothen, T. 2019. "21st Century Assessment: Online Proctoring, Test Anxiety, and Student Performance." *International Journal of E-Learning & Distance Education* 34 (1): 1–10. https://files.eric.ed.gov/fulltext/EJ1227595.pdf.

11

STUDENT EQUITY IN THE AGE OF AI-ENABLED ASSESSMENT

Towards a politics of inclusion

Bret Stephenson and Andrew Harvey

Introduction

Artificial intelligence (AI) in education is now prevalent, and as Cope, Kalantzis, and Searsmith (2020) have argued, "assessment is perhaps the most significant area of opportunity offered by artificial intelligence for transformative change in education" (5). For both good and ill, this wave of change is occurring as countless AI-enabled assessment products, and eager commercial edtech vendors, make their way into schools and universities globally (González-Calatayud, Prendes-Espinosa, and Roig-Vila 2021; Williamson and Eynon 2020). The deployment of AI-enabled assessments within the university landscape extends to assessments of all kinds, including formative and summative (Gardner, O'Leary, and Yuan 2021), as well as high-stakes and low-stakes assessment. In addition, it incorporates AI "solutions" aimed at addressing perceived threats to academic integrity (Coghlan, Miller, and Paterson 2020).

Critically, however, this rapid proliferation comes at a time when the computer and data sciences are undergoing a significant reckoning with their own complicity in perpetuating social discrimination and disadvantage through features inherent to AI and machine learning (ML) techniques and practices (Barocas, Hardt, and Narayanan 2020). AI-enabled assessment practices can contribute to this disadvantage by introducing, and often concealing, inequitable and discriminatory outcomes. After defining AI and questioning its often-triumphalist narrative, in this chapter we examine several examples of AI-enabled assessment and explore the ways in which each may produce inequitable or exclusionary outcomes for students.

We further aim to problematise recent attempts to utilise AI and ML techniques themselves to minimise or detect inequitable or unfair outcomes through the largely technological and statistical focus of the growing fairness, accountability,

DOI: 10.4324/9781003293101-14

and transparency movement in the data sciences. Our central argument is that technological solutions to equity and inclusion are of limited value, but particularly when educational institutions fail to engage in genuine political negotiation with a range of stakeholders and domain experts. Universities, we argue, should not cede their ethical and legal responsibility for ensuring inclusive AI-enabled assessment practices to third-party vendors, ill-equipped teaching staff, or to technological "solutions" such as algorithmic tests for "fairness". We conclude by outlining how, in the rapidly evolving age of AI-enabled education, universities can begin to engage in a politics of inclusion that rests upon robust democratic and ethical decision-making architectures.

Artificial intelligence (AI): Hype and hazards

More than 65 years since the term "artificial intelligence" was coined by McCarthy et al. (2006 [1955]), a commonly accepted definition of the term remains elusive. In a sweeping review of AI definitions from across the research literature, Wang (2019) argues that: "The current field of AI is actually a mixture of multiple research fields, each with its own goal, methods, applicable situations, etc., and they are called "AI" mainly for historical, rather than theoretical, reasons" (28). Given the tremendous diversity and complexity of modern AI methods, we argue that educators should be minimally familiar with the *two key stages of automation* that are fundamental to nearly all AI systems. Understanding these key stages will aid educators in developing the critical mindsets that are required if discriminatory outcomes are to be anticipated, discovered, and remediated:

1. *Automation of algorithmic learning* – Utilising an historical or "training" dataset, machine learning (ML) algorithms are *automatically* "trained" to find, or "learn", useful correlations between numerous variables and a "target variable" or "label" – the thing being predicted, categorised, or scored.
2. *Automation of algorithmic decision-making* – The AI system then uses these data-trained and optimised algorithms to *automate decisions* (classifications, predictions, scores, feedback, etc.) on new data in a way that imitates human-like judgements and decision-making processes.

These two key stages of automation are central to the brief description of AI provided by Gardner, O'Leary, and Yuan (2021): "The essence of artificial intelligence (AI) in both summative and formative [assessment] contexts is the concept of machine "learning" – where the computer is "taught" how to interpret patterns in data and "trained" to undertake predetermined actions according to those interpretations" (1207–1208). Even within this truncated sketch of the typical AI/ML lifecycle, we find three important points where it is widely recognised that biased outcomes may be unintentionally introduced into the process: (1) with the underlying training data that may lack diversity thereby causing representational harms; (2) at the stage of algorithmic "training" which can be a notoriously opaque and uninterpretable process; and (3) during the real-world model deployment stage (Barocas, Hardt, and Narayanan 2020).

A definition which focuses on these two fundamental stages of automation also works to take some of the unrealistic "magic" out of the AI mythology that is currently working to inflate public perceptions of AI's capabilities. We argue that demystifying AI is an important task, but particularly in educational environments where there is a need to relieve ourselves of notions that AI can currently "think", "understand", or deploy "knowledge" as humans do (Smith 2018). The often overly idealistic tone of AI's current wave of hype has been widely adopted by a university sector that has long been searching for cost-cutting measures, while also working to improve student success, retention, and completion outcomes. This drive for technologically powered "efficiencies" and "solutions" has been made much more acute by the COVID-19 crisis and the global emergency shift to computer-mediated "pandemic pedagogies" (Williamson, Eynon, and Potter 2020).

We should not lose sight, however, of the immense pressures of privatisation and profit that drives the rapid proliferation of educational technology (edtech) companies and the "Silicon Valley narrative" that they bring to higher education (Weller 2015). Matched with what Morozow (2013) describes as Silicon Valley's "technological solutionism", universities are in the midst of a sweeping movement of "edtech market-making" and a "private re-infrastructuring of public education" (Williamson and Hogan 2020). In the midst of this milieu of "Digital Enchantment" (Yeung 2022), it is important that we adopt a critical mindset in response to the triumphalist narrative of AI's remaking of higher education learning and teaching practice. The overtly techno-optimistic tone of public and academic discourse concerning AI's advancements – in the absence of critical evaluation – too easily serves to obscure the potential for AI to perpetuate disadvantage and exclusion based on, for example: disability (Lillywhite and Wolbring 2020), race and ethnicity (Leavy, Siapera, and O'Sullivan 2021), sex and gender (D'Ignazio and Klein 2020), economic status (O'Neil 2016), or linguistic background (Mayfield et al. 2019).

Examples of AI-enabled assessment and threats to equity and inclusion

While this chapter cannot offer a full overview of AI-enabled assessment practices, we will instead explore the risks they pose to principles of equity and inclusion through three representative examples. In the interest of brevity, we can think of these risks as being of two kinds: (1) the inherent risks posed by AI/ML processes themselves, such as "data bias", "algorithmic bias", or the lack of process transparency and "explainability", and (2) those created or exacerbated by commercial or governmental claims to confidentiality. In the realms of commercial edtech and AI, these two risks often present themselves jointly.

First, the recent A-level "exams fiasco" (Kippin and Cairney 2021) in England is perhaps the most recent and high-profile example of algorithmic bias finding its way into a high-stakes assessment process. Due to COVID-19 lockdowns in 2020, students were unable to sit for A-Level exams which weigh heavily in university admissions decisions. As an emergency measure, the Office of Qualifications and Examinations Regulations (Ofqual) opted to use teacher predictions of student results, along with the teachers' rank orderings, that were then standardised by an algorithmic process in the hopes of controlling for grade inflation. Designed with great haste, the selected algorithm unintentionally, but perhaps predictably, introduced a familiar set of inequitable outcomes that are commonly found in algorithmic decision-making processes. In their "attempt to match historical distributions, the algorithm increased predicted grades at small, private schools and lowered grades at larger, state-run schools that have historically educated a larger proportion of Black, Asian and Minority Ethnic (BAME) students" (Wachter, Mittelstadt, and Russell 2021, 737).

The public backlash against Ofqual's algorithm-produced grades was widespread and made more severe due to perceptions that both the algorithm, and the political process that created it, represented "a 'black box' of politically motivated manipulation" (Kelly 2021, 3). These claims were not baseless. Few technical details of the algorithm were shared with the public and only after the algorithmically adjusted grades were published. It was also later revealed that the Royal Statistical Society (RSS) had offered to help Ofqual with its algorithm, but ultimately opted not to participate after being asked to sign a restrictive non-disclosure agreement (Kelly 2021, 5). The inequitable results of the Ofqual algorithm, coupled with the strong public outcry, were enough for the government to decide to eventually scrap the results. Perhaps the most important lesson to take from the UK "exams fiasco", as Kelly (2021) has reflected, is that numerous non-algorithmic solutions were available to decision-makers but too quickly overlooked.

As algorithms go, the Ofqual algorithm was rather simple in its construction. And while media reports frequently blamed the fiasco on "AI" itself, only at a stretch could we class it as a true AI/ML algorithm. While its creators likely used elements of data mining in its production, there is no indication that the two key stages of AI automation that we described earlier were a part of the process. The key point is, however, that even within this comparatively low-tech algorithmic "solution" we find common hallmarks of discriminatory AI/ML algorithms. In the Ofqual example, the algorithmic sources of discrimination could be readily identified by experts once they were given full access to the algorithm itself. Had Ofqual opted for a true AI/ML algorithm – one that "learns" for itself through complex automated processes – the result could have been much worse and far more inscrutable.

Secondly, we can also look to examples of automated essay scoring (AES) systems which are now a common form of AI-enabled assessment practices within schools and universities. AES systems utilise natural language processing (NLP), a subfield of AI/ML, to automate formative feedback and summative "scoring" of a student's written text, such as essays and short answers (Gardner, O'Leary, and Yuan 2021). To be certain, AES technologies and products can hold tremendous comercial value as they are frequently used to score the written portion of millions of high-stakes standardised aptitude tests such as the Scholastic Aptitude Test (SAT) and Graduate Record Examinations (GRE) in the North American context (Ke and Ng 2019).

Using a recent and highly controversial proposal for an AES use case in Australia, we can briefly explore how AI's own inherent threats to equity can be further complicated by claims to commercial privacy. In 2018, it was proposed that the written portion of the National Assessment Program – Literacy and Numeracy tests (NAPLAN) – historically assessed and marked by highly trained human assessors – be "robo-scored" by AI software. While the Australian Curriculum, Assessment and Reporting Authority's (ACARA) internal research team claimed that the AES system developed by Pearson was valid and reliable (Lazendic, Justus, and Rabinowitz 2018), the NSW Teachers" Federation commissioned AES expert Les Perelman to review the research. Perelman was ultimately denied access to Pearson's proprietary software and ACARA declined to provide the underlying data used for their own assessment, yet Perelman's (2018) independent evaluation still proved devastating, and the program was scrapped for 2018.

Of particular interest for our purposes, Perelman noted the threat to cultural linguistic "fairness" presented by AES systems of this kind. "Whatever the explanation", he writes, "unfairness by machines in inflating the marks of some linguistic groups and artificially lowering the marks of others is morally indefensible and, possibly, illegal" (Perelman 2018, 5). Bias of this kind often makes its way into AI systems via culturally, linguistically, and even racially homogenous training data (Mayfield et al. 2019), or what is described as representational bias in the training data themselves. These equity and inclusion concerns are particularly salient as AI-enabled scoring is also currently deployed in the assessment of English proficiency for international university students via the Test of English as a Foreign Language (TOEFL), Post Enrolment Language Assessments (PELAs), and other high-stakes exams (Zimitat 2019).

Third, while university staff and students are well familiarised with the AI-enabled functionality of plagiarism checking services, such as Turnitin, AI is also increasingly being deployed for the purposes of ensuring academic integrity in online exam proctoring. The use of these online proctoring (OP) systems, or "robot invigilators" (Mubin et al. 2020), has seen a rapid rise amid the COVID-19 pandemic and numerous edtech providers have now flooded into the space. In their effort to detect instances of student cheating, OP systems frequently rely on a suite of "multimodal AI" capabilities which, for example, combine multiple AI systems, including facial and voice recognition/detection, object detection, as well as remote computer system surveillance. As Coghlan, Miller, and Paterson (2020) have explained, "OP software contains artificial intelligence (AI) and machine learning (ML) components that analyse exam recordings to identify suspicious examinee behaviours or suspicious items in their immediate environment" (1), or unexpected eye and body movements.

The threats posed by AI-powered OP systems to equity and inclusion concerns, not to mention privacy objections, are vast. As Swauger (2020) has detailed, algorithmic test proctoring can disadvantage, or simply not work, for people who lack access to suitable testing spaces, safe home environments, or who lack the necessary computer equipment. Critically, people who do not present as able-bodied or neurotypical to the OP algrithms are also likely to be flagged as cheating threats. For instance, many "robo-proctors" utilise eye-tracking software that may flag as suspicous test takers who are blind or express atypical eye movements due to a range of conditions. Facial recognition AI systems have also become notorious for their bias and inacuracy in relation to particular demographics, namely, people of colour and women (Lohr 2018). (See Chapter 10 for an account of inclusion, cheating, and academic integrity.)

Finally, we must also recognise that students and institutions who are already well resourced stand to benefit most from AI-enabled assessments and educational technologies. These are also the institutions that are most likely to have the greatest agency in making unconstrained decisions between which computer and human labours they wish to deploy. For instance, the utilisation of less advantageous AI technologies may be forced upon some students or institutions as a means of cost savings. As Selwyn (2019) has warned, "AI will impact on an Ivy League university such as Harvard in very different ways to a community college in Hudson County. In all these ways, then, we need to remain mindful of the politics of technology" (23). For this, and other reasons, we should be highly sceptical of edtech marketing claims concerning "equitable" AI technologies that provide greater "access" through scalability alone. As Selwyn et al. (2020) have argued, digital in/exclusion is not simply a matter of creating access to digital learning technologies. Uncritically accepting what we might call the "equality = access" narrative, they argue, problematically accepts educational technologies "as an inherently "good thing" that merely offers educational opportunities" to those in need. A focus on access, they argue, remains "an "easy" way for policy makers to signal that they are "dealing with" inequality" (Selwyn et al. 2020, 2).

Confronting AI-enabled disadvantage and discrimination

While the efficacy and performance of AI-enabled assessments, and their likelihood of meeting true parity with human assessors, has been critiqued and reviewed elsewhere (Cope, Kalantzis, and Searsmith 2020; Gardner, O'Leary, and Yuan 2021; Selwyn et al. 2020), our primary concern is with how institutions may protect against (unintended) AI-enabled discrimination and exclusion. The potential avenues for AI-enabled assessments, software, and platforms to quietly smuggle disadvantage and bias into the assessment process are numerous and complex. Their complexity is to be found in their technological and commercial aspects, certainly, but also in the inescapably complex political, ethical, and social contexts in which they are deployed.

To their credit, computer and data science academics have not remained aloof to the problems of AI-enabled disadvantage and discrimination, or to the pernicious ways that advanced data analytics can obscure inequitable outcomes.

The past ten years have seen an explosion of research in new fields such as Fairness, Accountability and Transparency in Machine Learning (FATML), Explainable Artificial Intelligence (XAI), and what is broadly called Responsible Artificial Intelligence (RAI) (Barocas, Hardt, and Narayanan 2020; Gilpin et al. 2018). There have been tremendous advancements made in these fields towards producing technical tools and strategies aimed at, for example, calculating the statistical "fairness" of AI systems or adding "explainability" outputs to otherwise inscrutable algorithmic decisions. As we have argued elsewhere, these technical advancements in AI fairness monitoring and transparency are necessary, but ultimately not sufficient, in our effort to maintain equitable and inclusive deployments of AI in educational settings (Stephenson, Harvey, and Huang 2022, 28–30).

For example, mathematical tests for "algorithmic fairness", of which there are now dozens to choose from, are frequently contradictory and fundamentally fail to be instructive in the absence of applied domain expertise, or where ethical and political negotiations of "the good" are not confronted (Green and Hu 2018). For example, an AI cannot tell us which fairness test, or which fairness definition, is ethically superior in each use case. Nor can an AI process tell us which course of action to take if an agreed principle of fairness is found to be violated. Equally, the goal of bringing interpretability and transparency to extremely complex algorithmic processes – that is, to open the "black box" of AI inscrutability – has also come under considerable critique (Gilpin et al. 2018). While the creation of tools which seek to make algorithmic decisions more comprehensible to human users is a necessary pursuit, it is not sufficient to guaranteeing equitable outcomes. There are ethical and political questions that must first be negotiated. To whom should the algorithm, or the student's AI-assessed feedback or grade, be interpretable to? Who will be the human-in-the-loop who possesses the necessary disciplinary content specialisation, coupled with AI understanding? Ultimately, we argue that determining the shape of fairness and inclusivity in educational contexts requires in-house ethical human judgements that should be made through rigorous political negotiation, not algorithmic quantification.

Towards an inclusive AI-enabled assessment policy and practice for institutions

Given the pressures exerted upon universities and teaching academics to create money and time-saving "efficiencies", we need to find ways to engage fully in the politics of technology and inclusivity in our institutions. Along with Zuboff (2019, 181), we must ask "Who knows? Who decides? Who decides who decides?". Who decides when an AI-enabled assessment is adequately protective of equity and inclusivity? Who is the sufficiently knowledgeable "human-in-the-loop" who can explain an AI-enabled assessment tool's scoring of a student's work? How can institutions construct robust and democratic decision architectures that protect equity and inclusion interests during rapid technological change?

Chaudhry and Kazim (2021) have claimed that teachers can play the role of human-in-the-loop, and that "the final decision makers are teachers" (1). But will all teachers be able to understand the algorithmic decision making of the AI? Teachers are, of course, content specialists, but few are specialists in AI and ML or familiar with its potential shortcomings. In a systematic review of research relating to data literacies and the training of university faculty, Raffaghelli and Stewart (2020) found that where training was taking place it was largely concerned with mastery of accepted, and unproblematised, technical practices. This finding indicates that many university teachers are unlikely to be prepared to be the critical-minded "human-in-the-loop", but particularly when commercial and proprietary AI are deployed within a veil of opacity and secrecy.

Ultimately, we agree with Elish and Boyd (2018) who have argued that "[a]cknowledging the limits of Big Data and AI should not result in their dismissal, but rather enable a more grounded and ultimately more useful set of conversations about the appropriate and effective design of such technologies" (73). But to protect equity and inclusivity goals, we must have transparency in university technology procurement processes (Zeide 2020), we should normalise the production of AI or algorithm impact assessments (Reisman et al. 2018), and we need to engage in a discussion about the outsourcing or insourcing of AI oversight. For instance, some have argued for the creation of a new industry of external algorithmic auditing professionals who might ensure legal protection for companies and institutions (Koshiyama et al. 2021).

We argue, however, that responsibility for AI oversight and monitoring should be made a standard part of internal institutional policy and practice. One approach could involve the creation of specialised institutional review boards that are of a similar composition to human research ethics committees. Such institutional governance bodies could draw on the evolving "responsible innovation" research literature (Jarmai 2020). In a university context, something like a Responsible Innovation Committee would require broad representation from equity cohorts, computer science/analytics experts, teaching and learning experts, ethicists, legal professionals, and student representatives. In this way universities may be able to better guarantee that the adoption of AI/ML processes will undergo a full engagement with the politics of technology and inclusion in a transparent and democratic manner. More broadly, the rise of AI-enabled assessment highlights the need for broad professional development that can then form a critical bulwark against many forms of digital enchantment (Yeung 2022) that put inclusivity at risk.

References

Barocas, S., Hardt, M., and Narayanan, A. 2020. *Fairness in Machine Learning: Limitations and Opportunities*. https://fairmlbook.org/.

Chaudhry, M. A., and Kazim, E. 2021. "Artificial Intelligence in Education (AIEd): A High-Level Academic and Industry Note 2021." *AI and Ethics* 2: 157–165. https://doi.org/10.1007/s43681-021-00074-z.

Coghlan, S., Miller, T., and Paterson, J. 2020. "Good Proctor or "Big Brother"?" AI Ethics and Online Exam Supervision Technologies." *ArXiv, abs/2011.07647*. http://doi.org/10.48550/arXiv.2011.07647.

Cope, B., Kalantzis, M., and Searsmith, D. 2020. "Artificial Intelligence for Education: Knowledge and Its Assessment in AI-Enabled Learning Ecologies." *Educational Philosophy and Theory* 53 (12): 1229–1245. https://doi.org/10.1080/00131857.2020.1728732.

D'Ignazio, C., and Klein, L. F. 2020. *Data Feminism*. Cambridge, MA: MIT Press.

Elish, M. C., and Boyd, D. 2018. "Situating Methods in the Magic of Big Data and AI." *Communication Monographs* 85 (1): 57–80.

Gardner, J., O'Leary, M., and Yuan, L. 2021. "Artificial Intelligence in Educational Assessment: "Breakthrough? or Buncombe and Ballyhoo?"" *Journal of Computer Assisted Learning* 37 (5): 1207–1216. https://doi.org/10.1111/jcal.12577.

Gilpin, L. H., Bau, D., Yuan, B. Z., Bajwa, A., Specter, M., and Kagal, L. 2018. "Explaining Explanations: An Overview of Interpretability of Machine Learning." In *The 5th International Conference on Data Science and Advanced Analytics (DSAA 2018)*. http://doi.org/10.48550/arXiv.1806.00069.

González-Calatayud, V., Prendes-Espinosa, P., and Roig-Vila, R. 2021. "Artificial Intelligence for Student Assessment: A Systematic Review." *Applied Sciences* 11 (12): 5467. https://doi.org/10.3390/app11125467.

Green, B., and Hu, L. 2018. "The Myth in the Methodology: Towards a Recontextualization of Fairness in Machine Learning." In *The Debates workshop at the 35th International Conference on Machine Learning*. Stockholm, Sweden.

Jarmai, K., ed. 2020. *Responsible Innovation: Business Opportunities and Strategies for Implementation*. Dordrecht, The Netherlands: Springer Open.

Ke, Z., and Ng, V. 2019. "Automated Essay Scoring: A Survey of the State of the Art." In *Proceedings of the Twenty-Eighth International Joint Conference on Artificial Intelligence (IJCAI-19)*.

Kelly, A. 2021. "A Tale of Two Algorithms: The Appeal and Repeal of Calculated Grades Systems in England and Ireland in 2020." *British Educational Research Journal* 47 (3): 725–741. https://doi.org/10.1002/berj.3705.

Kippin, S., and Cairney, P. 2021. "The COVID-19 Exams Fiasco across the UK: Four Nations and Two Windows of Opportunity." *British Politics* 17: 1–23. https://doi.org/10.1057/s41293-021-00162-y.

Koshiyama, A., Kazim, E., Treleaven, P., Rai, P., Szpruch, L., Pavey, G., Ahamat, G., Leutner, F., Goebel, R., Knight, A., et al. 2021. "Towards Algorithm Auditing: A Survey on Managing Legal, Ethical and Technological Risks of AI, ML and Associated Algorithms." *SSRN*. http://dx.doi.org/10.2139/ssrn.3778998.

Lazendic, G., Justus, J., and Rabinowitz, S. 2018. *NAPLAN Online Automated Scoring Research Program: Research Report*. Australian Curriculum, Assessment and Reporting Authority (ACARA), Tech. Rep. https://nap.edu.au/docs/default-source/default-document-library/naplan-online-aes-research-report-final.pdf?sfvrsn=0.

Leavy, S., Siapera, E., and O'Sullivan, B. 2021. "Ethical Data Curation for AI: An Approach Based on Feminist Epistemology and Critical Theories of Race." In *Proceedings of the 2021 AAAI/ACM Conference on AI, Ethics, and Society*.

Lillywhite, A., and Wolbring, G. 2020. "Coverage of Artificial Intelligence and Machine Learning within Academic Literature, Canadian Newspapers, and Twitter Tweets: The Case of Disabled People." *Societies* 10 (1): 23. https://www.mdpi.com/2075-4698/10/1/23.

Lohr, S. 2018. "Facial Recognition Is Accurate, If You're a White Guy." In *Ethics of Data and Analytics*, edited by Kirsten Martin, 143–147. New York: Auerbach Publications.

Mayfield, E., Madaio, M., Prabhumoye, S., Gerritsen, D., McLaughlin, B., Dixon-Román, E., and Black, A. W. 2019. "Equity beyond Bias in Language Technologies for Education." In *Proceedings of the Fourteenth Workshop on Innovative Use of NLP for Building Educational Applications*.

McCarthy, J., Minsky, M. L., Rochester, N., and Shannon, C. E. 2006 [1955]. "A Proposal for the Dartmouth Summer Research Project on Artificial Intelligence, August 31, 1955." *AI Magazine* 27 (4): 12. https://doi.org/10.1609/aimag.v27i4.1904.

Morozow, E. 2013. *To Save Everything, Click Here: Technology, Solutionism, and the Urge to Fix Problems that Don't Exist*. London: Penguin Press.

Mubin, O., Cappuccio, M., Alnajjar, F., Ahmad, M. I., and Shahid, S. 2020. "Can a Robot Invigilator Prevent Cheating?" *AI & Society* 35 (4). http://doi.org/10.1007/s00146-020-00954-8.

O'Neil, C. 2016. *Weapons of Math Destruction: How Big Data Increases Inequality and Threatens Democracy*. London: Penguin Press.

Perelman, L. 2018. "Robot Marking: Automated Essay Scoring and NAPLAN – A Summary Report." *Journal of Professional Learning*, Semester 1. https://cpl.asn.au/journal/semester-1-2018/robot-marking-automated-essay-scoring-and-naplan-a-summary-report.

Raffaghelli, J. E., and Stewart, B. 2020. "Centering Complexity in "Educators" Data Literacy" to Support Future Practices in Faculty Development: A Systematic Review of the Literature." *Teaching in Higher Education* 25 (4): 435–455. https://doi.org/10.1080/13562517.2019.1696301.

Reisman, D., Schultz, J., Crawford, K., and Whittaker, M. 2018. *Algorithmic Impact Assessments: A Practical Framework for Public Agency Accountability*. AI Now. https://ainowinstitute.org/aiareport2018.pdf.

Selwyn, N. 2019. *Should Robots Replace Teachers?* Cambridge, UK: Polity Press.

Selwyn, N., Hillman, T., Eynon, R., Ferreira, G., Knox, J., Macgilchrist, F., and Sancho-Gil, J. M. 2020. "What's Next for Ed-Tech? Critical Hopes and Concerns for the 2020s." *Learning, Media and Technology* 45 (1): 1–6. https://doi.org/10.1080/17439884.2020.1694945.

Smith, G. 2018. *The AI Delusion*. Oxford: Oxford University Press.

Stephenson, B., Harvey, A., and Huang, Q. 2022. *Towards an Inclusive Analytics for Australian Higher Education*. https://www.ncsehe.edu.au/publications/inclusive-analytics-australian-higher-education/.

Swauger, S. 2020. "Our Bodies Encoded: Algorithmic Test Proctoring in Higher Education." In *Critical Digital Pedagogy: A Collection*, edited by Jesse Stommel, Chris Friend, and Sean M. Morris. Washington, DC: Pressbooks.

Wachter, S., Mittelstadt, B., and Russell, C. 2021. "Bias Preservation in Machine Learning: The Legality of Fairness Metrics under EU Non-Discrimination Law." *West Virginia Law Review* 123 (3): 735–790. https://dx.doi.org/10.2139/ssrn.3792772.

Wang, P. 2019. "On Defining Artificial Intelligence." *Journal of Artificial General Intelligence* 10 (2): 1–37. http://doi.org/10.2478/jagi-2019-0002.

Weller, M. 2015. "MOOCs and the Silicon Valley Narrative." *Journal of Interactive Media in Education* 1 (5): 1–7. http://dx.doi.org/10.5334/jime.am.

Williamson, B., and Eynon, R. 2020. "Historical Threads, Missing Links, and Future Directions in AI in Education." *Learning, Media and Technology* 45 (3): 223–235. https://doi.org/10.1080/17439884.2020.1798995.

Williamson, B., Eynon, R., and Potter, J. 2020. "Pandemic Politics, Pedagogies and Practices: Digital Technologies and Distance Education during the Coronavirus Emergency." *Learning, Media and Technology* 45 (2): 107–114. https://doi.org/10.1080/17439884.2020.1761641.

Williamson, B., and Hogan, A. 2020. *Commercialisation and Privatisation in/of Education in the Context of Covid-19.* Brussels, Belgium: Education International. https://www.ei-ie.org/file/130.

Yeung, K. 2022. "Dispelling the Digital Enchantment." Futures Lecture, Edinburgh Futures Institute, the University of Edinburgh. https://www.birmingham.ac.uk/news/2022/cal-law-digital-enchantment.

Zeide, E. 2020. "Robot Teaching, Pedagogy, and Policy." In *The Oxford Handbook of Ethics of AI (Online Edition)*, edited by Markus D. Dubber, Frank Pasquale, and Sunit Das, 1–17. Oxford University Press. https://doi.org/10.1093/oxfordhb/9780190067397.013.51.

Zimitat, C. 2019. "Scalable English Language Screening in a Multi-Campus University." In *TEQSA 4th Annual Conference.* Melbourne, Victoria http://teqsa-2019.p.asnevents.com.au/days/2019-11-28/abstract/66733.

Zuboff, S. 2019. *The Age of Surveillance Capitalism: The Fight for a Human Future at the New Frontier of Power.* New York: Public Affairs.

12

OPPORTUNITIES AND LIMITATIONS OF ACCOMMODATIONS AND ACCESSIBILITY IN HIGHER EDUCATION ASSESSMENT

Christopher Johnstone, Leanne R. Ketterlin Geller, and Martha Thurlow

Introduction

A mechanism for understanding if students are learning in universities is classroom assessments. The practice of assessment has wide-ranging understandings that vary from classroom to classroom and instructor to instructor. This chapter considers assessment within the context of the United States, but lessons may be applicable in other parts of the world. In the United States, entrance examinations (those that are designed to inform admissions decisions in higher education institutions) are highly standardised, but beyond this there is little to no standardisation of assessment practice in higher education settings in the United States. For example, two instructors in the same department may take two entirely different approaches to assessment. Instructor A may define the goal of their class as factual or procedural knowledge, and thus rely heavily on quizzes and exams as mechanisms for students to demonstrate knowledge. Instructor B may be more concerned about applications and use written papers or authentic application activities (i.e., projects) to examine student course outputs.

The lack of consistency surrounding assessment in the United States can be challenging for students to navigate. A typical semester course load requires students to take 4–5 classes with instructors who each have their own vision of assessment. Students in higher education settings, then, are required to navigate due dates, instructors' assessment expectations, and (for many undergraduates) independent living skills during their university experience. The level of support that students receive for navigating higher education expectations also varies widely. In the next section, we will focus on support mechanisms for students with disabilities as an example of how assessment practice is constructed for a particular population within a larger decentralised higher education ecosystem.

DOI: 10.4324/9781003293101-15

Students with disabilities in higher education in the United States

A recent report by the National Center for Education Statistics (NCES) revealed that as many as 19% of undergraduate students and 12% of graduate students self-reported a disability (US Department of Education 2021). According to the survey, students could select "yes" to having a disability if they self-identified as having any of the following circumstances: blindness or visual impairment that cannot be corrected by wearing glasses; hearing impairment (e.g., deaf or hard of hearing); orthopaedic or mobility impairment; speech or language impairment; learning, mental, emotional, or psychiatric condition such as a serious learning disability, depression, ADD, or ADHD); or other health impairment.

Students identifying as having a disability, however, do not automatically receive any form of disability-related service from their home universities. According to US policy, if students wish to receive any form of disability services from their home institution, they must make an appointment with a designated disability resource office, disclose their disability, and provide accurate documentation of the disability. These processes can be stigmatising to students and many students may fail to receive services if they are uncomfortable with self-disclosure of a disability. Despite the stigmatising barriers that may prevent students from disclosing their disability to receive services, many students effectively advocate for themselves through disability resource offices in universities. In relation to assessment, students who register at disability resource offices are frequently entitled to accommodations in assessments. Because resource offices are mandated to serve students under US disability laws, once instructional and assessment accommodations decisions are finalised, instructors are mandated to implement them in classes.

Accommodations in higher education

Accommodations are any change to the presentation or response/action requirements of an assessment for an individual student if the conditions of the assessment create an accessibility barrier unrelated to the construct taught or assessed. Accommodations are a common global practice in higher education, primarily designed to provide opportunities for all students to participate in assessment. Accommodations practice and research aim to ensure inclusion in whatever assessment is given to students, but do not typically critique the utility, applicability, or authenticity of assessments themselves (Nieminen 2022). (See Chapter 6 for a broader discussion of the limitations of accommodations.)

Although accommodations can be provided for any type of assessment or any student, they are often applied in higher education settings as "testing accommodations", and frequently utilised by students with disabilities. For example, the *Americans with Disabilities Act* (1990) defines testing accommodations as:

- Braille or large-print exam booklets
- Screen reading technology

- Scribes to transfer answers to Scantron bubble sheets or record dictated notes and essays
- Extended time
- Wheelchair-accessible testing stations
- Distraction-free rooms
- Physical prompts (such as for individuals with hearing impairments)
- Permission to bring and take medications during the exam (e.g., for individuals with diabetes who must monitor their blood sugar and administer insulin)

In general, accommodations are designed to provide access to an assessment, without changing its constructs, when the standard presentation or response conditions introduce a barrier (Thurlow and Bolt 2001). In addition to testing accommodations, disability resource offices also provide documentation and require accommodations for non-exam assessments (such as papers and projects). Typical accommodations include extended time, allowances for alternative presentation (i.e., not in front of a large group), allowances for additional resources, grammar checks if projects are completed in class, and a host of other accommodations based on students' disability profiles.

As noted above, accommodations are a widespread practice worldwide and are often supported by national or institutional policies (see Hanafin et al. 2007). In the United States, accommodations are protected by educational rights and represent a clear pathway for student access in assessment. If disability resource centres document a need for accommodations, instructors must provide them or be in violation of US law. The language of accommodations is clear and non-debatable. Because of the procedural requirements for accommodations that require diagnosis data, appointments with disability resource offices, and the effort required to seek official letters, a relatively small number of students in universities benefit from them. For example, we are all highly committed to providing legally mandated accommodations in our classrooms, yet sometimes go entire semesters without official accommodations requests.

Increased attention to the provision of accommodations for higher education assessments emerged, in part, from the extensive increases in the provision of assessment accommodations in primary and secondary schools. In the United States, for example, some states reported more than 95% of high school students with disabilities received assessment accommodations during the 2018–2019 school year (Wu et al. 2021). As these students move on to higher education, they often expect to receive the same accommodations.

A report to the US Congress, however, foresaw the challenges in providing testing accommodations in higher education (Scott 2011). Although the report focused on assessments provided by testing companies, it was clear about the need for the Department of Justice to take a more strategic approach to enforcement of regulations governing testing accommodations in higher education settings. As a result, new guidance on testing accommodations was released (US Department of Justice 2014). It applied to tests related to "applications, licensing, certification, or credentialing for secondary or postsecondary education, professional, or trade purposes" (US Department of Justice 2014, 1) yet had implications for higher education in general. The following are among some of the many points made in the guidance:

- A person with a history of academic success may still be a person with a disability who is entitled to testing accommodations under the *Americans with Disabilities Act*. (3)
- Proof of past testing accommodations in similar test settings is generally sufficient to support a request for the same testing accommodations for a current standardised exam or other high-stakes test. (5)
- If a candidate previously received testing accommodations under an Individualized Education Program (IEP) or a Section 504 Plan,[1] he or she should generally receive the same testing accommodations for a current standardised exam or high-stakes test. (6)
- Testing entities should defer to documentation from a qualified professional who has made an individualised assessment of the candidate that supports the need for the requested testing accommodations. (7)

Although the above report's recommendations apply specifically to a narrow set of tests, consistency in approaches across instructional and assessment situations suggests that they have important implications for higher education testing situations in general.

The legal and contractual focus of accommodations provides an opportunity for students with disabilities to experience greater accessibility in assessment experiences but is limited in its reach and potential. Similarly, recent research on the effects of accommodations in higher education has been limited, and often not consistent in research findings. As noted by Weis and Beauchemin (2019), researchers have found positive effects (e.g., Kim and Lee 2016), negative effects (e.g., Lewandowski, Wood, and Lambert 2015), or no effect (e.g., Lombardi, Murray, and Gerdes 2012) of similar accommodations. Despite overall positive effects, Weis and Beauchemin (2019) themselves found negative results, indicating no performance advantage of a private room for examinations. A limitation of many of the findings of these and other studies is that the accommodations were not administered to students for whom there was an identified individualised need for the accommodation. A further limitation is that "assessment" in higher education is often conflated with testing, which is a narrowed imaginary of how students might demonstrate knowledge and how accommodations might support such a process.

Instructors are required to provide accommodations for students with identified disabilities who have chosen to seek assistance from disability services offices but may have additional students with and without disabilities in their classes who may benefit from individualised accommodations. In US higher education settings, there is little policy guidance that focuses on individual instructors providing accommodations based on their own knowledge of students and course assessments. We will revisit this limitation in our final section but will now introduce a second mechanism for increasing accessibility of assessments - Universal Design for Assessment (UDA).

Universal design for assessment

Although the previous section focused on accommodations and the legal right of students with disabilities to receive them, many students without disabilities may encounter barriers when in tests and other assessments that are rooted in similar reasons as those experienced by students with disabilities. Namely, there are some aspects of the assessment process that are not accessible to them based on the interactions between personal characteristics and the structure of assessments. Institutions of higher education host a wide range of students of different ages, cultural experiences, prior education background, continuity in formal schooling, and other histories that shape how they experience assessment. Some students may experience anxiety in certain subjects or settings that is based on prior experiences. For example, many students across the grades as well as in postsecondary settings experience math anxiety. While often not significant enough to be diagnosed as a disability, it may impact their learning as well as their ability to demonstrate their knowledge on assessment tasks. Students who experience math anxiety may have emotional, cognitive, and physiological reactions that reduce their ability to concentrate, impact their working memory, and physical symptoms such as an increased heart rate, upset stomach and light-headedness (Luttenberger, Wimmer, and Paechter 2018). Although students who experience these or similar situations may not have a disability that requires accommodations, their personal experiences coupled with the often-narrow range of assessments in mathematics may impact their performance in ways that are not related to their potential on the mathematics constructs in question. Under current US law, accommodations would not be allowable for these students. To improve accessibility for these and other students, many instructors have begun to design their assessments following the principles of UDA.

UDA began to be conceptualised in the early 2000s in the United States by scholars and practitioners concerned with accessibility of tests. Thompson, Johnstone, and Thurlow (2002) first attempted to make a linkage between Universal Design architectural principles and accessible assessment (see Center for Universal Design 1997, for an overview of these architectural principles, which focus on accessibility of the build environment). Thompson, Johnstone, and Thurlow's (2002) elements focused on (1) inclusive test populations, (2) precisely defined constructs, (3) accessible, non-biased items, (4) amenable to accommodations, (5) simple, clear, and intuitive instructions and procedures, (6) maximum readability and comprehensibility, and (7) maximum legibility. The policy context for accessibility advocacy at the time was the United States' No Child Left Behind Act, which increased assessment for accountability requirements in primary and secondary schools to the highest point in US history. Assessment experts responded by pushing for further evidence that test formats did not introduce barriers for students or assess skills that were outside of the intended construct. Both Ketterlin Geller et al. (2012) and Kettler (2012) warned that sometimes assessments had access requirements (i.e., decoding the words of a math word problem) that inhibited students from demonstrating knowledge of a construct (i.e., mathematical reasoning and problem solving).

Early twenty-first century UDA research focused heavily on assessment theory and understanding the interactions between assessment barriers and student abilities, capabilities, and disabilities. Around the same time, the Center for Applied Special Technologies (CAST) began conceptualising Universal Design for Learning (UDL) (Rose and Meyer 2002) as learning opportunities that included (1) multiple means of engagement, (2) multiple means of response/action, and (3) multiple means of representation. UDL became an important concept in the United States and beyond and was acknowledged in the 2008 US Higher Education Act to promote accessibility in higher education classrooms. Specifically, the guidance notes important features of UDL as: "(A) provides flexibility in the ways information is presented, in the ways students respond or demonstrate knowledge and skills, and in the ways students are engaged; and (B) reduces barriers in instruction, provides appropriate accommodations, supports, and challenges, and maintains high achievement expectations for all students, including students with disabilities and students who are limited English proficient" (US Department of Education 2008, sec. 103). Scholars also posited that UDL guidelines could improve the assessment experience for all students and allow for "built-in" accommodations that all students could access (Dolan et al. 2013). Sheryl Burgstahler and colleagues at the University of Washington Disabilities, Opportunities, Internetworking, and Technologies (DO-IT) Center have been at the forefront of promoting and conducting UDL research in higher education settings (see https://www.washington.edu/doit/).

The framing of UDA as an extension of UDL is an intuitive linkage for assessment in higher education. Although much of the early UDA research focused on paper- and later technology-based tests, in higher education contexts UDA can be applied to a variety of assessment approaches. The overall consideration for "multiple means" has provided instructors in higher education settings with a degree of freedom to allow their students to engage with material in ways that are most accessible. However, identifying ways to improve the accessibility of assessments may be difficult for some instructors. These instructors may be unaware of the barriers that students face, likely because they did not have similar experiences or receive training on assessments. As such, specific assessment practices are often perpetuated by instructors themselves or within disciplines with little understanding of student needs. Focusing on providing "multiple means" can help faculty recognise that students may express their knowledge in a variety of ways and varying their approach to assessment may draw out different levels of understanding.

Although the CAST guidelines associated with providing multiple means of action and expression tend to naturally apply to assessments, drawing on the range of modalities can enhance accessibility of assessments in higher education.

Examples of incorporating multiple means of engagement in assessment design include providing students with choice from a given set of situations, for instance, choice of context, choice of exercises to complete (see Chapter 18), increase the relevance of items or tasks to align with their interests, and build in ways for students to assess their own learning. Multiple means of action and expression can be embedded in assessments by allowing students to respond using different methods (e.g., a written response, a photo essay, or audio presentation), including different item formats that elicit different methods of expression, and scoring the processes (in addition to the products) that students use to engage in problem solving. Finally, multiple means of representation may include providing students with explanations and elaborations on aspects of the task that are not related to the construct, allowing language supports such as dictionaries or translation tools, and provide different ways in which the items are perceived (e.g., written, auditory). Important to all these accessibility features are that they do not change the underlying learning objectives.

Another important consideration when applying UDL to assessment is the way in which feedback information is provided to students. Within the assessment cycle, receiving results and acting on those data is as important as taking the assessment itself. As such, increasing the accessibility of feedback is an important consideration. "Multiple means" can be applied to the way in which feedback information is provided by annotating the scoring of worked samples, providing audio recordings of the instructor's comments, illustrating comments with specific examples, and building in opportunities for self-reflection on outcomes.

Universal Design in higher education in the United States, thanks to policy attention through the Higher Education Act, researchers, and other university disability resource centres, is a relatively well-known approach. UDL (and UDA as an emergent, yet small component of UDL) are now featured in training programs by centres for teaching excellence around the country. Instructors participate in training programs to help them understand that a singular concept may have multiple pathways to understanding and demonstration of knowledge for students. Training and implementation, however, most often occur at the goodwill of instructors, and there is little to compel instructors to take on UDL/UDA approaches except their own interest. Therefore, a student may, in the same semester, experience an instructor who begrudgingly implements accommodations as required but does little more, and another instructor who focuses on multiple means of engagement, response/action, and representation in a class. In the United States, academic freedom is often conflated with pedagogical freedom, which leads students to experience higher education in very different ways.

A proposal

Evidence from around the world indicates that accommodations provide a pathway for individual changes to higher education assessments. These changes are helpful to receiving students, and if they are administered via a disability services office, they are required by law. The procedural implementation of accommodations holds individual instructors accountable for providing changes to assessments for students, whether these assessments are examinations or applied activities. However, the number of students who disclose their disability and seek out accommodations in higher education institutions worldwide is likely far fewer than the actual number of students with disabilities (Griful-Freixenet et al. 2017). This creates a service gap and a barrier to accessible educational opportunities for students.

UDA provides greater flexibility and allows for accessibility measures to be implemented at any time for any student, regardless of disability status. A limitation of UDA, however, is that it largely depends on the interest and goodwill of individual instructors. In the United States there are ample professional development opportunities through university-based teaching centres of excellence and webinars from national organisations like DO-IT, but these opportunities are often underutilised. Further, although UDL is mentioned in the Higher Education Act, neither UDL nor UDA are mandated.

Our proposal for assessment for inclusion in higher education, then, is to draw upon the strengths of accommodations and UDA models to address the weaknesses of each other's model. There have previously been calls by scholars to facilitate greater accessibility in higher education assessment (see Hanafin et al. 2007), but in this chapter we propose a dialectical approach that considers both accommodations and UDA as separate approaches that are complementary, but also could be influential to one another. For example, accommodations are an excellent way to provide individualised changes for students on an as-needed basis. Accommodations, however, are often limited by instructors' perceptions that they must be sanctioned by a disability service office to be allowable. In fact, some disability services offices are now recommending that disability service office accommodations should be the *minimum* approach to accommodations, and instructors should feel empowered to provide accommodations as students' needs dictate (University of Minnesota Disability Resource Center, personal communication 2021).

In this way, accommodations might become a part of general practice, rather than be treated as a precious resource that can only be administered in rare instances (see Wong 2020). In such circumstances, new lines of research may emerge that would characterise accommodations as a practical and individualised solution to educational barriers, not a procedural action. In such scenarios new guidelines would likely need to be developed to ensure minimum, legally mandated accommodations were not overlooked.

Alternatively, UDA is a flexible strategy that can enhance educational accessibility for *all* students, but its implementation may be limited because there is a lack of policy mandates. Stronger guidance or required evidence of UDL/UDA implementation in instructors' portfolios is a policy lever that could increase accessibility for all students, including students with disabilities. Including UDL/UDA in tenure and merit reviews, or associating UDL/UDA principles as part of "quality teaching" expectations, for example, would mandate greater use in higher education classrooms.

In summary, there are two tools that are currently used to increase accessibility in assessments - whether those assessments are tests, authentic expressions of knowledge, or applied activities. Accommodations and UDA each provide useful pathways to accessibility, but also have limitations. One way to address these limitations is to better understand and articulate how accommodations and UDA can be used to inform one another. By drawing on the strengths of accommodations, institutions may become more accountable to their students by making accessibility of assessments an indicator of quality against which instructors' efforts are judged. At the same time, UDA can inform accommodations practice, unlocking greater potential for instructors to utilise and experiment with accommodations, rather than rely solely on minimum requirements outlined in accommodations letters. In the latter case, transparency by instructors on the decisions they make will be critical so that students can track instructor expectations of students, as well as what students can expect of their instructors, across multiple courses.

Further research in these areas is needed, both at the policy and pedagogical level. Little is known about how flexible administration of accommodations impacts the learning and assessment experiences of students, but we suspect such administration might improve students' motivation, decrease anxieties, and allow for greater focus on the core constructs of courses. At the same time, there are few case studies about the impact of institutional reform efforts focused on accessible learning and assessments. We suspect, however, that such changes may improve students' ability to demonstrate how they have understood and reflected on the material in their courses. To this end, we conclude by broadly arguing that enhanced accessibility of assessments aligns with the public good mission of higher education. By removing the access barriers students face in learning and assessment, students may have enhanced opportunity to enjoy all that higher education may provide for them as individuals and enhance their potential for making an impact on their communities and world.

Note

1 IEPs and Section 504 plans are educational planning documents required by law for students in primary and secondary schools in the United States. IEPs are generated by multidisciplinary teams and not used in postsecondary settings, but Section 504 Plans (which identify student accommodation needs based on their disability) are applicable in postsecondary settings).

References

Americans with Disabilities Act. 1990. 28 C.F.R. §§ 36.303(b), 36.309(b)(3).

Center for Universal Design. 1997. *The Principles of Universal Design.* Center for Universal Design, North Carolina State University. https://projects.ncsu.edu/ncsu/design/cud/pubs_p/docs/poster.pdf.

Dolan, R. P., Burling, K., Harms, M., Strain-Seymour, E., Way, W., and Rose, D. H. 2013. *A Universal Design for Learning-Based Framework for Designing Accessible Technology-Enhanced Assessments*. New Jersey: Pearson. http://doi.org/10.13140/RG.2.2.16823.85922.

Griful-Freixenet, J., Struyven, K., Verstichele, M., and Andries, C. 2017. "Higher Education Students with Disabilities Speaking Out: Perceived Barriers and Opportunities of the Universal Design for Learning Framework." *Disability and Society* 32 (10): 1627–1649. http://doi.org/10.1080/09687599.2017.1365695.

Hanafin, J., Shevlin, M., Kenny, M., and McNeela, E. 2007. "Including Young People with Disabilities. Assessment Challenges in Higher Education." *Higher Education* 54 (3): 435–488. http://doi.org/10.1007/s10734-006-9005-9.

Ketterlin Geller, L. R., Jamgochian, E. M., Nelson-Walker, N. J., and Geller, J. P. 2012. "Disentangling Mathematics Target and Access Skills: Implications for Accommodation Assignment Practices." *Learning Disabilities Research and Practice* 27 (4): 178–188. http://doi.org/10.1111/j.1540-5826.2012.00365.x.

Kettler, R. J. 2012. "Testing Accommodations: Theory and Research to Inform Practice." *International Journal of Disability, Development, and Education* 5 (1): 53–66. http://doi.org/10.1080/1034912X.2012.654952.

Kim, W. H., and Lee, J. 2016. "The Effect of Accommodations on Academic Performance of College Students with Disabilities." *Rehabilitation Counseling Bulletin* 60 (1): 40–50. http://doi.org/10.1177/0034355215605259.

Lewandowski, L., Wood, W, and Lambert, T. 2015. "Private Room as a Test Accommodation." *Assessment and Evaluation in Higher Education* 40 (2): 279–285. https://doi.org/10.1080/02602938.2014.911243.

Lombardi, A. R., Murray, C., and Gerdes, H. 2012. "Academic Performance of First Generation College Students with Disabilities." *Journal of College Student Development* 53 (6): 811–826. http://doi.org/10.1353/csd.2012.0082.

Luttenberger, S., Wimmer, S., and Paechter, M. 2018. "Spotlight on Math Anxiety." *Psychology Research and Behavior Management* 11: 311–322. http://doi.org/10.2147/PRBM.S141421.

Nieminen, J. H. 2022. "Governing the 'Disabled Assessee': A Critical Reframing of Assessment Accommodations as Sociocultural Practices." *Disability and Society* 37(8): 1293–1320. https://doi.org/10.1080/09687599.2021.1874304.

Rose, D. H., and Meyer, A. 2002. *Teaching Every Student in the Digital Age: Universal Design for Learning*. Alexandria, VA: Association for Supervision and Curriculum Development.

Scott, G. A. 2011. *Higher Education and Disability: Improved Federal Enforcement Needed to Better Protect Students' Rights to Testing Accommodations. Report to Congressional Requesters. GAO-12-40*. Washington, DC: US Government Accountability Office.

Thompson, S. J., Johnstone, C. J., and Thurlow, M. L. 2002. *Universal Design Applied to Large Scale Assessments. Synthesis Report 44*. Minneapolis, MN: National Center on Educational Outcomes.

Thurlow, M., and Bolt, S. 2001. *Empirical Support for Accommodations Most Often Allowed in State Policy* (Synthesis Report 41). Minneapolis, MN: University of Minnesota, National Center on Educational Outcomes.

US Department of Education, National Center for Education Statistics. 2021. *Digest of Education Statistics, 2019* (NCES 2021-009). https://nces.ed.gov/programs/digest/d19/tables/dt19_311.10.asp.

US Department of Education. 2008, sec. 103. The Higher Education Opportunity Act. Universal Design for Learning. 20 USC § 1003(24).

US Department of Justice. 2014. *ADA Requirements: Testing Accommodations*. https://www.ada.gov/regs2014/testing-accommodations.pdf.

Weis, R., and Beauchemin, E. L. 2019. "Are Separate Room Accommodations Effective for College Students with Disabilities? *Assessment and Evaluation in Higher Education* 45 (5): 794–809. https://doi.org/10.1080/02602938.2019.1702922.

Wong, A., ed. 2020. *Disability Visibility: First-Person Stories from the Twenty-First Century*. New York: Vintage Books.

Wu, Y.-C., Liu, K. K., Lazarus, S. S., and Thurlow, M. L. 2021. *2018–2019 APR Snapshot #26: Students in Special Education Assigned Assessment Accommodations*. National Center on Educational Outcomes. https://ici.umn.edu/products/ODcfUaAbRUm1nIr5nftRaQ.

13

MORE THAN ASSESSMENT TASK DESIGN

Promoting equity for students from low socio-economic status backgrounds

Trina Jorre de St Jorre and David Boud

What is the problem?

Investment in widening participation initiatives has significantly improved the participation of students from low socio-economic status (SES) backgrounds (Raciti 2019), but they continue to have poorer educational outcomes, both in terms of academic achievement and graduate employment (Harvey et al. 2017). As students, they face challenges related to belonging and engagement throughout their degree (Burke et al. 2016), and are more likely to discontinue study and achieve poorer grades (Harvey et al. 2017). As graduates they benefit less in the labour market than their peers from medium and high SES backgrounds (Li and Carroll 2019; O'Shea 2016; Richardson, Bennett, and Roberts 2016), having poorer rates of overall and full-time employment, and reduced salaries after graduation (4–6 months, QILT 2019; 5–15 years, Tomaszewski et al. 2019). Some causes have been identified, but more research is needed to fully understand and address inequities that cause disadvantage, especially with regards to the suitability of assessment.

Attempts to address inequalities for students from low SES backgrounds have primarily focussed on their transition into university, including transition pedagogies to address gaps in academic preparedness, self-efficacy and belonging as students move into and through their degrees (Devlin and McKay 2017; Kift 2015). This has led to improvements in understanding and practice, but gaps in academic achievement and retention remain, and few studies have focussed on the equally challenging transition that the same vulnerable cohorts face as they enter the highly competitive graduate workforce. Surprisingly, little attention has been paid to the contribution of assessment to gaps in retention, success or employment outcomes.

There is ample evidence that the ways in which universities represent the achievement of graduates provides poor evidence of capabilities and outcomes valued in the workplace (Jorre de St Jorre, Boud, and Johnson 2021). This presents

DOI: 10.4324/9781003293101-16

challenges for all graduates, because they need to look to experiences beyond what is assessed to convey their capabilities to employers (Jorre de St Jorre, Boud, and Johnson 2021). However, the shortcomings of assessment pose a greater problem for students from low SES backgrounds because they tend to be less aware of opportunities to improve their employability (Doyle 2011; Greenbank and Hepworth 2008; Harvey et al. 2017), and this contributes to disadvantage in the graduate labour market (Li and Carroll 2019; O'Shea 2016; QILT 2019; Richardson, Bennett, and Roberts 2016; Tomaszewski et al. 2019). Equitable employment opportunities are essential to improving social mobility and stopping cycles of intergenerational disadvantage for students from low SES backgrounds, so this aspect of assessment needs to be addressed urgently.

Why does assessment matter?

Assessment impacts what students learn and serves as a gateway to progression and entry into professions. Despite its importance, numerous scholars have expressed concerns about assessment failing to meet its potential and lagging other curriculum reform (Jorre de St Jorre, Boud, and Johnson 2021; Knight 2002; Shay 2008). Of equal concern, is the unchallenged influence that assessment has in legitimising certain capabilities, knowledge, and ways of knowing (Bullen and Flavell 2022; Leathwood 2005; Shay 2008). Assessment is a socially constructed practice, that is interwoven with relations of power (Leathwood 2005; Shay 2008). With that in mind, it is appropriate that we carefully examine the purpose of assessment and whose interest it serves.

There is growing evidence that assessment perpetuates dominant social structures and power relations. For example, stereotype threat (the predicament in which individuals from a stigmatised social group are or feel at risk of confirming a negative stereotype) is known to negatively impact the test performance of people from minorities groups and women (Nguyen and Ryan 2008), and it is well documented that unconscious bias in the assessment of learner performance disadvantages minority performance in medical education (Lucey et al. 2020). Thus, it is somewhat surprising, that assessment has not been scrutinised more as a source of the inequity that contributes to persistent gaps in academic achievement and employment outcomes for students from low SES backgrounds.

The shortcomings of current assessment strategies and how they might be addressed

Assessment privileges dominant cultural practices and perspectives

Assessment supports individualism and competition, and those who "understand the game" are advantaged by that knowledge and encouraged by early success. Whereas those who don't, need to learn the rules, and overcome the de-motivating potential of negative emotions associated with failure or disappointing grades (Leathwood 2005). These experiences impact some individuals more than others, but more concerningly, they can systemically discriminate against entire groups in ways that are insidious and predictable given common experiences of past inequalities.

Assessors strive for consistency and accuracy in the judgement of student work. However, they are rarely experts in assessment design, and grade integrity is compromised both by the scope and soundness of assessment design, and the subjectivity of judgements made about performance (Hailikari et al. 2014; Sadler 2009a). In reality, assessment is largely informed by long-standing disciplinary norms, and what educators have themselves experienced (Bearman et al. 2017). As such, it is designed and constructed in accordance with the social and cultural backgrounds of academics, whose experience of higher education may differ considerably from how it is experienced by contemporary students, or those from other sociocultural backgrounds (HEFCE 2015).

Qualitative research shows that students often feel that what they see in the curriculum, and thus assessment, does not reflect their identities (HEFCE 2015). However, students from middle and high SES backgrounds are more likely to be familiar with, and therefore be advantaged by, dominant cultural codes and practices (cultural capital) and social relationships which provide access to resources (social capital) relevant to their navigating assessment. Thus assessment "norms" and traditions advantage those who can relate to, or are familiar with, the values and practices reflected in standards and assessment tasks, particularly aspects that involve subjective elements (Sadler 2009a, 2009b; Yorke 2011).

The articulation of standards and criteria are meant to help with assuring accuracy and transparency in assessment. However, the way in which criteria are formulated and communicated provides insufficient clarity for students or those who contribute to assessment, leading to inconsistencies and inaccuracies in the judgement of achievement (Woolf 2004). Some argue that to strive for greater accuracy is fruitless, because the application of criteria necessarily requires subjective interpretation, and understanding therefore needs to be co-constructed (Shay 2008). This is especially important for students from low SES backgrounds, because they often feel underprepared academically and less assured in co-constructing knowledge. There is evidence that both university staff and students recognise the importance of accessible language and examples, especially with respect to assessment requirements (Devlin et al. 2012).

Assessment that is not inclusive is demotivating and enables social closure

Where students from low SES backgrounds are confused by assessment requirements, doubt their ability to succeed, or compare themselves to more advantaged peers, they are likely to be demotivated. Students who are demotivated are likely to engage less with activities of importance to assessment because expectations and personal efficacy are mediators of achievement related choices. Individuals are more inclined to engage with activities when they have high expectations of success and their own self-efficacy (Eccles 2009). Achievement-related choices are also influenced by internal and external comparison processes: people assess their skills across different tasks or contexts, and in comparison to others (Eccles 2009). Interpretive processes, such as the amount of effort attributed to success or failure, and social influences (people who reinforce whether they are good or not) are also important (Eccles 2009).

In addition to limitations imposed by students' perceptions of themselves and how they relate to assessment tasks, their aspirations can be further limited by how they are treated by others. "Social closure" is a phenomenon which describes the tendency of privileged groups to limit access to resources and opportunities in ways that sustain social hierarchies (Harvey et al. 2017). Harvey et al. (2017) raise concerns about social closure in relation to the employability strategies implemented by universities. They argue that institutions need to think more carefully about what, and who, are rewarded by such strategies. For example, it is well established that students from low SES backgrounds are less likely to engage with opportunities to gain experience relevant to employment – using career services, non-compulsory work-integrated learning, extra-curricular experiences valued by employers, and student clubs and societies – that can provide valuable networks and experience (Doyle 2011; Greenbank and Hepworth 2008; Harvey et al. 2017).

Concerns about the impact of social closure are equally relevant to assessment. Students who interact more with their teachers tend to do better, but students from low SES backgrounds are more reluctant to seek academic support than their more privileged peers, because they often lack confidence and self-esteem, and are more likely to question the validity of their questions and how staff might respond (Devlin et al. 2012). Greater focus on inclusive assessment could help to address inequities that lead to disparities in both academic achievement and employment outcomes. For example, scaffolded low stakes early assessment, enables students to develop skills and confidence, and formative feedback and self and peer review can be embedded into assessment processes to ensure that all students have opportunities to learn the rules of the game. Assessment can also be used to ensure that all students engage with learning relevant to developing their vocational aspirations and understanding of the skills and experience relevant to gaining those opportunities (Jorre de St Jorre, Boud, and Johnson 2021; Jorre de St Jorre and Oliver 2018).

"Fairness" at the expense of equity

The notion of fairness is integral to the design and improvement of assessment practices, but scholars have primarily been concerned with the challenge of constructing "neutral" and "objective" assessment tools (Leathwood 2005). For reasons of fairness, assessment strives to consistently measure student achievement of learning outcomes, irrespective of the student assessed or the assessor responsible. Historically, and ironically, examinations have been explicitly introduced to eliminate patronage and mitigate advantage afforded by social standing. However, the conditions under which assessment takes place are not identical and assessment that treats all students the same, is by definition, not equitable (Stowell 2004). Students have unique personal histories and lived realities which influence what they know (including their familiarity with the assessment processes) and can do, and opportunities for growth and expression. Those differences influence how students experience and perform during assessment.

Under some circumstances, inequities associated with assessing all students the same are acknowledged, for example, special arrangements are put in place to provide students with obvious and accepted disabilities with fairer opportunities to demonstrate achievement. Likewise, ill-health, family bereavements, and personal crises are commonly regarded as legitimate reasons for special arrangements, such as deferral or reassessment (Stowell 2004). However, other circumstances which are more likely to adversely affect the performance of students from low SES backgrounds are not acknowledged or written into policy. These include the impact of competing family and work responsibilities, which persist throughout a student's enrolment, or the impact of geographical distance which makes it more difficult and time consuming for students to access learning resources and environments. With these examples, one could argue that students have opportunities to adjust their own enrolment to accommodate competing demands (e.g., they can enrol in part-time study). However, other inequalities are not so easily dismissed. For example, students from low SES backgrounds commonly have less educational opportunity prior to entering higher education, and those who are first-in-family, have less support for understanding the "rules of the game".

It is not necessary for students to undertake identical assessment tasks or to produce identical artefacts to demonstrate equivalent achievement of the same learning outcomes, but that is the way in which assessment is most often designed (Jorre de St Jorre, Boud, and Johnson 2021). While it is commonplace for students to generate a variety of outputs with respect to project work, the same thinking is needed with all major summative assessment tasks. Assessment must enable judgement of whether a student has met the necessary learning outcomes, but the mechanisms or tasks they use to demonstrate those can vary.

Lack of opportunity to understand and portray meaningful achievements

Assessment for learning is a well-established concept, which recognises that assessment can, and should be used to direct students' attention to the achievement of important learning outcomes. Numerous authors have pointed to assessment as a means through which educators can engage students with learning important to employability (Jorre de St Jorre and Oliver 2018; Kinash, McGillivray, and Crane 2017), and this is especially relevant for students from low SES backgrounds because they more often lack awareness of the skills and experiences employers value, or networks that can provide careers advice or connect them with relevant opportunities (Doyle 2011; Richardson, Bennett, and Roberts 2016). Thus, it is especially important that assessment is designed to direct this vulnerable cohort to learning of importance to careers. Unfortunately, research has also shown that students rarely link assessment to employability (Ajjawi et al. 2020; Kinash, McGillivray, and Crane 2017).

As more students graduate from large cohorts, assessment that fails to capture unique achievements becomes increasingly questionable. In addition to failing to account for differences in opportunity and expression, homogenised assessment that involves identical tasks for all, provides students with poor opportunities to demonstrate achievements that distinguish them from peers or predecessors with the same or similar qualifications (Jorre de St Jorre, Boud, and Johnson 2021; Jorre de St Jorre and Oliver 2018). Instead of providing opportunities for distinctive achievement, common assessment practices encourage "sameness" which, beyond the necessary purpose of assuring threshold achievements, has little additional value to students, employers, or society.

Graduates with the same or similar qualifications do not all need to have the same strengths, because they will inevitably gain different roles in which different subsets of skills and personal attributes are most valued. Unlike assessment, employers judge graduates based on different characteristics and standards, because their preferences and the requirements of different job roles and organisations are highly variable. Thus, the ideal candidate for one employer will not necessarily be the best candidate for another.

Given that assessment signals that which is important, what does assessment that values sameness, say about the value of diversity in the workplace, our society and our learning environments? In requiring that students perform the same tasks and be judged against the same standards, homogenised assessment fails to acknowledge the value of different perspectives, skills, personal attributes and experience. This is in direct contrast with professional contexts in which individual differences can be a valuable source of competitive advantage, and diverse collaborations can be leveraged to solve complex problems, drive innovation and build new knowledge (Adams et al. 2011; Brown, Hesketh, and Williams 2004).

To enable students to utilise assessment for distinctiveness, we also need to rethink the ways in which we enable students to verify and portray their personal achievements to different audiences, for different purposes (Jorre St Jorre, Boud, and Johnson 2021). For example, representation of achievement through academic transcripts provides insufficient detail to enable identification of what a graduate can do. Likewise, where university awards are solely grades based (e.g., based on a Grade Point Average), they provide no context for what was achieved, and only recognise a small number of students, rather than all of those who meet a specific standard. Digital credentials can, however, be constructed to convey the context of achievement, including the standards assessed, and rich artefacts curated by students to evidence their achievements, such as portfolios or videos

(Miller et al. 2017). Valuing distinctiveness may require students from non-traditional backgrounds to be reassured that they do not need to always conform to the norm.

Fostering engagement with assessment

While the shortcomings of assessment can inappropriately limit students, other attributes can foster fuller engagement. The subjective value attributed to a task is important to motivation and the decisions made about engagement with specific tasks (Eccles 2009). Student engagement is bi-directional: curricula that increase achievement and satisfaction through fostering interest, enthusiasm and effort can lead to more of the same, that is, "engagement breeds engagement" (Kahu 2013). Thus, to be inclusive, assessment needs not only to provide equal opportunities for students to succeed, but it also needs to be equally meaningful to them. This requires that students understand the relevance of intended learning outcomes, and that these consider the values and aspirations of learners, and the communities to which they seek to belong. Eccles (2009, 82) suggest that four components contribute to the value of a task: (1) interest value: interest in, or enjoyment gained from the task itself; (2) attainment value: the value an activity has for affirming one's personal and collective identities; (3) utility value: utility of the task to achieving long term goals or to obtaining rewards; (4) perceived cost: the financial and emotional costs associated with engaging with the activity, as well as the potential opportunity cost, and the potential meaning of the behavior for confirming or disconfirming a salient personal or social identity.

The components proposed by Eccles align with factors known to be important to the retention and success of students. Being intellectually engaged with study, feeling a sense of belonging and feeling supported and able to succeed, are factors that incentivise students to study, whereas fear of failure, emotional health and financial stress, contribute to attrition (Naylor, Baik, and Arkoudis 2018). The costs associated with study tend to be less for students from middle and high SES backgrounds. Such students also have more opportunities to develop identities which support their expectations of success, their sense of belonging in higher education and help to develop their aspirations for life beyond higher education: factors which are likely to contribute to advantage in regards to retention, academic achievement and graduate employment outcomes.

We suggest that assessment which helps students develop their professional identity and understand the relevance of the curriculum and other opportunities to their future aspirations, can help to engage and address gaps in achievement for students from low SES backgrounds. Student-focussed research has shown that students perceive the involvement of industry or the professions in the design or delivery of their learning with credibility and relevance, and suggests that involvement of employers, professionals and recent graduates, and exposure to industry-related experiences can make the curriculum and the achievement of learning outcomes more meaningful (Jorre de St Jorre and Oliver 2018). Other studies have shown that experiences in the workplace can change how students approach learning on campus, because they help students to understand the relevance of their skills and knowledge, and orientate them to careers (Johnson and Rice 2016). Other research examining students experience of extra-curricular strategies designed to recognise and engage students in articulating and evidencing capabilities of importance to employability (i.e. video pitches and digital credentials requiring students to curate portfolios) has shown that students can gain confidence – in themselves, their employability and in their ability to articulate themselves to employers – and greater appreciation for learning throughout their degree (Jorre de St Jorre, Johnson, and O'Dea 2017). While the majority of students enrol in higher education for employment related reasons, employment outcomes are particularly important to students from low SES backgrounds (Raciti 2019).

Assessment that emphasises the relevance of learning outcomes to careers may also contribute to students' sense of belonging. Students have been shown to perceive teachers who emphasise employability as caring (Jorre de St Jorre and Oliver 2018). Positive correlations have been observed between students' perceptions of their employability, and their perception of their employability skills, knowledge and attitudes acquired through completing their degree (de Oliveira Silva et al. 2019). Thus, in addition to ensuring that students from low SES backgrounds proactively engage in activities that are important to expanding their understanding and development of employability, assessment which develops students' professional identity, such as through simulation or modelling activities, will likely also contribute to how they value and engage with their broader learning experience and with the assessment itself.

Conclusion

Assessment needs to ensure that all students meet appropriate high standards. However, it must do so in ways that do not provide additional privilege to certain social groups, or which place unnecessary barriers in the way of students meeting these standards. Inclusive assessment means not giving hidden advantage to those who have already benefited. Consideration of assessment for inclusion also provides an opportunity to rethink what is needed to motivate students and engage them in activities which aid their employability.

References

Adams, R., Evangelou, D., English, L., Fugueiredo, A., Mousoulides, N., Pawley, A. L., and Schiefellite, C. et al. 2011. "Multiple Perspectives on Engaging Future Engineers." *Journal of Engineering Education* 100 (1): 48–88. https://doi.org/10.1002/j.2168-9830.2011.tb00004.x.

Ajjawi, R., Tai, J., Huu Nghia, T. L., Boud, D., Johnson, L., and Patrick, C.-J. 2020. "Aligning Assessment with the Needs of Work-Integrated Learning: The Challenges of Authentic Assessment in a Complex Context." *Assessment and Evaluation in Higher Education* 45 (2): 304–316. http://doi.org/10.1080/02602938.2019.1639613.

Bearman, M., Dawson, P., Bennett, S., Hall, M., Molloy, E., Boud, D., and Joughin, G. 2017. "How University Teachers Design Assessments: A Cross-Disciplinary Study." *Higher Education* (1): 49–64. http://doi.org/10.1007/s10734-016-0027-7.

Brown, P., Hesketh, A., and Williams, S. 2004. *The Mismanagement of Talent: Employability and Jobs in the Knowledge Economy*. New York: Oxford University Press.

Bullen, J., and Flavell, H. 2022. "Decolonising the Indigenised Curricula: Preparing Australian Graduates for a Workplace and World in Flux." *Higher Education Research and Development* 41(5): 1402–1416. http://doi.org/10.1080/07294360.2021.1927998.

Burke, P. J., Bennett, A., Burgess, C., Gray, K., and Southgate, E. 2016. *Capability, Belonging and Equity in Higher Education: Developing Inclusive Approaches*. Accessed 23 September 2021. https://www.ncsehe.edu.au/publications/capability-belonging-and-equity-in-higher-education-developing-inclusive-approaches/.

de Oliveira Silva, J. H., de Sousa Mendes, G. H., Ganga, G. M. D., Mergulhão, R. C., and Lizarelli, F. L. 2019. "Antecedents and Consequents of Student Satisfaction in Higher Technical-Vocational Education: Evidence from Brazil." *International Journal for Educational and Vocational Guidance*. http://doi.org/10.1007/s10775-019-09407-1.

Devlin, M., Kift, S., Nelson, K., Smith, L., and McKay, J. 2012. *Effective Teaching and Support of Students from Low Socioeconomic Status Backgrounds: Practical Advice for Teaching Staff*. Accessed September 23, 2021. https://www.lowses.edu.au/assets/Practical%20Advice%20for%20Teaching%20Staff.pdf.

Devlin, M., and McKay, J. 2017. *Facilitating Success for Students from Low Socioeconomic Status Backgrounds at Regional Universities*. Ballarat: Federation University Australia. https://www.ncsehe.edu.au/wp-content/uploads/2018/05/55_Federation_MarciaDevlin_Accessible_PDF.pdf.

Doyle, E. 2011. "Career Development Needs of Low Socio-Economic Status University Students." *Australian Journal of Career Development* 20 (3): 56–65. http://doi.org/10.1177/103841621102000309.

Eccles, J. 2009. "Who Am I and What Am I Going to Do with My Life? Personal and Collective Identities as Motivators of Action." *Educational Psychologist* 44 (2): 78–89. http://doi.org/10.1080/00461520902832368.

Greenbank, P., and Hepworth, S. 2008. *Working Class Students and the Career Decision-Making Process: A Qualitative Study*. Great Britain: Higher Education Careers Services Unit (HECSU). http://hdl.voced.edu.au/10707/195946.

Hailikari, T., Postareff, L., Tuonone, T., Räisänen, M., and Lindblom-Ylänne, S. 2014. "Students' and Teachers' Perceptions of Fairness of Assessment." In *Advances and Innovations in University Assessment and Feedback: A Festchrift in Honour of Professor Dai Hounsell*, edited by Caroline Kreber, Charles Anderson, Noel Entwistle, and Jan McArthur, 99–113. Edinburgh: Edinburgh University Press. http://doi.org/10.3366/edinburgh/9780748694549.003.0006.

Harvey, A., Andrewartha, L., Edwards, D., Clarke, J., and Reyes, K. 2017. *Student Equity and Employability in Higher Education*. Melbourne: Centre for Higher Education Equity and Diversity Research. https://www.ncsehe.edu.au/wp-content/uploads/2018/06/73_LaTrobe_AndrewHarvey_Accessible_PDF.pdf.

HEFCE. 2015. *Causes of Differences in Student Outcomes*. Report to HEFCE by Kings College London, ARC Network and The University of Manchester. https://dera.ioe.ac.uk/23653/1/HEFCE2015_diffout.pdf.

Johnson, E., and Rice, J. 2016. *WIL in Science: Leadership for WIL Final Report*. https://www.chiefscientist.gov.au/2017/05/report-work-integrated-learning-in-science-leadership-for-wil/.

Jorre de St Jorre, T., Boud, D., and Johnson, E. D. 2021. "Assessment for Distinctiveness: Recognising Diversity of Accomplishments." *Studies in Higher Education* 46 (7): 1371–1382. http://doi.org/:10.1080/03075079.2019.1689385.

Jorre de St Jorre, T., Johnson, L., and O'Dea, G. 2017. "Me in a Minute: A Simple Strategy for Developing and Showcasing Personal Employability." In *The Me, Us, IT! Proceedings ASCILITE2017: 34th International Conference on Innovation, Practice and Research in the Use of Educational Technologies in Tertiary Education*. Toowomba.

Jorre de St Jorre, T., and Oliver, B. 2018. "Want Students to Engage? Contextualise Graduate Learning Outcomes and Assess for Employability." *Higher Education Research and Development* 37 (1): 44–57. https://doi.org/10.1080/07294360.2017.1339183.

Kahu, E. R. 2013. "Framing Student Engagement in Higher Education." *Studies in Higher Education* 38 (5): 758–773. https://doi.org/10.1080/03075079.2011.598505.

Kift, S. 2015. "A Decade of Transition Pedagogy: A Quantum Leap in Conceptualising the First Year Experience." *HERDSA Review of Higher Education* 2: 51–86. www.herdsa.org.au/publications/journals/herdsa-review-higher-education-vol-2.

Kinash, S., McGillivray, L., and Crane, L. 2017. "Do University Students, Alumni, Educators and Employers Link Assessment and Graduate Employability?" *Higher Education Research and Development* 37 (2): 301–315. http://doi.org/10.1080/07294360.2017.1370439.

Knight, P. T. 2002. "The Achilles Heel of Quality: The Assessment of Student Learning." *Quality in Higher Education* 8 (1): 107–116. https://doi.org/10.1080/13538320220127506.

Leathwood, C. 2005. "Assessment Policy and Practice in Higher Education: Purpose, Standards and Equity." *Assessment and Evaluation in Higher Education* 30 (3): 307–324. https://doi.org/10.1080/02602930500063876.

Li, I. W., and Carroll, D. R. 2019. "Factors Influencing Dropout and Academic Performance: An Australian Higher Education Equity Perspective." *Journal of Higher Education Policy and Management* 42 (1): 14–30. https://doi.org/10.1080/1360080X.2019.1649993.

Lucey, C. R., Hauer, K. E., Boatright, D., and Fernandez, A. 2020. "Medical Education's Wicked Problem: Achieving Equity in Assessment for Medical Learners." *Academic Medicine* 95 (12S): S98–S108. http://doi.org/10.1097/ACM.0000000000003717.

Miller, K. K., Jorre de St Jorre, T., West, J. M., and Elizabeth, D. J. 2017. "The Potential of Digital Credentials to Engage Students with Capabilities of Importance to Scholars and Citizens." *Active Learning in Higher Education* 21 (1): 11–22. http://doi.org/10.1177/1469787417742021.

Naylor, R., Baik, C., and Arkoudis, S. 2018. "Identifying Attrition Risk Based on the First Year Experience." *Higher Education Research and Development* 37 (2): 328–342. http://doi.org/10.1080/07294360.2017.1370438.

Nguyen, H.-H. D., and Ryan, A. M. 2008. "Does Stereotype Threat Affect Test Performance of Minorities and Women? A Meta-Analysis of Experimental Evidence." *Journal of Applied Psychology* 93 (6): 1314–1334. http://doi.org/10.1037/a0012702.

O'Shea, S. 2016. *'Mind the Gap!' Exploring the Postgraduation Outcomes and Employment Mobility of Individuals Who Are First in Their Family to Complete a University Degree*. Perth: National Centre for Student Equity in Higher Education. https://www.ncsehe.edu.au/wp-content/uploads/2020/01/OShea_ResearchFellowship_FINALREPORT_.pdf.

QILT. 2019. 2018 *Graduate Outcomes Survey*. National Report. https://www.qilt.edu.au/resources?survey=GOS&type=Reports.

Raciti, M. 2019. *Career Construction, Future Work and the Perceived Risks of Going to University for Young People from Low SES Backgrounds*. Research Fellowship Final Report. Perth: National Centre for Student Equity in Higher Education (NCSEHE).

Richardson, S., Bennett, D., and Roberts, L. 2016. *Investigating the Relationship between Equity and Graduate Outcomes in Australia*. Perth: National Centre for Student Equity in Higher Education.

Sadler, D. R. 2009a. "Grade Integrity and the Representation of Academic Achievement." *Studies in Higher Education* 34 (7): 807–826. http://doi.org/10.1080/03075070802706553.

Sadler, D. R. 2009b. "Indeterminacy in the Use of Preset Criteria for Assessment and Grading." *Assessment and Evaluation in Higher Education* 34 (2): 159–179. http://doi.org/10.1080/02602930801956059.

Shay, S. 2008. "Beyond Social Constructivist Perspectives on Assessment: The Centring of Knowledge." *Teaching in Higher Education* 13 (5): 595–605. http://doi.org/10.1080/13562510802334970.

Stowell, M. 2004. "Equity, Justice and Standards: Assessment Decision Making in Higher Education." *Assessment and Evaluation in Higher Education* 29 (4): 495–510. http://doi.org/10.1080/02602930310001689055.

Tomaszewski, W., Perales, F., Xiang, N., and Kubler, M. 2019. *Beyond Graduation: Long-Term Socioeconomic Outcomes Amongst Equity Students*. https://www.ncsehe.edu.au/wp-content/uploads/2019/08/Tomaszewski_UQ_Final_Accessible_9_8.pdf.

Woolf, H. 2004. "Assessment Criteria: Reflections on Current Practices." *Assessment and Evaluation in Higher Education* 29 (4): 479–493. http://doi.org/10.1080/02602930310001689046.

Yorke, M. 2011. "Summative Assessment: Dealing with the 'Measurement Fallacy.'" *Studies in Higher Education* 36 (3): 251–273. https://doi.org/10.1080/03075070903545082.

14

ASSESSING EMPLOYABILITY SKILLS

How are current assessment practices "fair" for international students?

Thanh Pham

Introduction

International education plays a significant role in Australia's economy. The sector contributed A$40.3 billion to Australia's economy in 2019 (UK Department of Education 2019). However, Australia's position in the international education market has been threatened because both traditional (e.g., the UK) and non-traditional (e.g., Asian countries) immigration countries have actively launched policies to attract and retain highly skilled migrants (Czaika 2018). Post-study career prospects are a key goal for many international students. Therefore, to become more competitive in the international education market, Australian higher education needs to better ensure international students' employability outcomes.

In fact, the Australian Government has recently targeted graduate employability as its key priority by linking university performance-based funding directly to employment outcomes (Wellings et al. 2019). Universities have taken the skills-based approach that emphasises the need for students to learn a range of professional skills (e.g., communication, teamwork) as a "solution" to enhance students' education-to-work transition. Although this approach has been widely applied, professional skills are still perceived as supplementary to the curriculum or part of work-integrated learning units. Consequently, insufficient attention has been paid to how students' professional skills could be assessed properly. Importantly, current practices designed to assess students' professional skills disadvantage international students in various ways.

This chapter aims to critically discuss how current assessment practices of employability skills disadvantage international students. The chapter has three main parts. It starts with a discussion about how employability skills have been implemented and assessed in higher education. It then discusses common

DOI: 10.4324/9781003293101-17

limitations in employability skills facing international students. Finally, the chapter critically discusses how current assessment practices disadvantage international students.

Employability skills and assessing employability skills of international students in higher education

Employability is a contested concept. Predominantly, researchers have argued that employability refers to skills and capacities of students to obtain and gain employment and be successful in their chosen occupations (Yorke 2004) and the capability to move self-sufficiently within the labour market to realise potential through sustainable employment (Hillage and Pollard 1998). Recently, an increasing number of researchers have argued for the need to examine employability as a phenomenon that is supported and constrained by various capitals (e.g., human, social, cultural, identity, psychological, agentic) rather than as a skill (Pham 2021b; Tomlinson 2017).

Due to the predominance of the skills-based approach, in Australia, for the last two decades universities have attempted to identify specific graduate attributes that they believe university students need to develop during their studies. There has been an array of terminology used to describe employability skills. The common terms are "competencies", "generic skills", "professional skills", "graduate outcomes", "graduate capabilities", "transferable skills", and recently "professional skills" (Clanchy and Ballard 1995; Jones 2010; Pham and Saito 2019). In general, "employability skills" refers to the skills – beyond disciplinary knowledge and technical skills – considered necessary and relevant for the workplace. A wide range of employability skills have been identified and emphasised differently in different disciplines. However, the most common skills are communication (verbal and written), problem solving, analysis, critical thinking, and teamwork.

To assess students' employability skills, recently, more and more researchers have argued for a novel test format known as competence-oriented examinations, also referred to as "performance-based" or "competence-oriented tests" (Braun 2021). This type of assessment aims to test the individual's capabilities to act holistically (Blomeke, Gustafsson, and Shavelson 2015; Shavelson, Zlatkin-Troitschanskaia, and Mariño 2018). Competence-oriented examinations emphasise the specificity of the situation and the student's capacity to adapt. They measure skills by introducing situations that involve complex interactions that are as authentic as possible (Braun and Mishra 2016). This means that employability skills are not assessed by standardised written tests but in scenarios where students need to show their technical knowledge and skills so that they can respond to the situation.

Although this employability skills approach and competence-oriented examination have been predominant in higher education, the approach has received a range of criticisms. One of the main critiques is that the concepts of skills are vague (Lowden et al. 2011; Mason, Williams, and Cramner 2009). Jackson (2012) evidenced that there was a range of different interpretations of an attribute or a skill depending on the context, background, expertise and position of the interpreter. In the workplace, the process of matching expert knowledge with occupational recruitment and roles does not take place in a social vacuum, with all skills and attributes heavily raced, classed, and gendered (Brown 1995; Morrison 2014; Tholen 2015). This means the skills that students learn in higher education are often interpreted and used differently in the workplace although the name might be the same.

In the case of international students, a range of studies exploring international students' employability have reported a wide range of problems related to employability skills facing this cohort. They have been evidenced to have limited English proficiency, low-level communication skills and limitations in a range of Western personal values like being proactive, critical, innovative, and independent (Blackmore, Gribble, and Rahimi 2017). They therefore need additional assistance in order to excel in their studies and to gain the most of their overseas study experiences (Briguglio and Smith 2012). When international graduates enter the workforce, they have been described as having similar problems. For instance, common comments about international, especially Asian, students are that they are "not active", "unconfident", and "not critical". Specifically, Howells, Westerveld, and Garvis (2017) found that workplace supervisors complained that international students, particularly those from Asia, were disengaged because they did not ask questions.

Amongst employability skills, the skill that international students have received the most complaints about is communication (Pham 2021a). Communication skills are often interpreted as linguistic skills, so understood as cognitive dispositions (Blomeke, Gustafsson, and Shavelson 2015). Communication skills are, therefore, measured using standardised written and oral tests. In these tests, common problems facing international students are their "heavy" accents and limited terminologies. They often cannot pronounce sounds and phonemes that do not exist in their language accurately. For instance, Asian students from certain regions often have difficulty with, and inaccurate pronunciation of "r", "th", and "w" sounds. Some students are notedto have an "awkward" accent which can be hard to understand (Barton et al. 2017). This is because British and American English are the most preferable. These accents are reported as "clear", "intelligible", and representative of "world standards" (Ngoc 2016). Those who do not possess an accent familiar to British and American English speakers often experience difficulties in interacting with other people. The second problem often facing international students is their limited writing and technical terminologies. Consequently, it is hard for them to write and communicate in a natural way. In daily practices, their difficulties are amplified because the native English speakers often use slang terms such as "grab a cuppa", "calling the roll", and "put your hands up" (Barton et al. 2017), which are not taught in official teaching and learning programs.

Another line of research argues that communication competencies should include a range of factors including discourse (capacity to speak and write in a suitable context), actional (capacity to convey communicative intent), sociocultural (capacity to use culturally appropriate language), and strategic (capacity to learn the language in the context) (Celce-Murcia, Dörnyei, and Thurrell 1995). In brief, this perspective argues for the need to examine the non-verbal aspect as an important part of communication. Non-verbal signals are also crucial to successful communication. They include all the physical signals that occur when a person talks, apart from actual words (Braun 2021). It is how something is said, independent of the content. Röhner and Schütz (2015) claimed that common physical signals are haptic (e.g., touching), body language (e.g., posture, mimicry), proxemics (e.g., the chosen spatial proximity to one another), or physical characteristics (e.g., clothing and cosmetics). Body language in particular is relevant to communication (Röhner and Schütz 2015). Sharing a similar view, Blomeke, Gustafsson, and Shavelson (2015) argued that communication should include competence to act. This competence refers to the ability to adapt effectively to one's social environment or to behave appropriately according to the situation. According to this notion of competence, individuals are perceived to have good communication if they have socially accepted behaviours. This means this line of research argues for the use of competence-oriented examinations so that multifaceted aspects of communication could be assessed.

Pham (2021a) reported evidence about a range of issues that international graduates often face in scenarios like competence-oriented examinations. They often divulge a sense of difficulty in obtaining the right knowledge, appropriate communication skills, and sensitivity to cultural differences to respond to real-life scenarios, so fail to conduct natural and smooth conversations. Issues associated with smoothness and confidence did not arise from the graduates' English proficiency, but from the context in which they performed their interactions. This point is illustrated in an excerpt of an international graduate in this study as follows:

> I do not know why, it was the same "me" who had the same level of English, but sometimes I could talk and sometimes I could not. I always got tongue-tied when meeting my colleagues. They never tried to understand me, but kept saying "pardon", which made me lose confidence in my English.

How does employability skills assessment disadvantage international students?

As discussed above, international students have been reported as having various limitations in employment skills assessment. However, a critical question that needs further discussion and more attention is: Why are only international students blamed for these problems?

Pham (2021b) claims that the local society is divided into various discourses; of these, the main discourses are discourses of local people and international students. The former is featured by expectations of Western culture and habitus. Therefore, at university and in workplaces, desirable knowledge, skills, and behaviours are English proficiency, high-level communication skills, local work experience, and a range of Western personal values like being proactive, critical, innovative, and independent (Blackmore, Gribble, and Rahimi 2017). International students are categorised in another discourse where their position is defined as "inferior others" (Leask 2004, 186) who need to be filled with Euro-American knowledge (Sancho 2008), or "complex others" who have their own identities but still need to assimilate into Australian academic conventions (Magyar and Robinson-Pant 2011). International students tend to be expected to adjust themselves to fit the conventions of programs.

When assessment of employability skills is applied, common comments about international, especially Asian, students are that they are "not active", "unconfident", and "not critical". Specifically, Howells, Westerveld, and Garvis (2017) found that international students, particularly those from Asia, were perceived as being disengaged because they did not ask questions. This is because asking questions has been considered as an indicator of being critical in Western classrooms (Ryan and Louie 2006). In interactions, local people have a strong desire for critical thinking because it shows how people question current practices and challenge the status quo to generate newer ways of thinking. Unfortunately, international students have difficulty engaging with this process (Clements and Cord 2013) because they often struggle with being self-critical and reflecting on personal experience (Campbell and Zegwaard 2011). Local people may therefore interpret Asian students as lacking engagement or interest in what they are doing when they do not ask questions.

In fact, issues perceived as "problems" of Asian students, as discussed above, are more related to cultural norms in different contexts. Asian students consider asking their supervisor a question as an act of challenging them and a lack of deference to authority (Elliott and Reynolds 2014). In fact, the concepts of "active", "passive", and "critical" have attracted lots of attention from researchers. Jin and Cortazzi (1995) point out that these terms are often interpreted differently, depending on the expectations of the "culture of learning" into which one has been socialised. In recent times the idea of using Vygotskian notions of language as the tool for thought has become very popular, especially in Western discourses. In Western classrooms, talk or verbal participation are seen as pathways to a critical questioning approach (Ryan and Louie 2006) and "learner-centred" pedagogies are designed to encourage students to "learn by participating, through talking and active involvement" (Jin and Cortazzi 1995, 6). This explains why Western employers have implicit and explicit preferences for these activities and expect their employees to actively engage in these practices. If students and employees are not verbally participatory, they are very likely to be seen as problematic. Such a view of "effective" learning contrasts with the more cognitive-centred, learning–listening approach that is largely favoured by Asian learners (Jin and Cortazzi 1995). Within this tradition, being "active" suggests cognitive involvement, lesson preparation, reflection and review, thinking, memorisation and self-study (Cortazzi and Jin 1996).

Therefore, Littlewood (2000) claims that Asian classrooms may indeed appear relatively "static" in comparison to those of the Anglophone West. However, just because the students operate in a receptive mode does not imply that they are any less engaged. Conversely, just because students in Anglophone Western classrooms are seen to be verbally participatory, this does not necessarily guarantee that learning is actually taking place. For instance, in her study, Pham (2014) reported that Asian students found it astonishing and culturally inappropriate when Australian students interrupted someone who was talking to make a point or ask a very simple question when they could just have kept quiet and found out from their classmates at a later time. As such, it appears that each specific learning context has its own explicit and tacit rules to define what should be called "active", "critical", and "confident".

When competence-oriented examinations are applied, these assessment practices disadvantage international students because they rarely embrace deep cultural values of international students but spotlight their limited understanding of multiple aspects of what Bourdieu (1986) calls "cultural capital". Specifically, Bourdieu (1986) discusses two aspects of cultural capital. He claims that cultural capital carries standardised values, which are legalised and institutionalised, and embodied values, which refer to one's preference or perception of the "correct" way of doing things. While people may possess the same standardised values, it is often the case that only the dominant groups' embodied values are acknowledged and validated. Regarding communication, Bourdieu (1992) highlighted two components: linguistic skill, which refers to the use of standardised grammatical structure, and legitimate language skills, which describes "the social capacity to use the linguistic capacity adequately in a determinate situation" (as cited in Cederberg 2015, 41). International students might be aware of the embodied values and used legitimate language skills. However, they cannot often read non-verbal language when they work with people from different backgrounds, which leads to more problems in their communication ability. Therefore, it is very common that they struggle to find "proper" behaviours, shared interests, and values when conducting conversations with local people. They often experience mishaps, described by Cultural Savvy (2003) as "hitting [an] iceberg", when venturing into different cultures without adequate preparation. This leads to international students feeling left out and failing to engage their local friends in small talk to build relationships. Such failures are not necessarily due to limited English proficiencies but more about preferences and "ways of doing things".

Moving forward: Developing assessment practices that are "fair" for international students

Australian universities are under great pressure to produce employable graduates, so have widely adopted the skills-based approach. However, this approach has been widely criticised due to a number of limitations. In the case of international students, assessment practices that have been used in higher education have been evidenced to disadvantage them in various ways. There is a need to rethink how much international students should be assessed based on Western values. To address this issue, it is important to work on internationalising curricula. Although internationalising the curriculum has been implemented for decades, most activities related to this agenda have only stopped at introducing cultural topics such as foods and clothes to domestic students, but have not embedded intellectual resources of other countries (i.e., concepts, ideologies) in current pedagogies and curricula (Singh 2009). Without considering deep cultural values and intellectual heritages of different cultures, assessment practices keep creating gaps between different groups of students and disadvantage international students.

To truly internationalise curricula and pedagogies and create more suitable and fairer assessment practices for international students, there is a need for Australian universities to be more engaged with forms of pedagogies related to legitimatising marginalised knowledge. For example, Moll et al. (1992) developed the "funds of knowledge" approach requiring teachers to bring minority students' prior knowledge into the mainstream curriculum. Other researchers, by using the socio-cultural perspective, further argue for the deployment of culturally appropriate pedagogies to transfer new knowledges into the existing curriculum (e.g., Pham 2014; Zipin 2005). It has been widely reported that so-called marginalised countries have a rich body of philosophical and ethical socio-political thought. India is a clear example of being widely recognised for its rich science, philosophy, literature, and critical theories. These intellectual qualities are helping many of these countries develop their economies over Western nations – China is a clear example. International students are nurtured with these intellectual heritages, so surely they possess and could access them while working in Australia. It is timely for current and future employers in Australia to rethink and make use of these marginalised ways of thinking and working.

International students should also engage in social interactions so that they could have better chances to understand the expectations of the people they are communicating with. This would help them avoid asking "odd" questions. It is also noted that the international graduates' ability to recognise subtle codes in order to perform "acceptable" behaviours is premised on them being active, observant, and reflective, because many of these "soft" aspects cannot be taught by their host institutions. This also means that the predominant skills-based approach – which emphasises the enhancement of communication skills through English tests such as IELTS, additional language support services, and embedding language within the disciplinary study – excludes students and is therefore, inadequate to prepare and measure international students' communication.

References

Barton, G., Hartwig, K., Joseph, D., and Podorova, A. 2017. "Practicum for International Students in Teacher Education Programs: An Investigation of Three University Sites through Multisocialisation, Interculturalisation and Reflection." In *Professional Learning in the Work Place for International Students: Exploring Theory and Practice*, edited by Georgina Barton and Kay Hartwig, 129–146. Cham: Springer.

Blackmore, J., Gribble, C., and Rahimi, M. 2017. "International Education, the Formation of Capital and Graduate Employment: Chinese Accounting Graduates' Experiences of the Australian Labour Market." *Critical Studies in Education* 58 (1): 69–88. http://doi.org/10.1080/17508487.2015.1117505.

Blomeke, S., Gustafsson, J.-E., and Shavelson, R. 2015. "Beyond Dichotomies: Competence Viewed as a Continuum." *Zeitschrift fur Psychologie* 223 (1): 3–13. http://doi.org/10.1027/2151-2604/a000194.

Bourdieu, P. 1986. "The Forms of Capital." In *Handbook of Theory and Research for the Sociology of Education*, edited by John G. Richardson, 241–259. New York: Greenwood Press.

Bourdieu, P. 1992. *Language and Symbolic Power.* Cambridge, UK: Polity.

Braun, E. 2021. "Performance-Based Assessment of Students' Communication Skills." *International Journal of Chinese Education* 10 (1): 1–12. https://doi.org/10.1177/22125868211006202.

Braun, E., and Mishra, S. 2016. "Methods for Assessing Competences in Higher Education: A Comparative Review" In *Theory and Method in Higher Education Research Vol. 2*, edited by Jeroen Huisman and Malcolm Tight, 47–68. Bingley: Emerald Group. https://doi.org/10.1108/S2056-375220160000002003.

Briguglio, C., and Smith, R. 2012. "Perceptions of Chinese Students in an Australian University: Are We Meeting Their Needs?" *Asia Pacific Journal of Education* 32 (1): 17–33. https://doi.org/10.1080/02188791.2012.655237.

Brown, P. 1995. "Cultural Capital and Social Exclusion: Some Observations on Recent Trends in Education, Employment and the Labour Market." *Work, Employment and Society* 9 (1): 29–51. https://doi.org/10.1177/095001709591002.

Campbell, M., and Zegwaard, K. E. 2011. "Ethical Considerations and Workplace Values in Cooperative and Work-Integrated Education." In *International Handbook for Cooperative and Work-Integrated Education: International Perspectives of Theory, Research and Practice*, rev. ed., edited by Richard K. Coll, and Karsten E. Zegwaard, 363–369. Lowell, MA: World Association for Cooperative Education.

Cederberg, M. 2015. "Embodied Cultural Capital and the Study of Ethnic Inequalities." In *Migrant Capital: Networks, Identities and Strategies*, edited by Louise Ryan, Umut Erel, and Alessio D"Angelo, 33–47. Basingstoke, Hampshire; New York, NY: Palgrave Macmillan.

Celce-Murcia, M., Dörnyei, Z., and Thurrell, S. 1995. "Communicative Competence: A Pedagogically Motivated Model with Content Specifications." *Issues in Applied Linguist* 6 (2): 5–35. https://doi.org/10.5070/L462005216.

Clanchy, J., and Ballard, B. 1995. "Generic Skills in the Context of Higher Education." *Higher Education Research and Development* 14 (2): 156–166. https://doi.org/10.1080/0729436950140202.

Clements, M. D., and Cord, B. A. 2013. "Assessment Guiding Learning: Developing Graduate Qualities in an Experiential Learning Program." *Assessment and Evaluation in Higher Education* 38 (1): 114–124. http://doi.org/10.1080/02602938.2011.609314.

Cortazzi, M., and Jin, L. 1996. "Cultures of Learning: Language Classrooms in China." In *Society and the Language Classroom*, edited by Hywel Coleman, 169–206. New York: Cambridge University Press.

Cultural Savvy. 2003. "What is Culture? How Does It Impact Everything We Do?" Accessed July 23, 2022. http://www.culturalsavvy.com/culture.htm.

Czaika, M. 2018. "High-Skilled Migration." In *High-Skilled Migration: Drivers and Policies*, edited by Mathias Czaika, 1–20. Oxford Scholarship. http://doi.org/10.1093/oso/9780198815273.003.0001.

Elliott, C. J., and Reynolds, M. 2014. "Participative Pedagogies, Group Work and International Classroom: An Account of Students" and Tutors" Experiences." *Studies in Higher Education* 39 (2): 307–320. http://doi.org/10.1080/03075079.2012.709492.

Hillage, J., and Pollard, E. 1998. "Employability: Developing a Framework for Policy Analysis". Department for Education and Employment, London. https://www.researchgate.net/publication/225083565_Employability_Developing_a_framework_for_policy_analysis_London_DfEE

Howells, S., Westerveld, M., and Garvis, S. 2017. "Revisiting Cultural and Linguistic Diversity in Speech Pathology Programs in Australia: Listening to the Voices of Staff and International Students." In *Professional Learning in the Work Place for International Students: Exploring Theory and Practice*, edited by Georgina Barton and Kay Hartwig, 165–182. Cham: Springer International.

Jackson, D. 2012. "Business Undergraduates" Perceptions of Their Capabilities in Employability Skills Implications for Industry and Higher Education." *Industry and Higher Education* 26 (5): 345–356. http://doi.org/10.5367/ihe.2012.0117.

Jin, L., and Cortazzi, M. 1995. "A Cultural Synergy Model for Academic Language Use." In *Explorations in English for Professional Communication*, edited by Paul Bruthiaux, Tim Boswood, and Bertha Du-Babcock, 41–56. Hong Kong: City University of Hong Kong.

Jones, A. 2010. "Generic Attributes in Accounting: The Significance of the Disciplinary Context." *Education: An International Journal* 19 (1–2): 5–21. https://doi.org/10.1080/09639280902875523.

Leask, B. 2004. "Transnational Education and Intercultural Learning: Reconstructing the Offshore Teaching Team to Enhance Internationalisation." In *Proceedings of the Australian Universities Quality Forum 2004*. Australia: AUQA Occasional Publication. http://citeseerx.ist.psu.edu/viewdoc/download?doi=10.1.1.114.9090&rep=rep1&type=pdf.

Littlewood, W. 2000. "Do Asian Students Really Want to Listen and Obey?" *ELT Journal* 54 (1): 31–36. https://doi.org/10.1093/elt/54.1.31.

Lowden, K., Hall, S., Elliot, D., and Lewin, J. 2011. *Employers" Perceptions of the Employability Skills of New Graduates*. Glasgow: University of Glasgow SCRE Centre and Edge Foundation.

Magyar, A., and Robinson-Pant, A. 2011. "Special Issue on University Internationalisation – Towards Transformative Change in Higher Education. Internationalising Doctoral Research: Developing Theoretical Perspectives on Practice." *Teachers and Teaching: Theory and Practice* 17 (6): 663–677. https://doi.org/10.1080/13540602.2011.625189.

Mason, G., Williams, G., and Cramner, S. 2009. "Employability Skills Initiatives in Higher Education: What Effects Do They Have on Graduate Labour Market Outcomes?" *Education Economics* 17 (1): 1–30. https://doi.org/10.1080/09645290802028315.

Moll, L., Amanti, C., Neff, D., and Gonzalez, N. 1992. "Funds of Knowledge for Teaching: Using a Qualitative Approach to Connect Homes and Classrooms." *Theory into Practice* 31 (2): 132–141. https://www.jstor.org/stable/1476399.

Morrison, A. 2014. "A Class Act? Lecturers" Views on Undergraduates" Employability." *British Journal of Sociology of Education* 35 (4): 487–505. http://doi.org/10.1080/01425692.2013.802420.

Ngoc, B. D. 2016. "To Employ or Not to Employ Expatriate Non-Native Speaker Teachers: Views from within." *Asian Englishes* 18 (1): 67–79. http://doi.org/10.1080/13488678.2015.1132112.

Pham, T. 2014. *Implementing Cross-Culture Pedagogies: Cooperative Learning at Confucian Heritage Cultures*. Singapore: Springer.

Pham, T. 2021a. "Communication Competencies and International Graduates" Employability Outcomes: Strategies to Navigate the Host Labour Market." *Journal of International Migration and Integration* 23: 733–749. https://doi.org/10.1007/s12134-021-00869-3.

Pham, T. 2021b. "Conceptualising the Employability Agency of International Graduates." Working Paper 75, Centre for Global Higher Education. Oxford: University of Oxford. https://www.researchcghe.org/perch/resources/publications/working-paper-75-1.pdf.

Pham, T. 2021c. "Developing Effective Global Pedagogies in Western Classrooms: A Need to Understand the Internationalization Process of Confucian Heritage Cultures (CHC) Students." In *Transforming Pedagogies through Engagement with Learners, Teachers and Communities*, edited by Bao Dat and Thanh Pham, 37–52. Singapore: Springer.

Pham, T., and Saito, E. 2019. "Teaching towards Graduates Attributes: Is This a Solution for Employability of University Students in Australia?" *In Innovate Higher Education to Enhance Graduate Employability*, edited by Hong T. M. Bui, Hoa T. M. Nguyen, and Doug Cole, 109–121. NY: Routledge.

Röhner, J., and Schütz, A. 2015. *Psychologie der Kommunikation*. Wiesbaden: Springer VS. http://doi.org/10.1007/978-3-531-18891-1.

Ryan, J., and Louie, K. 2006. "False Dichotomy? "Western" and "Confucian" Concepts of Scholarship and Learning." *Educational Philosophy and Theory* 39 (4): 404–417. http://doi.org/10.1111/j.1469-5812.2007.00347.x.

Sancho, J. M. 2008. "Opening Students' Minds". In *Researching International Pedagogies*, edited by Meeri Hellstén, and Anna Reid, 259–276. Dordrecht, The Netherlands: Springer. https://doi.org/10.1007/978-1-4020-8858-2_16.

Shavelson, R. J., Zlatkin-Troitschanskaia, O., and Mariño, J. P. 2018. "International Performance Assessment of Learning in Higher Education (iPAL): Research and Development." In *Assessment of Learning Outcomes in Higher Education: Cross-National Comparisons and Perspectives Assessment*, edited by Olga Zlatkin-Troitschanskaia, Miriam Toepper, Hans Anand Pant, Corinna Lautenbach, and Christiane Kuhn, 193–214. Cham: Springer International. http://doi.org/10.1007/978-3-319-74338-7_10.

Singh, M. 2009. "Connecting Intellectual Projects in China and Australia." *Australian Journal of Education* 54 (1): 31–45. http://doi.org/10.1177/000494411005400104.

Tholen, G. 2015. "What Can Research into Graduate Employability Tell Us about Agency and Structure?" *British Journal of Sociology of Education* 36 (5): 766–784. https://doi.org/10.1080/01425692.2013.847782.

Tomlinson, M. 2017. "Forms of Graduate Capital and Their Relationship to Graduate Employability." *Education + Training* 59 (4): 338–352. http://doi.org/10.1108/ET-05-2016-0090.

UK Department of Education. 2019. *International Education Strategy: Global Potential, Global Growth*. https://www.gov.uk/government/publications/international-education-strategy-global-potential-global-growth/international-education-strategy-global-potential-global-growth.

Wellings, P., Black, R., Craven, G., Freshwater, D., and Harding, S. 2019. *Performance-Based Funding for the Commonwealth Grant Scheme*. Accessed January 20, 2022. https://www.dese.gov.au/higher-education-funding/performancebased-funding-commonwealth-grant-scheme.

Yorke, M. 2004. *Employability and Higher Education: What It Is – and What It Is Not*. York, England: Higher Education Academy. https://www.advance-he.ac.uk/knowledge-hub/employability-higher-education-what-it-what-it-not.

Zipin, L. 2005. "Dark Funds of Knowledge, Deep Funds of Pedagogy: Exploring Boundaries between Lifeworlds and Schools." *Discourse: Studies in the Cultural Politics of Education* 30 (3): 317–331. https://doi.org/10.1080/01596300903037044.

SECTION III

Micro contexts of assessment for inclusion: Educators, students, and interpersonal perspectives

15

HOW DO WE ASSESS FOR "SUCCESS"? CHALLENGING ASSUMPTIONS OF SUCCESS IN THE PURSUIT OF INCLUSIVE ASSESSMENT

Sarah O'Shea and Janine Delahunty

Introduction

"Success" at university is largely focused on calculations of "high" marks or grades derived from assessable academic activities. While there is a sense of personal achievement in "passing" assessments, these measures of academic success alone have become too narrow; yet they remain largely unquestioned within the higher education environment. The relationship between "success" and grades needs further interrogation, particularly for students who have returned to university after a significant break in formal study. For older learners, "success" is not exclusively academic, but often defined through complex combinations involving life experience and alternative rationales for participating in university.

In a recent national study, we asked students how they personally defined "success" at university. Their answers were illuminating, revealing that "success", as a taken-for-granted term, is very diverse in its application including how it is perceived and valued. Surprisingly, in educational literature there is limited explicit focus on how the concept of success is individually understood, translated, and enacted. Drawing attention to this, the chapter provides a summary overview of how success was constructed and defined through the reflections of first in family students. Only by focussing on, and unpacking the value of, higher education participation as defined by students themselves, can we begin to trouble the ways in which assessment is traditionally constructed and designed. In revealing tensions around understandings of "success", this chapter is designed to prompt thinking about how, as teaching and learning practitioners, we might redefine assessment practices that consider success in more multi-faceted and inclusive ways.

DOI: 10.4324/9781003293101-19

Success as a construction

Understandings of academic success are largely unquestioned within higher education. Success has been problematically constructed as academic achievement, progression through a degree, overlayed with expectations of a linear, uninterrupted barrier-free passage to completion armed with a knowledge of the implicit "rules" of the game (Bathmaker, Ingram, and Waller 2013; Tinto 2021). However, given the diversity of our student populations and the sometimes complex circumstances they exist within, unpacking and deconstructing taken-for-granted notions of "success" can help identify and eliminate potential barriers. Rather than perceiving "success" as a contractual arrangement that requires judging the value or merit of a student's performance, more nuanced, individualised notions of success are needed.

Research and literature on success indicate highly subjective variations in meaning. Conceptions of academic success can deviate between teaching staff and students, such as polarised understandings on barriers to achieving success as highlighted by Dean and Camp (1998). These authors identified how academic staff considered success to be determined by students' attitudes and motivations, while for students, it was the external factors that were the biggest influencers on success, with success more akin to "general life satisfaction" (10). In a similar vein, Tinto (2021) highlights the internal-external tension of students "wanting to persist" as distinct from "being able to persist" (7) and the responsibility of institutional support in removing barriers that thwart students' actual capacity to achieve.

Whilst research indicates some of the complexities of what constitutes success, we argue that this complexity is exacerbated for students from equity backgrounds accessing various pathways into higher education. For example, pathways such as open access colleges may emphasise non-normative measures of student success or academic achievement. In recognition of this variety, there have been calls for alternative understandings or measures of success, which "acknowledge the unique complexities, challenges and material conditions" of specific student groups (Sullivan 2008, 629). Undoubtedly perceptions of success are intertwined with preconceived ideas of what constitutes a "good" grade or the ways in which success is measured (Yazedjian et al. 2008). This chapter seeks to consider how alternative conceptions of success should inform and influence the objectives and design of assessment items. Building upon previous publications which have unpacked notions of academic success from the perspectives of equity intersected learners, the term success cannot be assumed to have a common meaning nor be embedded within normalised discourses of meritocracy (Delahunty and O'Shea 2019; O'Shea and Delahunty 2018).

Data collection and analysis

Given the implicit complexity of "success", this chapter now explores how students themselves considered and articulated notions of success to better understand implications for constructing assessment in university. The research

TABLE 15.1 Equity factors

Equity factors	*Survey respondents (n = 208)*		*Interviewees (n = 20)*	
First in family	208	100%	20	100%
Aboriginal or Torres Strait Islander	9	4%	1	5%
Disability	11	5%	4	20%
Low socio-economic status (LSES)	71	34%	11	55%
Rural/Isolated	67	32%	3	15%
Non-English-speaking background (NESB)	12	6%	3	15%
Refugee	2	1%	1	5%
TOTAL self-selected equity factors	**380**	**183%**	**43**	**215%**
Other (e.g., extra information/ clarification of category(ies))	208	100%	20	100%

was conducted under the auspices of an Australian Research Council (ARC) Discovery Project (2017–2021) that explored the ways in which students who are the first in their family to attend university enacted persistence during their undergraduate studies. A total of 376 students across eight institutions participated in either interviews or surveys, designed to encourage broad reflection on experiences of sustaining their studies in often complex and challenging circumstances. All participants were asked if they regarded themselves as "successful students" and this chapter focuses on a selection of qualitative data from 228 participants who responded to the question: *How do you define success at university?* Self-selected demographic details in Table 15.1 highlight the diversity of equity factors of this mostly female (85%), mature-aged group (83% aged 21+) as chosen by participants (indicated by >100% totals).

Responses were imported into NVivo and line-by-line coding was undertaken to unpack how success manifested and specifically how these understandings informed persistence in higher education. These learners reflected upon a broader conceptualisation of success including as a form of validation, a highly emotional or embodied state as well as understandings of failure and what "success was not".

Themes generated defined success variously with thematic analysis identifying subjective alternatives to success which were: success as personal outcomes (55%), learning or gaining/applying knowledge (20%), and what success is not (7%); with the theme "grades/passing" comprising 16%. The following section briefly highlights these themes, before providing implications for assessment for inclusion.

Alternative conceptions of success

This study contested the often unquestioned concept of success and assumed common or global definitions, with participants evoking instead a range of emotional and structural considerations. Alternative conceptions of success became apparent through the absence of reference to "marks" or "grades" (and their synonyms) by over half the participants ($n = 118$). Interestingly, in the grades/passing theme, general reference to "passing" (e.g., "scores that reflect your best effort", "marks I'm proud of") was made by 23 participants, rather than as a specific goal (e.g., "success is achieving high grades/GPA/distinction average"). Thus, we turn attention to the more contested nature of success. These first in family learners repeatedly linked their own success to the satisfaction they gained, often articulated in emotional terms through the embodiment of persevering or achieving personal goals, rather than through detached academic measures:

> I finished my degree, that is my measure of success, I made it through many obstacles including physical/mental/financial health challenges
>
> *(Female Survey Respondent, 31–40, Disability, LSES)*

> Success is finding something that you passionate about, could be easy or hard and going after it until you get it. That's success
>
> *(Female Survey Respondent, 21–25, 2nd year, Refugee)*

This is not to say that grades or marks were considered unimportant or irrelevant. Interestingly, for some students grading provided a form of "external" validation of their entitlement to be enrolled and many were performing as well as, if not better, than they had anticipated. Similar to others, Danielle was unsure about openly defining herself as successful, preferring instead to defer to external validations gained from lecturers, peers, and assignment feedback as "proof" of her success in achieving an acceptable academic standard, as the following insight shows,

> Having lecturers say ..."This piece of work was so good that you should actually use it in real life, like submit that to a government committee"; that's the best feedback that I could ever get in my life and then that makes me think that yeah, you know, I am actually really successful in what I'm doing
>
> *(Danielle, 32, 3rd year, Online, LSES)*

Significantly, it was the additional, personalised feedback that helped Danielle to meaningfully translate her marks. This is an important consideration for equity students who may experience a level of uncertainly about how "success" is translated within a university setting especially if grading is not contextualised within constructive feedback. Notably, receiving some kind of validation was how these students measured their successful selves. As first in family, without familial biographies to draw upon, it is common to feel like an outsider or experience imposter syndrome. This sense of dislocation was sometimes revealed via the level of discomfort in identifying as successful, such as Danielle's unwilling admission,

> I don't really like to toot my horn but looking at what I've done and achieved and how much people have said to me, like, 'You're doing really, really well'. Yes, I do [define myself as successful].

There can also be an element of resistance to placing too much emphasis on grades, even though many participants were self-confessed high achievers. Instead, a focus on retaining "your sense of self" is the advice from this female survey respondent who also admits that,

> I do aim for HDs, but I think it's important to realise that sometimes, not achieving in line with your expectations is a lesson in humility
>
> *(Female Survey Respondent, 31–40, 3rd year)*

Repeatedly, there was a delineation between how success was constructed by individual learners compared to institutional or political discourses. For these participants, success was contextualised and informed by wider social and economic factors, rather than simply attributed to the meritocratic skill set of the learner. The dichotomous nature of this term most clearly articulated when participants reflected on what success was not, or even defining the act of failing in terms of success.

What success-is-not and failure-as-success

The term "failure" was contested by participants. Some students agreed that success could come from failure and so was not failure at all. For example, withdrawing from a course was considered a chance to redefine self or focus on another area of life, rather than "failing". A number of participants reflected how the act of failing was key to learning and also, developing as a person, as shown in these statements:

> I have only failed one class and then from failing that one class, I have got distinctions or high distinctions in all my other classes and also that class when I redid it plus I'm finishing uni which I think is quite an achievement with two children and working full-time.
>
> *(Dyahn, 25, 4th Year, LSES)*

> Success in the university environment is trying your hardest and passing well (although I think if you try your hardest and fail the first time but try again that can still be success).
>
> *(Female Survey Respondent, 21–25, 3rd Year, LSES)*

Failing was intricately bound up with success, one seemingly could not exist independent of the other. For some not failing was an indication of success: "Yeah I guess [I am successful], I've never failed anything" (Lisa, 21, 4th year). However, experience of failure was sometimes a "wake-up call" which acted as a catalyst for change,

> I was going to major in Economics but I actually didn't do very well with the prerequisite classes last year so I failed Management and Finance which was all part of that wake-up call of thinking "Yeah, I'm going to be a lot

> more happy if I just follow my passion and don't worry about other people's perceptions of me so much.
>
> *(Thomas, 20, final year)*

Being successful was also defined by what it is not, defying normative assumptions of success by taking a particular stance against these. For one student success was "not about getting a job … it's about completing something that I never thought possible" (Heather, 59, final year); for another: "I don't think success is 2.5 kids and a house" (Female Survey Respondent, 26–30, 5th year, LSES, Rural). Other success-is-not definitions included downplaying grades as the most important measure,

> Not just going to university because you have to, but going because you learn things that make you curious and inspired. It's not necessarily about getting great grades or succeeding all the time, but about learning from your mistakes and becoming more resilient
>
> *(Female Survey Respondent, 26–30, 5th year)*

> I may not have HD marks on paper, but I have HD life experience!
>
> *(Female Survey Respondent, 21–25, 5th year part-time)*

> Success…is not about living up to the 'norms' but to be resilient to tough paths ahead and to be able to overcome these barriers
>
> *(Female Survey Respondent, 21–25, 4th year, Rural)*

Considerations for assessment for inclusion

In light of the strong deviation from traditional, measurable indicators as sole identifiers of success, these first in family participants point us to alternatives on how success at university and beyond needs to better align to student conceptions. Personal definitions of success far outweigh others, such as gaining a sense of satisfaction and enjoyment both individually and socially, working towards personal aims and gaining the respect of others. Being successful was also identified through the experience of learning, such as being engaged and active in learning, being self-directed, and being able to apply skills and knowledge. Defining success in terms of "failure" or what it is not can also underpin development of alternative forms of assessment which are more learner and learning-centred, rather than grade-focused.

Undoubtedly, the aim of assessment should be for learning, but equally assessment designed for inclusion should encourage self-motivation, autonomous learners, and importantly, provide an opportunity to develop collective-minded individuals who are not solely defined as being in competition with each other. Grades are inadequate indicators of these qualities and represent narrowness if these are the sole or foregrounded definition of achievement.

Implications for assessment for inclusion

These diverse participants rarely focused on grades alone when defining their successful student selves, articulating alternative and broad notions of success. This presents a challenge to higher education institutions, namely, why "measuring" achievement, which fosters a competitive and individualised learning culture, continues to be highly valued, even while collaboration, communication, and collective knowledge are being demanded as key competencies for the future. The following sections explore alternatives to current assessment practices with a focus on building upon relational aspects to ensure that the student voice is key to facilitating change to assessment which more accurately reflects varied and relevant notions of success. This discussion will focus on two main themes, the need to de-emphasise grades within assessment practices, and the need to adopt students as partners approaches to involve learners themselves in the design of authentic and inclusive assessment.

Not grading: A brave starting point

Firstly, the idea of achieving particular grades as the main aim of assessment needs to be challenged when considering assessment for inclusion. It may be a brave, even radical, shift to imagine assessment designed without grading, one which Warner (2020) describes as,

> a leap of faith, and there is no guarantee that after the leap, you won't go splat, no matter the amount of preparation, enthusiasm, and confidence you bring to the task
>
> *(208)*

However, such a shift is needed in order to explore how we might create the best possible environments in which learning is emphasised, and where each student, regardless of background, has "equitable opportunities to demonstrate their mastery of course content and skills" (Chu 2020, 164).

Students, released from anxiety associated with a grade judgement of their performance, are likely to be more willing to exercise creativity, to be more adventurous and self-identify weaknesses or areas they would like to improve. Learners, not defined only by meritocracy, may also be more willing to seek feedback and consequently better understand the value of feedback. They may even "fail" or perform poorly sometimes, such as many diverse learners who have to make choices if other life priorities demand attention. There are few places in the higher education curriculum where learning and failure co-exist as opportunities for success; however, "failure" can present some of our most memorable and transformational learning experiences, particularly when failure is not framed as a source of embarrassment or fear.

Assessment for inclusion, therefore, must take account of intersecting equity factors that may impact on an assumed linear pathway through a program of study to completion. For many diverse students, the assumption of such linearity in their learning journeys is an unrealistic one (see Crawford, Chapter 16; Delahunty 2022; O'Shea 2014, 2020). Students leading complex lives may need to miss classes or limit time on tasks due to competing priorities and this should not be interpreted as lacking in academic abilities or motivation. As adults they are best placed to make such judgements regarding their commitments or personal care (Schulz-Bergin 2020), and should not be penalised for the impact that external pressures place on their time, well-being or capacity to achieve.

Bourke (Chapter 17) emphasises that in many assessment approaches students' attention is directed "to 'proving' what they know and can apply, rather than on 'improving' the way they learn" (p. 190). We know that grades-focus does not incentivise learning, nor motivate students towards deep learning, is not meaningful nor indicative of the learning taking place (Gibbs 2020; Stommel 2020), does not allow for failure (Chu 2020), leads to gaming-the-system or corner-cutting (Blum 2020), and does not encompass various goals for learning (Gibbs 2020). This critical perspective challenges educators to consider how current models of teaching and assessment that are apparently designed to support students in fact fail to "meet the needs of diverse students" and "fail to promote equity" (Blum 2020, 227).

Perhaps the biggest stumbling block to assessment for inclusion is assuming that assessment be coupled with grading. Stommel (2020) is careful to distinguish assessment and grading as distinctly different things, arguing that "spending less time on grading does not mean spending less time on assessment" (36) and that while assessment is inevitable, deeply considering the need to include grading forces us to question "our assumptions about what assessment looks like, how we do it, and who it is for" (36). Instead of preconceived grades or meritocratic rankings being provided, one alternative might be to embed students' own goals for the assessment within marking criteria. Providing rich qualitative comments to contextualise the feedback on execution of the task would be key to such an approach but equally, a focus on the process of assessment rather than only the end product is undoubtedly important.

Whatever the approach taken, it is clear that assessment needs to be embedded within and informed by student perspectives. The next section considers the necessity of student involvement in designing assessment to ensure inclusivity. In adopting student-centred approaches, the intent is to address power relations in the teaching-learning environment and ensure that assessment is embedded within student perspectives and worldviews.

Students as partners approaches to promote assessment as partnership

Students as partners (SaP) challenge hierarchical relations of power that traditional assessment practices often reflect. To counter such power imbalances, SaP approaches encourage a more equitable experience of education through genuine partnership. For educators, there are many benefits in taking a relational approach to teaching and learning but this is particularly the case in (re)designing assessment. Adopting a more relational approach foregrounds student perspectives and recognises that learners are the "best experts in their own learning" (Stommel 2020, 29). As a genuine partnership model, SaP enables educators and institutions to move beyond opinion-based surveys that may have traditionally included the "student voice" but retained limited scope for genuine student involvement in curriculum or pedagogy change. Instead, SaP re-positions students as agentic, where they can exert their influence (see Cook-Sather, Bovill, and Felten 2014; Healey, Flint, and Harrington 2014; Matthews 2017). Such repositioning is key for equity-related issues and can usefully inform an inclusive pedagogy across the higher education sector (O'Shea, Delahunty, and Gigliotti 2021)

In considering a "marriage" of assessment and inclusion, it makes little sense *not* to involve students, who have the most to gain (or lose). Partnerships between faculty, students, and other stakeholders hold the promise of richer and more meaningful assessment processes and outcomes, even though participants may not all contribute in the same ways, all can engage equally through the "collaborative, reciprocal process" (Cook-Sather, Bovill, and Felten 2014, 6). Actively seeking student engagement and collaboration in assessment (re)design not only raises the potential for enduring change that is meaningful to those for whom it matters most but also fosters much deeper engagement in learning in addition to benefits to teaching practice (Healey, Flint, and Harrington 2014).

However, productive student-faculty partnerships are not always easily negotiated in practice, as Dargusch, Harris, and Bearman (Chapter 19) describe. Power relations need to be acknowledged and explicitly addressed when considering SaP projects (O'Shea, Delahunty, and Gigliotti 2021). Importantly, Bovill, Matthews, and Hinchcliffe (2021) set out five key principles for co-creating assessment change using SaP as the approach. This includes developing assessment and feedback dialogue which is transparent and ongoing; sharing responsibility for assessment and feedback including acknowledgement that teacher-student power dynamics and roles will be disrupted; fostering trust through dialogue; nurturing inclusive assessment and feedback processes; and connecting partnership in assessment and feedback with curriculum and pedagogy.

At a practical level, a SaP approach could usefully inform the practical development of assessment including working with students to develop meaningful goals/outcomes, assessment formats, the assessment outline/brief and even, the assessment exemplars. Equally, creating assessment criteria that respond to the motivations and goals of the specific student cohort would ensure these activities are meaningful to those involved.

Concluding thoughts

Returning to the broad definitions of success articulated by our first in family participants; these prompted us to question the relevance of traditional assessment and its narrow focus on measurable indicators. Challenging the exclusionary nature and reward-punishment of grades-focused assessment is one step towards disrupting these practices. Such necessary disruption facilitates students from all backgrounds to have equitable opportunities to demonstrate their knowledge and skill mastery. Engaging students as partners in assessment and feedback is a next logical step in order to "advance relational pedagogies in the co-creation of learning, teaching and assessment" (Bovill, Matthews, and Hinchcliffe 2021, 5).

As a much needed innovation, assessment for inclusion will undoubtedly present challenges for educators. Some questions demanding consideration include: How can we build upon alternative non-meritocratic perspectives of success within assessment practices? How might assessment be redefined for students from equity backgrounds to better account for the diversity of their backgrounds? Exploring these and other related questions, as presented in this book, will hopefully instigate generative discussions that will rejuvenate assessment practices to take account of diverse student cohorts and assist in adapting to the post-pandemic educational environment.

References

Bathmaker, A.-M., Ingram, N., and Waller, R. 2013. "Higher Education, Social Class and the Mobilisation of Capitals: Recognising and Playing the Game." *British Journal of Sociology of Education* 34 (5–6): 723–743. http://doi.org/10.1080/01425692.2013.816041.

Blum, S. D. 2020. *Ungrading: Why Rating Students Undermines Learning (and What to Do Instead)*. Morgantown, WV: West Virginia University Press.

Bovill, C., Matthews, K., and Hinchcliffe, T. 2021. "Students as Partners in Assessment (SPiA)". https://www.advance-he.ac.uk/knowledge-hub/student-partnerships-assessment-spia.

Chu, G. 2020. "The Point-less Classroom: A Math Teacher's Ironic Choice in not Calculating Grades." In *Why Rating Students Undermines Learning (and What to Do Instead)*, edited by Susan D. Blum, 161–170. Morgantown, WV: West Virginia University Press.

Cook-Sather, A., Bovill, C., and Felten, P. 2014. *Engaging Students as Partners in Teaching and Learning: A Guide for Faculty*. San Francisco, CA: Jossey-Bass.

Dean, A., and Camp, W. 1998. "Defining and Achieving Student Success: University Faculty and Student Perspectives." In *the American Vocational Association Convention*. New Orleans, LA. https://files.eric.ed.gov/fulltext/ED428180.pdf.

Delahunty, J. 2022. *"You Going to Uni?": Exploring How People from Regional, Rural and Remote Areas Navigate into and through Higher Education*. Perth: National Centre for Student Equity in Higher Education. https://www.ncsehe.edu.au/publications/regional-rural-remote-navigate-higher-education/.

Delahunty, J., and O'Shea, S. 2019. ""I'm Happy, and I'm Passing. That's all that Matters!": Exploring Discourses of University Academic Success through Linguistic Analysis." *Language and Education* 33 (4): 302–321. https://doi.org/10.1080/09500782.2018.1562468.

Gibbs, L. 2020. "Let's Talk about Grading." In *Ungrading: Why Rating Students Undermines Learning (and What to Do Instead)*, edited by Susan Blum, 91–104. Morgantown, WV: West Virginia University Press.

Healey, M., Flint, A., and Harrington, K. 2014. *Engagement through Partnership: Students as Partners in Learning and Teaching in Higher Education*. London, UK: Higher Education Academy. https://www.advance-he.ac.uk/knowledge-hub/engagement-through-partnership-students-partners-learning-and-teaching-higher.

Matthews, K. E. 2017. "Five Propositions for Genuine Students as Partners Practice." *International Journal for Students as Partners* 1 (2): 1–9. https://doi.org/10.15173/ijsap.v1i2.3315.

O'Shea, S. 2014. "Transitions and Turning Points: How First in Family Female Students Story Their Transition to University and Student Identity Formation." *International Journal of Qualitative Studies in Education* 27 (2): 135–158. https://doi.org/10.1080/09518398.2013.771226.

O'Shea, S. 2020. "Crossing Boundaries: Rethinking the Ways that First in Family Students Navigate "Barriers" to Higher Education." *British Journal of Sociology of Education* 41 (1): 95–110. https://doi.org/10.1080/01425692.2019.1668746.

O'Shea, S., and Delahunty, J. 2018. "Getting through the Day and Still Having a Smile on My Face! How Do Students Define Success in the University Learning Environment?" *Higher Education Research and Development* 37 (5): 1062–1075. https://doi.org/10.1080/07294360.2018.1463973.

O'Shea, S., Delahunty, J., and Gigliotti, A. 2021. "Creating Collaborative Spaces: Applying a "Students as Partner" Approach to University Peer Mentoring Programs". In *Student Support Services*, edited by Henk Huijser, Megan Yih Chyn A. Kek, and Fernando F. Padró. Singapore: Springer. https://doi.org/10.1007/978-981-13-3364-4_7-1.

Schulz-Bergin, M. 2020. "Grade Anarchy in the Philosophy Classroom." In *Ungrading: Why Rating Students Undermines Learning (and What to Do Instead)*, edited by Susan Blum, 173–187. Morgantown, WV: West Virginia University Press.

Stommel, J. 2020. "How to Ungrade." In *Ungrading: Why Rating Students Undermines Learning (and What to Do Instead)*, edited by Susan Blum, 25–41. Morgantown, WV: West Virginia University Press.

Sullivan, P. 2008. "Opinion: Measuring "Success" at Open Admissions Institutions: Thinking Carefully about This Complex Question." *College English* 70 (6): 618–630. http://doi.org/10.2307/25472297.

Tinto, V. 2021. "Increasing Student Persistence: Wanting and Doing." In *Student Support Services*, edited by Henk Huijser, Megan Yih Chyn A. Kek, and Fernando F. Padró. Singapore: Springer. https://doi.org/10.1007/978-981-16-5852-5_33.

Warner, J. 2020. "Wile E. Coyote: The Hero of Ungrading." In *Ungrading: Why Rating Students Undermines Learning (and What to Do Instead)*, edited by Susan Blum, 25–41. Morgantown, WV: West Virginia University Press.

Yazedjian, A., Toews, M., Sevin, T., and Purswell, K. 2008. ""It's a Whole New World": A Qualitative Exploration of College Students Definitions of and Strategies for College Success." *Journal of College Student Development* 49 (2): 141–154. http://doi.org/10.1353/csd.2008.0009.

16

INCLUSIVE AND EXCLUSIVE ASSESSMENT

Exploring the experiences of mature-aged students in regional and remote Australia

Nicole Crawford, Sherridan Emery, and Allen Baird

Introduction

"Assessment" and "inclusion" are both recognised, albeit separately, in Australian higher education policy, within the Higher Education Standards Framework (Threshold Standards; HESF 2021). For instance, assessment is addressed in Section 1.4, "Learning outcomes and assessment", which sets up the foundations for assessment, stating: "Methods of assessment are consistent with the learning outcomes being assessed, are capable of confirming that all specified learning outcomes are achieved" (HESF 2021, 5). Inclusion is specifically addressed in Section 2.2.1 (HESF 2021, 7) as follows: "Institutional policies, practices and approaches to teaching and learning are designed to accommodate student diversity, including the under-representation and/or disadvantage experienced by identified groups, and create equivalent opportunities for academic success regardless of students' backgrounds". (See Chapter 9 for a policy analysis.) Despite these clear standards in the HESF and the potential role of inclusive assessment design to foster inclusion of students from diverse backgrounds and address their challenges, there is a gap in the literature, particularly in regards to the experiences of students in equity groups (Tai, Ajjawi, and Umarova 2021).

Assessment has been found to influence student well-being, which is a centrepiece of a recent national study that investigated the perspectives of mature-aged students in, and from, regional and remote areas in Australia about what impacts their mental well-being (Crawford 2021). A major finding of this research is the important role of teaching and support staff, and teaching and learning environments in enhancing or hindering students' mental well-being (Crawford 2021). The everyday interactions that students have with teaching and support staff; their peers; the unit/subject content and curriculum (including assessment tasks); and the physical or online learning environments were each found to impact

DOI: 10.4324/9781003293101-20

students' mental well-being. The research findings also suggest that entrenched attitudes and expectations that favour and privilege some students over others continue to prevail. For instance, challenges with course content or delivery, and with university rules and regulations, which were found to be unconsciously designed for so-called "ideal", "implied", and "traditional" students, exacerbated the already-challenging situations of students who did not fit this profile, such as mature-aged students in, and from, regional and remote areas, many of whom juggled parenting and work with their university studies (Crawford 2021; Crawford and Emery 2021).

One of the impacts on students' mental well-being was assessment tasks (Crawford 2021). In the study's survey of approximately 1,800 mature-aged students in, and from, regional and remote areas in Australia, 39.3% of respondents reported that assessment tasks impacted extremely negatively or negatively on their mental well-being; 31.2% reported an extremely positive or positive impact, while 29.5% were neutral (Crawford 2021, 37). To provide a nuanced picture behind these numbers, we explore the participants' experiences of assessment by analysing the qualitative data. We then employ Bronfenbrenner's (1995) ecological systems model to interrogate institutions' systemic and cultural influences on students' experiences of assessment. We conclude by proposing some approaches to moving towards more inclusive assessment.

Research methods

The larger project (Crawford 2021) from which this chapter draws followed a concurrent transformative mixed-methods design (Creswell 2014) and received ethics approval from the Tasmania Social Sciences Human Research Ethics Committee. The target population for this research was mature-aged undergraduate university students in, and from, regional and remote areas in Australia.[1] All data collection was completed in February 2020, just prior to COVID-19 arriving in Australia.

For this chapter, we returned to the 51 interview transcripts and the open-ended survey questions, and considered the following question: "How do mature-aged students in, and from, regional and remote Australia experience assessment?" We undertook reflexive thematic analysis of the qualitative data (Braun and Clarke 2022), interpreting and making meaning of the participants' experiences of assessments. We then considered impacts on students' varied experiences of assessment by employing Bronfenbrenner's (1995) ecological systems model to identify the layers of the ecological system and the array of influences.

Bronfenbrenner's ecological systems theory (illustrated in Figure 16.1) provides a way to view a student's everyday lifeworlds of university, home, work, and local community (that is, their micro-level systems), and the interactions between them (the mesosystem). It also enables consideration of the systemic and structural, and the social, cultural, political and historical factors that impact on an individual (that is, the exo, macro, and chrono-level systems), as well as the interactions and interplay between the various layers (Bronfenbrenner 1995).[2]

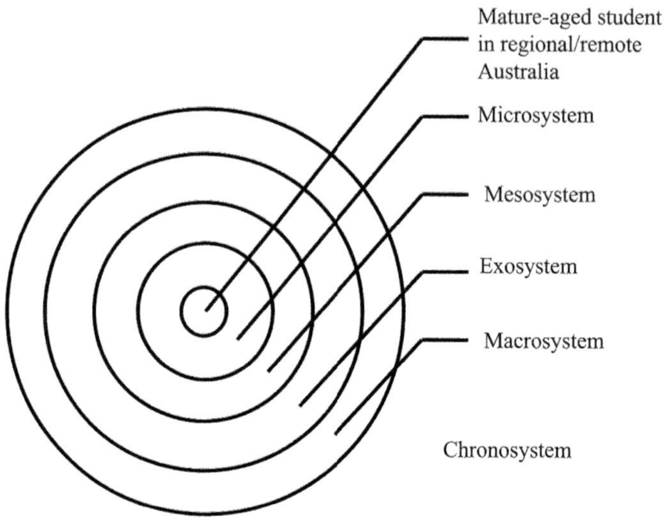

FIGURE 16.1 Bronfenbrenner's ecological systems (Crawford 2021, 18).

Students' experiences of assessment: qualitative findings

In this section, we focus on several themes to illustrate students' similar and varied experiences of assessment. Pseudonyms are used to maintain participants' anonymity; when cited, the student participants' gender, age-range, geographical location, study mode, and course are also included.

Unclear assessment tasks and not receiving timely responses to questions

The lack of clarity in assessment task descriptions was a major theme. For instance, Lara, an online student, experienced unclear assessment tasks throughout her five and a half years of part-time study:

> One thing that I find very difficult, and I know I'm not alone in this [is] the wording of a lot of the assessment tasks has really managed to get a lot of us confused. In fact, even just in the very last assessment task that I did, the wording was sort of a bit vague, and, so, certain students took it to mean one thing and other students took it to mean another. And, I found that all the way along – the wording for the assessment tasks can actually sometimes be very unclear. And, of course, you're not in a classroom situation where you can stick your hand up and say, "Look, this isn't making a lot of sense". So, then you've got to go onto the discussion boards and sort of say, "Look, I really am not getting this".
>
> *(Lara; female; 41–50; Inner Regional; online; Dementia care)*

Lara noted a disadvantage of being online is that she could not simply seek clarification during or at the end of a lecture or tutorial. She had to wait for an answer on a discussion board. With an approaching deadline, waiting for the task to be clarified adds to an already stressful situation.

Other online students, such as Alice, spoke of similar experiences:

> One of the biggest things that holds you up on assignments is that you've got a question and you post the question to the forum, and you have a look, and it hasn't been answered, or you don't really understand it still, and sometimes it can take a while to get a response from one of the teachers.
>
> *(Alice; female; 26–30; Outer Regional; online; Nursing)*

Design student Beverley's comments evoke her frustration at undertaking assessment tasks for which the skills or knowledge required had not yet been taught; she also recounted experiencing inconsistent information about a task in the assessment description, the rubric and from staff:

> I took a break this term because I had a subject in the previous term … how to put it? The way the materials were written was quite a mess. You were expected to have certain things in assignments that hadn't even been taught yet, because they came in the later lessons. So, obviously, there'd been changes made, but things hadn't been matched up properly. And then the assignment requirements are one thing, and then they'd be [another] thing in the marking rubric, which weren't in the assignment requirement, and then you got marked down because you didn't get it from the rubric or something. So, instead of having the full assignment requirements in the brief, that was spread around a bit. Then you had two or three tutors giving responses, and they weren't agreeing on things, and so it got very, very confusing.
>
> *(Beverly; female; 61–70; Outer Regional; online; Design)*

We found that experiences of not understanding assessment tasks and not receiving timely clarification were more commonly expressed by students who studied online. The inference here is that it is easier for on-campus students, by comparison, to seek clarification for an unclear assessment task as they have more incidental opportunities to ask questions of their lecturers, tutors, and peers face-to-face during a class, at break time, afterwards in the corridor or during their teachers' student consultation hours.

Deadlines and extensions

Undertaking assessment tasks can be a stressful experience at the best of times. This stress is often exacerbated when needing to meet deadlines along with family, parenting, or work challenges and commitments, as illustrated by John's experience of being overwhelmed when his wife gave birth to their second child:

> But during that time it was, just a few issues with the pregnancy before, and then obviously with the recovery after, and I still had to look after our

> daughter who was not quite two. And, I was, you know, in the hospital, running to and from, trying to maintain some sort of order in the house while visiting my wife and my new daughter in the hospital. Yeah, there was a uni assignment due in and around that time, obviously. Yeah, and there were times when I didn't get an opportunity to actually sit down and do any study until, you know, 11, 12 at night. And I would work until the early hours of the morning as much as I could until I needed sleep. But yeah, and I think I failed that subject because, yeah, I just couldn't. I just couldn't. [Laughs] I thought I'd be right because we had some help from family. But, yeah, it was just, the burden was just too much and it was just too late to pull out. And, I didn't fail by much, but I did fail, and it was just [a] really, really tough time.
>
> *(John; male; 31–40; Inner Regional; online; Education)*

A common complaint, as expressed in the following two comments, was the issue of several assignments being due at or around the same time, and how difficult it was to manage competing deadlines along with family, parenting, and work commitments:

> Assessments always tend to be due around the same time across units. I think with core units, at least, for each year of a degree, they could be coordinated together better because all students have to do them. With general electives, I understand this is probably difficult. Mature age students are likely working and/or parenting, as I am, and structure uni time around kids and work. The workload is never even throughout a semester. When there are multiple assessments due around the same time, the weekly workload increases significantly, and I find it hard to manage this around work and kids, even though I set aside time each week for uni.
>
> *(Student Survey)*

> I also had 3 large assessments all due on the same day, which not only affected my mental state but made me feel very alone.
>
> *(Student Survey)*

Some students experienced difficulties receiving extensions for unexpected natural disasters, family, or life events. One survey respondent highlighted the challenges of acquiring an extension when her children were unwell:

> I have found that most of my lecturers have been understanding. However, generally speaking most will not offer extensions etc. without medical certificates. This can add additional stress to mature age students who are also parents – sick kids and kids in general can add additional challenges to being a student. I believe that Universities need to be more considerate

> of this factor. Speaking personally, I am attempting to gain qualifications while I am still an at-home mum, so I am ready to re-enter the workforce when my children are older. As such, my children and their needs will always take priority over a due date for an assignment.
>
> *(Student Survey)*

Angela shared her humiliation around needing to disclose her divorce to seek an extension:

> When I first started my studies, I was divorcing. And I was struggling at the beginning, so I couldn't comprehend that that happened to me. I couldn't complete an assessment, and then I have to tell everyone what happened. What was the problem? You know? I mean, where can I find a certificate that says that "I'm struggling because I'm very depressed because I'm divorcing" … There is no such certificate … That was my situation, but I cannot prove it, so I have to tell my story to everyone… So, at that time, what I did, I just withdrew [from] the subject because I say, "I'm not going to cope and I can't do it".
>
> *(Angela; female; 41–50; Outer Regional; online; Hospitality Management)*

Angela's experience is an example of a traumatic life event that does not fit the typical list of reasons why a student might be granted an extension.

Students' experiences of receiving extensions for natural disasters were mixed. For instance, during the devastating 2019/2020 bushfires in Australia, some students reported having supportive teaching staff, and they received extensions without question, while others did not; some students reported inconsistent experiences within their university with one lecturer, for example, granting an extension in one unit, but the same request was denied in another (Crawford 2021).

The role of academic staff

Irrespective of attendance mode (online or on-campus), students shared experiences of varying degrees of support with assessments from academic staff:

> I struggled with it [assessment task], and both the lecturer and the tutor were brilliant. And, I spent, I think, an hour on the phone with both of them, at different times, to help with an assessment task. So, they were really good and happy to have that kind of conversation over the phone. Whereas some others just seemed to prefer either email contact or a drop-in session. It's like, "these are my hours". It's like, well, "that's great, but I'm not even in the same state as you".
>
> *(Sabrina; female; 41–50; Outer Regional; online; Health and community care)*

Numerous interviewees identified specific staff who spent time assisting them with assessment tasks; Simone shared one such example of the invaluable role played by a tutor:

> [I] would say she [the tutor] has been the most impactful on just building my confidence in myself and, like I said, giving me resources and showing me where to go for certain things, and when I came home and had to do assessments as part of that unit, I had this incredible amount of information that I could draw upon, and I did not feel like I was kind of stabbing in the dark. Yeah, I felt, actually, really confident with my knowledge on the subject
>
> *(Simone; female; 31–40; Outer Regional; online; Education)*

Simone also acknowledged that she received support for her assessments from a Facebook group of peers. Olivia commented positively on the role of teaching staff in contextualising assessments and understanding students' circumstances:

> The assessment, so, it means that information that we're given is contextualised for our area. And, it also means that the person that's teaching us, teaching me, marks my assessment ... It means that they understand, they have a deeper understanding of what you're trying to get at. It's really special.
>
> *(Olivia; female; 31–40; Remote area; online; Education)*

From the qualitative data analysis of the students' experiences of assessment, we interpreted that they did not always understand what was required in a task nor receive timely clarification of such tasks. They also had practical concerns around deadlines and challenges with receiving extensions. These experiences exacerbated the stress experienced in undertaking assessment tasks. Positive experiences were also reported – particularly, receiving support from academic staff, as well as assessment tasks being contextualised for a student's regional/remote location.

Impacts on students' experiences of assessment: An ecological systems perspective

The students' more negative experiences of assessment, reported above, can be explained, at first glance, at the individual level of a student's prior educational experiences and preparedness for university study. That is, their prior experiences and preparedness influence whether they understand the requirements of the task and have the expected academic skills and literacies to undertake the task. Similarly, responsibility can be placed on individual staff members, such as tutors and lecturers at the micro or classroom level of the university, for providing (or not providing) consistent information or timely responses to students' questions. These explanations have some relevance. However, they are deficit views of individual students and staff; they fail to consider systemic factors that impact on assessment design, staff workloads, an institution's culture and its expectations of students, and, thus, on students' experiences of assessment.

In this section, we broaden our lens from the individual and micro levels of the capacities and actions of individual students and staff to the systemic and structural factors – that is, to the influence of university cultures, rules and regulations and higher education policy – to provide a more holistic picture of what makes assessment inclusive or exclusive for mature-aged students in, and from, regional and remote areas in Australia. We explore some of the themes interpreted in the qualitative data from the perspective of Bronfenbrenner's ecological systems theory and identify the layers of the ecological system and the array of influences that impact on the students' experiences of assessment.

The lack of clarity in an assessment task description, inconsistency of information about the task within a subject/unit's documentation and between teaching staff, as well as students not receiving timely clarification of a task requirement, have, on the surface, straightforward solutions. Why, then, do students have these types of experiences? One reason is that casual teaching staff (for example, online tutors) are often not paid for the number of hours required to monitor the discussion forums (for instance, to be answering questions about assessment tasks) (Dodo-Balu 2017). From an ecological systems perspective, we can find explanations in the neoliberalisation of higher education (chronosystem impacts), the strain on higher education budgets (exosystem impacts) and the resultant casualisation of the university teaching workforce in Australia (May, Peetz, and Strachan 2013) to more fully explain the students' experiences; these influences originate in the outer layers of the ecological systems model (refer to Figure 16.1).

Students not receiving extensions for natural disasters, family illness, or life events can be explained by staff strictly following rules around extension requests (exosystem impacts). Some students, however, reported receiving extensions for situations not identified in documentation (for example, bushfires). In these cases, staff may have used their discretion and not steadfastly followed the rules because they had developed relationships with their students and knew their situations. When staff understand their students' circumstances (micro-level impacts) and follow their personal and/or teaching team's philosophy and expectations of students (micro-level and macrosystem impacts), they are well positioned to make appropriate personalised adjustments to assessment requests from students.

Not having previously been taught the discipline content and/or academic literacies and skills required to undertake an assessment task, as expressed by the interviewee Beverley, implies that "good practice" strategies in curriculum design and teaching are not always implemented, and also that assumptions are made about the academic skills and literacies expected of students enrolled at university. The "constructive alignment" in university teaching approach – which promotes alignment between i) a unit's intended learning outcomes; ii) what students learn in the teaching/learning activities; and iii) assessment tasks (Biggs 2014) – is of relevance here. Constructive alignment is a fundamental principle in university teaching and learning (exosystem impacts), but, as the students' experiences illustrate, it is not always implemented beyond a tick-box exercise. In their chapter on universal design for assessment, Ketterlin Geller, Johnstone, and Thurlow (2015) make a similar point; they refer to "access skills" – the skills required to actually undertake an assessment task (for example, how to write an academic essay or report including following referencing style guides; how to do an oral presentation), but which are often assumed and not taught (macrosystem impacts).

This point about "access skills" highlights the assumptions that are made about the types of academic knowledges, literacies, and skills that students arrive at university with, which are required to undertake assessment tasks. Such knowledges, literacies, and skills are not always made explicit to students upon commencement. In fact, they are often implicit, assumed, and form part of the hidden curriculum (macrosystem impacts) and are not always embedded in curriculum across courses.

Our analysis, from an ecological systems perspective, shows that the mature-aged students in regional and remote areas in this study – especially those who studied online – experienced numerous challenges with assessments. Along with curriculum design more broadly, assessment tasks are not always designed with all students – in all of their diversity – front of mind. We do not always know who we are teaching – that is, students' circumstances, strengths and challenges – and scholars have identified that default approaches have tended to privilege "traditional", "typical", "ideal", or "implied" students and/or follow disciplinary traditions (Crawford 2021; Ulriksen 2009). Despite endeavours to improve inclusion, diversity and equity in universities, entrenched attitudes and expectations prevail, which advantage some students (for example, school-leaver students with time and who study on-campus) over others (such as mature-aged students who juggle numerous commitments and study online) (Crawford 2021).

Moving towards more inclusive assessment

Within the sphere of teaching and learning, there is a variety of approaches that would help mitigate students' poor experiences of assessment. We argue that a first step would be for university leaders to reflect on their institution's mission, purpose, and values, asking who they intend to serve. It is paramount that universities and staff (academic and professional) know who their students are in all of their diversity – that is, their different circumstances, compounding challenges, and strengths (Crawford 2021). Gaining this understanding is foundational to implementing appropriate pedagogies (Crawford, Kift, and Jarvis 2019) and prompts consideration of the assumptions made about students and expectations of them. Implementing constructive alignment in unit design (genuinely and critically) would help to ensure that students are learning the knowledges, literacies and skills required to undertake their assessment tasks, as would embedding academic literacies across a course and/or providing transition courses, so that students commence their undergraduate degree on a more level playing field, having developed the academic literacies expected of them. Further approaches include implementing inclusive education principles (Houghton 2019) and/or universal design in higher education and universal design in assessment (Burgstahler 2015; Ketterlin Geller, Johnstone, and Thurlow 2015). As Jain argues in Chapter 3, any implementation of universal design needs to be undertaken critically and with ongoing reflection or risk inadvertently further marginalising the students who are already experiencing exclusion. (Chapter 12 also examines universal design for assessment.)

Assessment is one part of students' broader experiences of teaching and learning. The factors that are inclusionary or exclusionary often relate to the more peripheral layers of the ecological system, such as the culture of a university – its mission, values, philosophies, attitudes, and expectations – which influence who an institution really serves. As Burke et al. (2016, 8) recommend: "Schools and universities must proactively challenge stereotypes about the 'types' of students who are capable of university study". A social justice orientation (Gidley et al. 2010) applied to assessment in higher education would challenge the privileging of traditional knowledge hierarchies and of the "implied student" to value difference and diversity and to genuinely focus on engaged participation for all students. Such an approach would value and draw upon the numerous assets and expertise of, for instance, mature-aged students in regional and remote areas. Beyond specific assessment approaches, the discussion above highlights the need for cultural change and for teaching budget allocations in higher education to be addressed.

Notes

1 "Regional and remote" students is one of the six government-identified equity groups in Australia. Refer to Crawford (2021, 18–19) for definitions of "mature-aged" and "regional and remote" students.
2 The ecological systems are described in Table 9 in Crawford (2021, 70–71).

References

Biggs, J. 2014. "Constructive Alignment in University Teaching." *HERDSA Review of Higher Education* 1: 5–22. https://www.herdsa.org.au/herdsa-review-higher-education-vol-1/5-22.

Braun, V., and Clarke, V. 2022. "Conceptual and Design Thinking for Thematic Analysis." *Qualitative Psychology* 9 (1): 9–26. https://doi.org/10.1037/qup0000196.

Bronfenbrenner, U. 1995. "The Bioecological Model from a Life Course Perspective: Reflections of a Participant Observer." In *Examining Lives in Context: Perspectives on the Ecology of Human Development*, edited by Phyllis Moen, Glenn H. Elder, and Kurt Lüscher, 599–618. Washington, DC: American Psychological Association.

Burgstahler, S. 2015. "Universal Design in Higher Education." In *Universal Design in Higher Education: From Principles to Practice*, edited by Sheryl E. Burgstahler, 3–28. Cambridge, MA: Harvard Education Press.

Burke, P. J., Bennett, A., Burgess, C., Gray, K., and Southgate, E. 2016. *Capability, Belonging and Equity in Higher Education: Developing Inclusive Approaches.* Callaghan, NSW, Australia: The University of Newcastle. https://www.newcastle.edu.au/__data/assets/pdf_file/0011/243992/CAPABILITY-ONLINE.pdf.

Crawford, N. 2021. *"On the Radar": Supporting the Mental Wellbeing of Mature-Aged Students in Regional and Remote Australia.* Accessed 18 January 2022. https://www.ncsehe.edu.au/wp-content/uploads/2021/04/Crawford-Equity-Fellowship-Report_FINAL.pdf.

Crawford, N., and Emery, S. 2021. "'Shining a Light' on Mature-Aged Students in, and from, Regional and Remote Australia." *Student Success* 12 (2): 18–27. https://doi.org/10.5204/ssj.1919.

Crawford, N., Kift, S., and Jarvis, L. 2019. "Supporting Student Mental Wellbeing in Enabling Education: Practices, Pedagogies and a Philosophy of Care". In *Transitioning Students in Higher Education: Philosophy, Pedagogy and Practice*, edited by Angela Jones, Anita Olds, and Joanne G. Lisciandro, 161–170. London: Routledge.

Creswell, J. W. 2014. *Research Design: Qualitative, Quantitative, and Mixed Methods Approaches*, rev. ed. Thousand Oaks, CA: SAGE.

Dodo-Balu, A. 2017. "Students Flourish and Tutors Wither." *Australian Universities Review* 59 (1): 4–13. https://files.eric.ed.gov/fulltext/EJ1130301.pdf.

Gidley, J., Hampson, G., Wheeler, L., and Bereded-Samuel, E. 2010. "From Access to Success: An Integrated Approach to Quality Higher Education Informed by Social Inclusion Theory and Practice." *Higher Education Policy* 23 (1): 123–147. http://doi.org/10.1057/hep.2009.24.

Higher Education Standards Framework (Threshold Standards). 2021. Australian Government Federal Register of Legislation10. Accessed 18 January 2022. https://www.legislation.gov.au/Details/F2021L00488/Download.

Houghton, A.-M. 2019. "Academic and Departmental Support." In *Student Mental Health and Wellbeing in Higher Education: A Practical Guide*, edited by Nicola Barden, and Ruth Caleb, 125–144. London: SAGE.

Ketterlin Geller, L., Johnstone, C., and Thurlow, M. 2015. "Universal Design of Assessment." In *Universal Design in Higher Education: From Principles to Practice*, edited by Sheryl E. Burgstahler, 163–175. Cambridge, MA: Harvard Education Press.

May, R., Peetz, D., and Strachan, G. 2013. "The Casual Academic Workforce and Labour Market Segmentation in Australia." *Labour and Industry: A Journal of the Social and Economic Relations of Work* 23 (3): 258–275. https://doi.org/10.1080/10301763.2013.839085.

Tai, J., Ajjawi, R., and Umarova, A. 2021. "How Do Students Experience Inclusive Assessment? A Critical Review of Contemporary Literature." *International Journal of Inclusive Education.* https://doi.org/10.1080/13603116.2021.2011441.

Ulriksen, L. 2009. "The Implied Student." *Studies in Higher Education* 34 (5): 517–532. https://doi.org/10.1080/03075070802597135.

17

NORMALISING ALTERNATIVE ASSESSMENT APPROACHES FOR INCLUSION

Roseanna Bourke

Introduction

If assessment tasks are effective, they will serve as powerful mediating learning tools that enable students to demonstrate their knowledge, understanding, and application of their knowledge to real-world contexts. Assessments that capture the interest of students also support them to imagine their own possibilities and future applications after the course has finished. This chapter explores how alternative and atypical assessment practices, that are innovative or novel for students, can enhance their sense of engagement in a course, and can provide a more equitable means for students to demonstrate their learning.

Assessment tools in higher education that provide more equitable options for students will first involve novel approaches, that over time become normalised. Importantly, atypical approaches to assessment (such as self-assessment, ipsative assessment, and technology-based assessments) need to move beyond being considered "alternative" or "innovative and novel" forms of assessment in higher education. Clearly, there are challenges when introducing alternative forms of assessment in higher education (HE) especially in highly competitive university courses. Often students are keen to complete assessments that are traditionally known to them (e.g., essays, written assignments, examinations) because they have learned to optimise their grade through these traditional means. Another challenge when introducing alternative forms of assessment is that students "generally place a higher value on traditional assessment tools especially in terms of their validity and reliability" than more novel types of assessment (Phongsirikul 2018, 61). However, these alternative forms of assessment are fast becoming key approaches required by students in their preparation for a post-COVID, new world zeitgeist, premised on social justice, inclusiveness, cultural, and Indigenous understandings.

DOI: 10.4324/9781003293101-21

Background

Assessment methods traditionally used in university settings (essays, written assignments, tests, and examinations) tend to determine whether, and by how much, a student has learned against the learning outcomes of a course. Ironically, these assessment approaches direct the students' attention to "proving" what they know and can apply, rather than "improving" the way they learn or even to understand themselves better in relation to their learning and the world around them. Higher education policies, student wellbeing, and the type of pedagogical and assessment practices within any given course, all impact on how inclusive the course is orientated and experienced by the student. For example, researchers have shown the critical role that Indigenous pedagogies and practices play in higher education for all students to feel included and to succeed (e.g., Mayeda et al. 2014; Roberston, Smith, and Larkin 2021).

This means that an assessment tool (e.g., essay, critique, exam, self-assessment) cannot simply be pulled out of a suite of possible assessment methods, without a closer understanding of why, when, and how it is used, or a clear rationale for the *purpose* of the assessment. An inclusive assessment approach is one where *all* students can develop the skills to sustain their learning, and that can strengthen their motivation towards their *own* goals. This increases the likelihood that these assessment tasks will also be sustainable; sustainable assessment is where students incorporate the skills, knowledge, and attitude to continue using life-long assessment practices (Boud and Soler 2016).

In higher education, the assessment of students is often controlled through policies and regulations that can either *prevent* responsive changes to assessment tasks, or *promulgate* a vision for change. When a shift in rhetoric is pronounced, it becomes the starting point of a change-process to enable more inclusive, equitable assessment approaches to be used. In the context of the introduction of the YouTube clip assignment, the Assessment Handbook at Massey University (2019, 3) now includes the explicit intention:

> to promote sustainable assessment practices for lifelong learning, staff must focus on engaging students as active partners in their learning. By enabling students to continually assess while they learn, when they are exposed to novel situations outside the classroom, they will be able to self-assess and use evaluative judgements.

This is the key policy document that enabled the introduction of an assignment where students developed and trialled their own YouTube clips. A growing body of evidence shows that supporting students as partners in decisions that affect them, will increase student motivation, learning and likely success (Bovill, Jarvis, and Smith 2020; Cook-Sather, Bovill, and Felten 2014). Therefore, alternative and authentic assessments need to be developed alongside, and with students. When the YouTube clip assignment was first introduced, I worked in partnership with a student cohort to establish a marking rubric that they could see themselves in. For example, students explicitly rejected criteria associated with the technical aspects of the clip, and did not believe a "wow" factor should be part of the criteria. The rubrics were linked to learning outcomes for the course, and learning associated with using their knowledge in their everyday lives. The rubric also included how the clip demonstrated their knowledge and learning for the course. Assessment innovations in university contexts must work with students as partners to ensure "what works" represents the perspective of students and their learning. In this experience, incorporating partnership approaches in assessment with students using their own preferred modes of presenting their learning, challenges the "expert" and "outside" model of assessment, replaced with one underpinned by values of partnership, respect, and inclusion.

In developing ethically defensible assessment practices that are inclusive of all students, the impact of assessment on student wellbeing must be considered. Increasingly, the wellbeing of students is recognised as not being separate from their assessment experiences, and while this link has yet to be systematically examined, it has been argued that there is "a bidirectional relationship between wellbeing and assessment experiences" (Jones et al. 2021, 439). There is evidence for example, that even when examinations are adapted to become more authentic for students such as changing from norm-referenced assessment to one of criterion referenced, there is a beneficial impact on reducing student anxiety (Slavin, Schindler, and Chibnall 2014).

Examples of authentic assessment methods and impact on student learning

Authentic assessment methods come in a range of guises and can include varying forms such as iPortfolio, WeCreate Activity, and iLearn & Teach projects (Phongsirikul 2018), self-assessment (Bourke 2018), and ePortfolios (Kahn 2019; Slepcevic-Zach and Stock 2018). Generally, such assessment tasks will provide students with more autonomy and control over what they attend to and how they want to respond to the assessment task (Bourke, Rainier, and de Vries 2018). Practical experience in trialling these ideas, along with research on their impact, has shown that autonomy is valued by students: "The ePortfolio is about what I think is important. It is about my *own* autonomy of my *own* assessment" (Bourke, Rainier, and de Vries 2018, 4, emphasis added). Students are also aware that some assessments (such as ePortfolios) "bring a far broader benefit than just on the course of studies" (Slepcevic-Zach and Stock 2018, 305). Often these assessments encourage learners to intentionally focus on *their own* learning and *on the criteria for that learning*, and are more likely to be sustainable simply because students are afforded more agency to develop the ability to self-assess. Self-assessment is an example of an alternative assessment process that can be "normalised". It is best understood as a sustainable assessment approach that allows for "a way of rethinking outcomes, curriculum and pedagogy away from a focus on disciplinary knowledge to what students can do in the world" (Boud and Soler 2016, 401).

As an example of sustainable assessment, self-assessment is both a skill and competency required in professional life and for lifelong learning which prompts graduates to continue being reflective independent assessors of their own learning. This enables young people to place less reliance on external markers to affirm learning, and more on their own understanding of their learning. Aligning with future-driven self-assessment (as distinct from programme-driven self-assessment, or teacher-driven self-assessment) (Tan 2007), learners use their skills to assess their learning beyond course requirements. In this way self-assessment is markedly different from self-marking (e.g., Bourke 2018), and supports the intention of developing students' skills and expertise to be lifelong learners *and* lifelong assessors of their learning. Research shows self-assessment can be used to establish a greater sense of student identity as a learner and practitioner (Bourke 2018) where they develop capability with regard to self-regulation (Panadero and Alonso-Tapia 2013).

Research within health, education, and social sectors has identified that for most people, self-assessment is difficult and typically fundamentally flawed (Dunning, Heath, and Suls 2004). This creates an imperative to focus on developing skills and insight for young people to continue their "future" assessment once the course is over and to want to self-assess their learning without a teacher, grade or mark (Bourke 2018; Tan 2007, 2009). An argument is often made that individuals with specialist skills such as vets, doctors, teachers, dentists, and pilots need a strong knowledge base and demonstrated competency in order to pass courses. In a similar way, those in trades in specialised areas such as building, engineering, electricians, and hairdressing, must show they have the skills to do the job, and problem-solve unanticipated issues as they arise. So should these training programmes include self-assessment tasks or traditional forms of assessment? Clearly both are needed, and the evidence for self-assessment skills can be found in real life examples of how self-assessment has been used by experts faced with novel situations that they have not specifically been trained for, or have earlier practiced. An example is the response of Captain Sullenberger to a critical incident when flying over the Hudson River in New York after a double engine blow-out following a bird strike. He landed the plane on the river without loss of life, and at the time Captain Sullenberger explained he had mere seconds to assess the situation and determine what he needed to do, self-assess his skills and those around him, and what was required to land the plane. He later reported that this was not something he had trained to do. Another situation arose when a New Zealand broadcaster suffered a mild heart attack mid-flight. Without a doctor on board, it was a veterinarian who came to his aid, and used her skills albeit within a different professional context.[1] As she later reported, this was something she was not trained specifically for, but her self-assessment enabled her to use her skills in this new context. She noted wryly, unlike her typical animal patients "he didn't try to bite"!

The YouTube clip assessment

Given there is growing urgency in developing assessment tasks that (1) incorporate self-assessment skills, (2) empower students to demonstrate their learning in different and diverse ways, and (3) are more equitable in the sense of being able to showcase knowledge in a range of ways, this section presents the introduction of the YouTube clips as an assessment task. Students are aware of, and use YouTube clips in their formal and everyday learning, where they can upload, and share videos to learn everything from changing a tyre, learning a musical instrument or a new language, and to cooking a cake. The introduction of this assessment approach was staggered across three years, first at undergraduate and then subsequently at postgraduate level and Educational Psychology Internship courses.

The YouTube clip assignment was introduced to enable students to not only demonstrate their knowledge in new ways but also to learn skills such as communication of ideas, self-assessment, creation of digital clips to share and teach with others, and critical analysis of how major concepts can be simplified and actioned in practice; all skills associated with their introduction into professional practice. Three components to the assignment include: (1) development of a 3–4 minute YouTube clip; (2) sharing the YouTube clip with others and; (3) a 2000-word critical analysis of the trial of the clip on both their own and others' learning. Although the YouTube clips developed and presented by the students were diverse, they were all engaging and contained a wealth of ideas and application of knowledge. Some students used animation, others used slides and talk, and there were also ones that included a demonstration of a task or a skill. In all cases, the student was actively able to demonstrate their learning, and themselves in that learning.

Following completion of their respective courses, students who had submitted a YouTube assessment were asked to complete an online survey (university ethics approval was obtained). Responses from 110 students were received, and were representative across courses including undergraduate (34%); postgraduate (MEdDevPsych) (48%); and the EdPsych Internship year (18%). The survey asked students to rank their assessment preference for learning and were given a range of assessment options that they had encountered over their studies (essays, examinations, online tests, or open book tests, self-assessment, novel assessments, presentations, case studies, ePortfolio collections). Over half the students (63%) across both the undergraduate and postgraduate courses opted for a traditional form of assessment to support their learning, and arguably a safe way to complete their assessment requirements for course completion. Written assignments (i.e., essays 45% and tests 18%) were the two most preferred assessment approaches. However, respondents specifically identified aspects of the

YouTube clip assignment that they enjoyed, especially with regards to applying key concepts:

> The practical aspect of this assignment was really helpful and enabled me to understand what I was learning. I was able to see the effects of my YouTube clip on teaching and learning, reflect on this, and apply the knowledge gained from the course readings and teaching. I think it helped me to cement key concepts.
>
> *(Education undergraduate student, 2021)*

Sixty-five percent of the students believed the YouTube form of assessment was more equitable than other forms of assessment (37.33% Yes, and 28% in some ways), mainly because it enabled students to actively engage in their learning and assessment in an authentic way showing more of *themselves* through the assessment. For example, one student commented: "It provided [an] opportunity to show personality and humour which isn't necessarily accommodated in APA [American Psychological Association] writing". Students identified further equity benefits, such as supporting those with learning difficulties (e.g., dyslexia), and that the assessment task opened "thinking to being more creative and thinking on the spot, rather than it becoming a "tick the box" exercise and in ensuring all references have been covered". Importantly, students completed component parts by actively including others (either through technical support, or through watching and learning from the clip). One student reported: "The YouTube clip assignment was far more interactive, so I was more willing and able to share my learning with others in both formal and informal settings".

Are innovative assessment practices inclusive of all learners?

A dilemma arises when determining whether to pursue assessment approaches that students are not familiar with. These could feasibly detract from students' expectations and experiences of tertiary assessment, especially given that students seem to prefer traditional assessments (Jones et al. 2021). This ambivalence showed in a student's response in the YouTube clip: "It was nice to do something that didn't involve so much writing, but I did have to learn how to make and edit a YouTube video without understanding how it is relevant to our learning or future career". This shows the importance of student-staff partnership where teachers can "join the dots" for students who do not see the benefit in the longer term. Another consideration is that even though exams are reported by students as creating stress and anxiety, they are also viewed as familiar and expected. Jones et al. (2021) note that as students know the requirements of exams, and how to prepare, such methods of assessment are "potentially preferred in comparison with other less traditional forms of assessment" (442). In the present example where students developed YouTube clips, they learned a range of technical skills to demonstrate their learning, and while they did view the process as a learning experience, the question remains: do the gains outweigh the possible anxiety created through this novel approach?

Students were also asked whether they had learned something they did not expect through the YouTube assignment, and the responses showed that there were gains beyond the knowledge they learned. Students reported improving their personal learning and teaching skills, actively learning patience, and perseverance, gaining a thorough understanding of course content, gaining the ability to express learning in a new way, honing their problem-solving skills, elevating their knowledge from theoretical to practical, understanding YouTube as a form of learning, and time management skills. As one noted:

> I felt I gained a better understanding by undertaking this assignment because it was a new way of testing and presenting my learning. I also enjoyed the process more than a traditional assignment, especially compared to exams
>
> *(Education undergraduate student, 2021)*

However, other students might be more challenged by the task itself, rather than the learning:

> When trying to convey [my] learning I especially found it challenging to not only write something but video and edit it. I found it extremely time-consuming and felt I could be doing more valuable exercises instead. I found it stressful and found that it didn't really help convey my learning in any way
>
> *(Education undergraduate student, 2021)*

Some students reported they did not realise the extent of their learning, until after the course was completed:

> I've never uploaded anything to YouTube before so that was interesting. Now that I think about it, watching my participants use my video was my first ever observation, and I was observing through the lens informed by the literature such as community of practice, active participation, collaboration, and self-directed learning. Concepts I was unaware of prior to that learning experience. On reflection, there was actually a lot of valuable learning that I appear to have implicitly absorbed.
>
> *(Education postgraduate student, 2021)*

What does this mean for assessment for inclusion?

Simply giving students choice of assessment or alternative assessment tasks does not create equitable or inclusive assessment options. Initially when students experience novel approaches to assessments, they may be anxious until they understand there is no "one way" to present their knowledge and understanding. Jones et al. (2021, 443) report that for "students to become more independent, they needed to be given the space to develop their own strategies for completing assessments. While some students find this independence gives greater control and ownership of their work, less confident students experience it as stressful".

The results from the student survey indicated that they preferred traditional assessments, which highlights the complexity of giving students the "freedom to choose" assessments. Students will base their choices on their own historical, cultural, and social experiences of assessment and learning, and can be reluctant to move into new territory. Ironically as Rogoff (1990, 202) identified, learning involves "functioning at the edge of one's competence on the border of incompetence"; learning in this sense encourages students to explore the unknown and take risks in the belief they can, and will, achieve.

The survey also showed that the benefits gained from learning through alternative assessment methods were not fully realised and used by students, until after the course was completed. Sustainable assessment practices such as YouTube clips and self-assessment, while uncomfortable at the time, can have more impact on students' learning than traditional assessments. It also shows that assessment requires an element of *trust* between teachers and students, and therefore for staff-student partnership to work, power-sharing must result. Staff may have concerns about handing over power to students when they wish to cover substantial content and they are unconvinced that students know enough about the subject to be co-creating classes (Bovill, Jarvis, and Smith 2020, 37).

An interesting unintended consequence of the YouTube assessment activity was that it required students to *think* about their learning, rather than *prove* their learning. This meant there was an absence of plagiarism. Plagiarism can be examined through a policy, pedagogical, or moral lens (Eaton 2021), and institutions determine specific ways to "define, detect, prevent, and punish" students who are found to have plagiarised (Marsh 2007). In my experience, students tend to plagiarise when they remove themselves from the assessment, when they look to sources to cite, or have others complete aspects of their work. In contrast, authentic assessment approaches that engage learners in-depth, and over time, such as the YouTube clip development, self-assessment, and ePortfolios, can tell educators "much about how students view themselves as learners or emerging professionals; how they are perceiving, connecting, and interpreting their in- and out-of-class learning experiences; and why they may be struggling with particular content or concepts" (Kahn 2019, 138). As one student who completed a YouTube clip assignment noted:

> Some of my favourite assignments were ones where I was able to be myself, be creative and show my learning in a way that interests me. This is what we expect students to do in primary school so why does it suddenly stop during high school/university and then you're expected to regain creativity in your job/career?
>
> *(Education postgraduate student, 2021)*

Inclusive assessment practices enable increasingly diverse cohorts of students to succeed in multiple ways if educators extend options for students. Alternative assessment practices that become normalised in higher education allow for a greater choice over what inclusive assessment practices to employ. Teachers need to recognise students as both learners and assessors, trial innovative and sustainable assessment practices, develop an evidence-base on the impact of assessment on learners and support student assessment literacy. While the "learning outcomes race" (e.g., Douglass, Thomson, and Zhao 2012) is feasibly a barrier to redefining student success and inclusion, it remains important to remind students that it is *their* learning that counts. Over time universities have created a proliferation of policies that become unintentional barriers for staff and students alike; creating bureaucratised multi-layered processes for assessment, research integrity, and polices on learning and teaching. Increasingly though, unequivocal messages are emerging in both policy and practice that call for inclusion of students, sustainable assessment, values-based decisions, and professional autonomy; all essential components for inclusive assessment practices. An imperative for practice is to normalise assessments that challenge the status quo, by developing alternative assessment with students from the ground up.

Note

1 https://www.nowtolove.co.nz/news/latest-news/jason-gunn-treated-by-vet-on-plane-33701

References

Boud, D., and Soler, R. 2016. "Sustainable Assessment Revisited." *Assessment & Evaluation in Higher Education* 41 (3): 400–413. http://doi.org/10.1080/02602938.2015.1018133.

Bourke, R. 2018. "Self-Assessment to Incite Learning in Higher Education: Developing Ontological Awareness." *Assessment and Evaluation in Higher Education* 43 (5): 827–839. http://doi.org/10.1080/02602938.2017.1411881.

Bourke, R., Rainier, C., and de Vries, V. 2018. "Assessment and Learning Together in Higher Education." *International Journal of Student Voice* 25: 1–11. https://repository.brynmawr.edu/cgi/viewcontent.cgi?article=1194&context=tlthe.

Bovill, C., Jarvis, J., and Smith, K. 2020. *Co-Creating Learning and Teaching: Towards Relational Pedagogy in Higher Education*. Critical Publishing. https://www.criticalpublishing.com/asset/394452/1/Co_creating_Learning_and_Teaching_sample.pdf.

Cook-Sather, A., Bovill, C., and Felten, P. 2014. *Engaging Students as Partners in Learning and Teaching: A Guide for Faculty*. San Francisco: Jossey Bass.

Douglass, J. A., Thomson, G., and Zhao, Ch.-M. 2012. "The Learning Outcomes Race: The Value of Self-reported Gains in Large Research Universities." *Higher Education* 64: 317–335. http://doi.org/10.1007/s10734-011-9496-x.

Dunning, D., Heath, Ch., and Suls, J. M. 2004. "Flawed Self-Assessment. Implications for Health, Education, and the Workplace." *Psychological Science in the Public Interest* 5 (3): 69–106. https://doi.org/10.1111/j.1529-1006.2004.00018.x.

Eaton, S. E. 2021. *Plagiarism in Higher Education: Tackling Tough Topics in Academic Integrity*. Santa Barbara, CA: ABC-CLIO.

Jones, E., Priestley, M., Brewster, L., Wilbraham, S. J., Hughes, G., and Spanner, L. 2021. "Student Wellbeing and Assessment in Higher Education: The Balancing Act." *Assessment & Evaluation in Higher Education* 46 (3): 438–450. http://doi.org/10.1080/02602938.2020.1782344.

Kahn, S. 2019. "Transforming Assessment, Assessing Transformation: ePortfolio Assessment Trends." In *Trends in Assessment: Ideas, Opportunities, and Issues for Higher Education*, edited by Stephen. P. Hundley and Susan Kahn, 137–156. Bloomfield: Stylus Publishing.

Marsh, B. 2007. *Plagiarism: Alchemy and Remedy in Higher Education*. New York: SUNY Press.

Massey University. 2019. *Massey University Assessment Handbook. Principles, Guidelines, and Resources*.

Mayeda, D. T., Keil, M., Dutton, H. D., and Ofamo'oni, I. F-H. 2014. "You've Gotta Set a Precedent. Māori and Pacific Voices on Student Success in Higher Education." *AlterNative* 10 (2): 165–179. https://doi.org/10.1177/117718011401000206.

Panadero, E., and Alonso-Tapia, J. 2013. "Self-Assessment: Theoretical and Practical Connotations. When It Happens, How Is It Acquired and What to Do to Develop It in Our Students." *Electronic Journal of Research in Educational Psychology* 11 (2): 551–576. http://doi.org/10.14204/ejrep.30.12200.

Phongsirikul, M. 2018. "Traditional and Alternative Assessments in ELT: Students' and Teachers' Perceptions." *rEFLections* 25 (1): 61–84.

Roberston, K., Smith, J. A., and Larkin, S. 2021. "Improving Higher Education Success for Australian Indigenous Peoples. Examples of Promising Practice." In *Marginalised Communities in Higher Education*, edited by Neil Harrison and Graeme Atherton, 179–201. London: Routledge.

Rogoff, B. 1990. *Apprenticeship in Thinking. Cognitive Development in Social Context*. Oxford: Oxford University Press.

Slavin, S. J., Schindler, D. L., and Chibnall, J. T. 2014. "Medical Student Mental Health 3.0: Improving Student Wellness through Curricular Changes." *Academic Medicine* 89 (4): 573–577. http://doi.org/10.1097/ACM.0000000000000166.

Slepcevic-Zach, P., and Stock, M. 2018. "ePortfolio as a Tool for Reflection and Self-Reflection." *Reflective Practice* 19 (3): 291–307. http://doi.org/10.1080/14623943.2018.1437399.

Tan, K. 2007. "Conceptions of Self-Assessment: What Is Needed for Long-Term Learning?" In *Rethinking Assessment in Higher Education: Learning for the Long Term*, edited by David Boud and Nancy Falchikov, 114–127. London: Routledge.

Tan, K. 2009. "Meanings and Practices of Power in Academics' Conceptions of Student Self-Assessment." *Teaching in Higher Education* 14 (4): 361–373. http://doi.org/10.1080/13562510903050111.

18

STUDENT CHOICE OF ASSESSMENT METHODS

How can this approach become more mainstream and equitable?

Geraldine O'Neill

Introduction

In higher education some assessment approaches dominate the landscape. The end of semester unseen examination, for example, is widely used internationally (Brown 2015; National Forum 2016). However, this and other common approaches have been criticised for not allowing for all students to play to their strengths. Diversifying assessment methods in higher education is a logical step in supporting a more inclusive approach to assessment for diverse cohorts (O'Neill and Padden 2021). Diversifying assessment is also in keeping with the growing emphasis on universal design for learning (CAST 2018). Hundley and Kahn (2019, 207) identified that a meta-trend in higher education assessment internationally is "assessment strategies and approaches that are becoming more inclusive, equity-oriented and reflective of the diverse students our institutions serve".

While diversifying assessment to move away from dominant forms of assessment seems a positive step, if not approached appropriately it can put some students under pressure and may result in unintended outcomes such as poorer performance (Armstrong 2014; Bevitt 2015; Kirkland and Sutch 2009; Medland 2016). For example, in the case of international students "coping with novel assessment represents just one part of a much larger and slower process of adaptation" (Bevitt 2015, 116). One approach worth considering therefore is giving all students in a module[1] (course) a choice of assessment methods, thus increasing the chance of playing to the strengths of all students and minimising any potential disadvantage. Giving students a choice between two or more assessment methods within a module, appears to go some way towards supporting the concept of equity, often described as "fairness" (Easterbrook, Parker, and Waterfield 2005; Garside et al. 2009; O'Neill 2011, 2017; Waterfield and West 2006). In the case where there is a genuine opportunity for students to achieve better outcomes,

DOI: 10.4324/9781003293101-22

it supports the idea of assessment for social justice (McArthur 2016). However, using a choice of assessment approach is not without its challenges.

Over a 10-year period, as an academic staff member and an educational developer, I have engaged in a programme of research to design, implement, and evaluate student choice in assessment. My earlier work at institutional level resulted in the development of: a) disciplinary case studies, b) a design template to ensure equity between the choices given; c) a seven-step implementation process, and d) an evaluation tool that measures equity between the choices (O'Neill 2011, 2017). During my work at national level, I advocated the concept of student-as-partners, including the use of choice of assessment (National Forum 2016). Choice of assessment, in our recent research, although was shown to empower students in their learning there are concerns around equity between the choices and it was still relatively under-used (O'Neill and Padden 2021). This programme of research and the wider literature on choice of assessment therefore highlight key questions that are addressed in this chapter:

- How can staff ensure that there is equity between the choices given to the students?
- How can it become more mainstream in institutional policies and practice?
- How do staff implement this approach in their practices?

Developing equity between the choices: Procedures and outcomes

Choice of assessment is one approach that aims to level the playing field, supporting the idea of equity or fairness. In order to support a fairer approach to assessment in 2010 at University College Dublin (UCD), I co-ordinated a strategic institutional project with module co-ordinators across a variety of disciplines to implement choice of assessment in one of their modules (Nine modules; n = 370 students). However, a common theme identified at the start of the project, when staff came together to design their choice of assessment, was how does one ensure that there is fairness *between* the choices. Staff expected the assessments to be relatively equal in relation to workload (of both staff and students), feedback opportunities, alignment with teaching approaches, and opportunities to succeed. This is often called "procedural equity" (O'Neill 2017). Students in particular, as noted in the literature, are also concerned about fairness between the assessment choices (Craddock and Mathias 2009) and ensuring that they have sufficient examples and experience to make an "informed" choice.

Based on the earlier work by Easterbrook, Parker, and Waterfield (2005), who encourage students to reflect on their choices, as part of the project, I developed a template to ensure staff considered "procedural equity" between the choices. This also doubled up as a document that helped students make an informed choice (O'Neill 2011). This template encouraged staff to explore and describe to the students the assessment's equity under the heading of: its weighting to the overall grade; its traits (visual, type of writing); the learning outcome to be assessed; the criteria used; equity in approaches to marking/teaching/workload/feedback; and links to some examples of the assessment choice (O'Neill 2011, 2017).

The students' views on their experience of choice of assessment, in this institutional project in 2010, were gathered by a questionnaire (respondents, $n = 144/370$ students). An interesting finding was that students in later years and those pursuing postgraduate studies were more open to the use of choice of assessment (O'Neill 2011), a result that was supported by Francis (2008). This may be explained by their increased level of experience of different assessment that helps in them making an informed choice of assessment. Students also noted that the choice between two assessments was sufficient level of diversity of choice (O'Neill 2011). This speaks to an issue that was discussed in our more recent paper on the use of this approach – there can be such a thing as too much diversity and too much choice (O'Neill and Padden 2021).

Some of these findings are linked with "procedural equity", but staff on the project wanted to be sure that the different choices they are presenting to students would also allow all students an equal chance of succeeding in the outcomes of the assessment, that is, the grades. McArthur (2016) also emphasised that procedural fairness is not enough and that these don't always relate to "just outcomes", sometimes described as an aspect of "assessment for social justice". Irish students have indicated in a recent national project that "achieving high academic attainment" is a key measure of student success (National Forum 2019, 5). Grades matter to them. Stowell (2004) describes equity in performance not so much as "equity" but as "justice" which is more concerned with fairness in outcomes. In examining the pattern of grades between the choices of assessment in this institutional project, it was found that:

- Students performed better than previous years' cohorts in the module.
- Their median grade was higher (B+) than the institutional median grade (C grade).
- Particular student groups appeared to score higher when given an opportunity to play to their strengths – for example, students from different socio-economic groups.

(O'Neill 2017)

Wanner, Palmer, and Palmer (2021) reported in their study on *flexible assessment* that when they gave students some choices, students reported that it helped them get better marks. Wanner, Palmer, and Palmer (2021) study, however, also included choice of submission dates and weighting of assessment. Although improving student grades should be a positive outcome, a resulting tension that can arise with this approach is that staff become concerned with how to deal with what they describe as "grade inflation". In our recent institutional survey ($n = 160$ module co-ordinators) on diversifying assessment and use of choice of assessment, grade inflation was more of a concern for staff, when considering this approach, than fear of student failure (O'Neill and Padden 2021). Grade inflation is often described as perceived or actual rise in students' average grades.

This highlights challenges in institutional grading systems and the use of norm-referenced assessment in many institutions internationally. Tannock (2017) emphasised that grading to a normal curve can create "social division among students depending on where they stand in the grading hierarchy, and particularly destructive impacts on the learning, esteem and identity of students at the lower end of this hierarchy" (1350). If it is our intention for more students to succeed, it would make sense that more would do well, in particular if we are not disadvantaging other students in the process. This fear of grade inflation needs to be interrogated at institutional and national levels. We need to also explore the complexity of other influences on institutional grading approaches, for example, the impact of high student fees; comparability of international grading scales (Witte 2011); staff confidence in grading; staff accountability and the role of the "public" university (Tannock 2017). Staff fear of grade inflation appears to be running counter to student success. Efforts should be taken to ensure that it does not become a barrier to the introduction of choice of assessment.

Institutional policies on assessment, including aspects such as grade distribution, can be associated with the wider concept of social justice in assessment. McArthur (2016) explores the concept of social justice as it relates to fairness in assessment, she maintains that "that a preoccupation with fairness as sameness is one of the major factors constraining assessment playing a greater social justice role" (973). She describes the concept of the "assessment for social justice" as referring "both to the justice of assessment within higher education, and to the role of assessment in nurturing the forms of learning that will promote greater social justice within society as a whole" (McArthur 2016, 968). The development of student opportunities to play to their strengths and having an opportunity to improve their grades through the choice of assessment method, goes some way towards this understanding of social justice. (See Chapter 2 for reflections on assessment for social justice.)

Another positive impactful outcome was that the use of choice of assessment had empowered students in their learning (O'Neill and Padden 2021). This gave them some level of responsibility, trusting them to make a choice. Responsibility and trust are two aspects of "assessment for social justice", referred to in McArthur's recent description of this term (McArthur 2021). Taking responsibility was noted by Wanner, Palmer, and Palmer (2021) as an important skill for graduates in the workplace. Where choice of assessment methods falls short in relation to the wider concept of social justice is that the methods on their own do promote social justice within society as a whole. McArthur (2021) also highlights that assessment for social justice should be aspirational and transformative. She explores how assessment systems can be inherently unfair and not all students have an opportunity to succeed or indeed contribute to society more broadly.

Mainstreaming this approach

Choice of assessment, therefore, seems to have some positive impact on students, it supports student empowerment and the diversification of assessment. However, to what extent is it being used, how widespread is it nationally and internationally? In 2016, my work on a national project, in association with the Union of Students in Ireland (USI), advocated the concept of students-as-partners, including the use of choice of assessment (National Forum and USI 2016). Therefore, there appears to be an appetite, in the Irish context, for this approach, including from the student body. However, in exploring the literature and in a recent institutional survey (O'Neill and Padden 2021), although choice of assessment was shown to empower students in their learning it appears still relatively under-used. Why, if so inclusive, is this approach not more widespread in its use institutionally, nationally, and internationally? How could it become more mainstream?

A key challenge to any assessment change or innovation is staff resources. "Effective resourcing plays an important part in overcoming barriers to innovation" (Kirkland and Sutch 2009, 24). Lack of time and lack of resources (such as support) were the top two barriers cited by staff implementing choice of assessment in the recent research (O'Neill and Padden 2021). Wanner, Palmer, and Palmer (2021) explored some flexible approaches to the assessment of students (including choice of assessment task) in the University of Adelaide, Australia. They noted that flexible approaches to assessment can be time-consuming for the staff, it may also need institutions to develop staff capacities. Staff need to "overcome any feelings of loss of power, control and autonomy and have their time commitment acknowledged to implement the flexible and personalised assessment" (Wanner, Palmer, and Palmer 2021, 11). Therefore, mainstreaming this and other assessment innovations requires adequate resourcing and a freeing of staff time to allow for their development.

There is a growing international movement towards empowering students and diversification of assessment to support more: inclusive assessment (EUA 2020); innovative assessment (Kapsalis et al. 2019); student-centred learning (Jordan et al. 2014; Pham 2010); universal design (AHEAD 2021; CAST 2018; Mavrou and Symeonidou 2014); and students-as-partners (Cook-Sather, Bovill, and Felten 2014). However, despite this trend in assessment policies and practices, there are many staff who are not yet comfortable with handing over the reins of power (Jordan et al. 2014; McArthur 2016). Staff often model their practice on what they themselves experienced, which tends to have been a more teacher-centred approach. Jordan et al. (2014) highlighted that student-centred learning is a concept that is not embraced by all individual staff, students, and disciplines and needs to move away from pockets of practice to more institutional approaches to this learning paradigm. "Trusting" students and giving them some responsibility (McArthur 2016, 2021) appear to be a challenge for some staff.

Student-centred learning also needs to be supported as an approach with students. Wanner, Palmer, and Palmer (2021) found that most students had a strong appetite for flexibility in assessment, although they identified that it can also be stressful and they may regret the choices later. In particular, the students highlighted that it would only work "with the guidance and support of enthusiastic teachers" (Wanner, Palmer, and Palmer 2021, 11).

Supporting assessment processes that gives students more responsibility, therefore, can be slow to emerge as "assessment systems are rooted in academic cultures and institutional habitus" (Leathwood 2005, 315). The slowness of this turn towards student-centred practice has also led to a lack of examples from practice. "Lack of discipline examples" was cited as a barrier to staff implementing choice of assessment in the recent research (O'Neill and Padden 2021). Just as students need examples to make an informed choice, staff need examples of choice of assessment approaches in order to be confident in developing such approaches in their own contexts. Despite the increased interest in Universal Design for Learning (UDL), a search of the empirical literature reveals a relative absence of showcases or papers on choice of assessment and indeed on inclusive assessment more widely. In a recent critical review of literature from 2005 to 2020, the evidence base for inclusive assessment was noted to be quite small with only 13 empirical peer-reviewed studies (Tai, Ajjawi, and Umarova 2021). Therefore, a concerted effort is needed to encourage those using this approach to share examples of success and any lessons learned. There is also a need to share the process of implementation of this approach to guide module designers in the implementation of the approach.

A recommended design process

To assist in mainstreaming this approach, I therefore present the seven-step process that I developed as part of my research over the last few years (See Figure 18.1) (adapted from O'Neill 2011, 2017). It guides the design, implementation, and evaluation of choice of assessment.

The process is divided into three stages, the design stage (steps 1–4), the implementation stage (steps 5 and 6), and the evaluation stage (step 7) (see Figure 18.1).

Design stage

Consider which module (step 1): This step recommends that the module co-ordinator considers which modules might be best suited to empowering students with a choice. For example, it may suit modules that have students with a variety of learning needs; with different prior learning; or in modules with high numbers of special accommodations (O'Neill 2011). There may be modules where allowing a choice may not be suitable, for example, where the ability to communicate through the written word (such as through an essay) is a competency highlighted in the module's learning outcomes. A programmatic

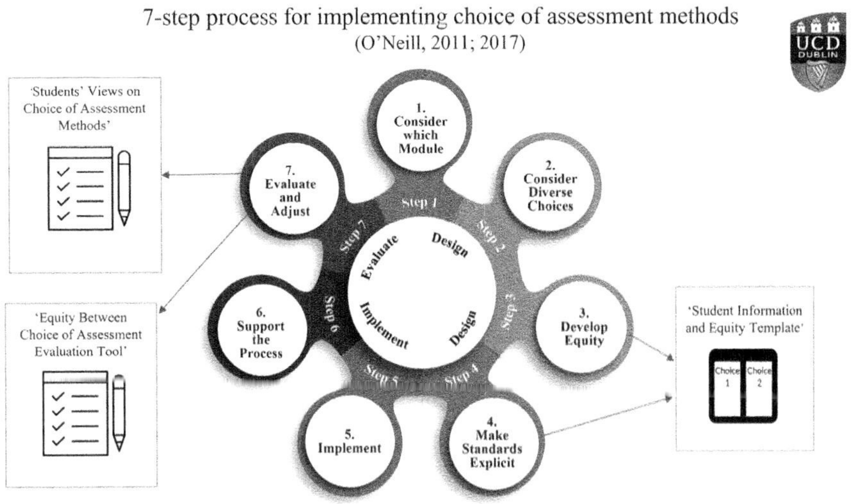

FIGURE 18.1 A process for implementing choice of assessment methods.

approach (Gibbs and Dunbar-Goddet 2009; National Forum 2017) to its use is one way forward, where some modules in the programme are identified as suitable and others where it may be less appropriate.

Consider diverse choices (step 2): This step advises the module coordinator to consider assessment methods that are dissimilar to each other, as this would maximise the choice for students with different strengths, approaches to learning, learning needs and from different contexts. Two options can often be sufficient choice (O'Neill 2011).

Develop equity (step 3): In addressing the issue of concern around fairness (equity) between the choices, the module coordinator needs to design for this in the assessment, as far as is reasonably practical. One tool that can support this is the "Student Information and Equity Template" (O'Neill 2017; UCD Teaching and Learning 2022a). This was designed to consider the equity between the choices in relation to, for example, student workload, teaching, and learning approaches, standards, feedback, etc. In addition, this can then be made available to the students at the beginning of the module to assists the students in making an informed choice.

Make standards explicit (step 4): In the case where students are unfamiliar with one or more of the choices, they need to see examples of assessment of these methods. Therefore, the module coordinators should share some examples of the assessment methods and make these available to the students at beginning of the module. In addition, it is good practice that the assessment criteria/rubrics for both assessment methods are also available for the students (Bennett 2016; O'Neill 2018).

Implementation stage

Implement (step 5): At the start of the module, the rationale for this choice of assessment methods should be made clear to the students, that is, to empower them in their learning, to allow them to play to their strengths. It needs to be clear to students how and when they need to communicate to the staff the decision on their assessment choice (O'Neill 2011). To streamline this, it may be useful to decide that one assessment method is the "default" assessment, if students have not informed staff of the choice. This could be the more familiar of the two assessments. Retaining one assessment that has some familiarity could reduce some of the challenges student experience with new and innovative assessment approaches (Armstrong 2014; Bevitt 2015; Kirkland and Sutch 2009; Medland 2016).

Support the process (step 6): At the early stage of the module, it may be useful to allow some in-class discussion on the choices, including opportunities for the students to discuss these with staff and/or with other students. Throughout the module's implementation, the teaching activities, support for feedback, and advice on the assessment must be relatively equitable (O'Neill 2011).

Evaluation stage

Evaluate and adjust (step 7): Finally, to ensure that there is some feedback on the approach, module coordinators should gather students, and where relevant staff, views on its implementation. In my original study, an evaluation tool was developed for the approach, the "*Students' views on Choice of Assessment Methods*" (O'Neill 2011, 76–77). In one section of this tool, five key themes were developed into a 20-item scale, that is, equity, anxiety, support, empowerment, and diversity. Four statements were created in each of these five themes (O'Neill 2011) This tool is available for use at UCD Teaching and Learning (2022c). I developed a sub-section of this tool (O'Neill 2017) using a factor analysis, now titled the *Equity Between Choice of Assessment Evaluation Tool* (available for use at UCD Teaching and Learning 2022b). This eight-item tool tool is more focused on the concept of equity between the choices given. It has good internal reliability (Cronbach's alpha = 0.792) and face validity. The key questions validated for use in this evaluation tool were:

- I felt I was given sufficient information required to choose the assessment method.
- I was confident in my choice of assessment method.
- The staff could have been more supportive in helping me choose my assessment method(s) (negatively worded).
- The assessment method I chose was not explained as well as the other assessment method (negatively worded).
- I felt I was given the support required while attempting this assessment method.

- I was satisfied with the level of feedback I had compared to the feedback in other assessment method.
- Over the course of the semester, the workload for my choice appeared similar to the other assessment method(s).
- I was satisfied with the examples available of my assessment method compared to the examples of the other assessment method.

(O'Neill 2017, 228; UCD Teaching and Learning 2022b)

In addition, to triangulate the students' views, further data could be gathered by qualitative interviews or focus groups of staff and students, as appropriate. The final aspect of this step is that based on any evaluations, the module co-ordinator should make improvements for the next reiteration of the module.

Conclusion

Moving away from a reliance on a narrow range of traditional methods of assessment can support the increasing diversity of student cohorts in higher education internationally. This movement is part of a wider trend towards inclusive assessment and supports the growing interest in universal design for learning (CAST 2018; Hundley and Kahn 2019). One approach to diversifying, which gives students some increased level of responsibility, is to allow students a choice of assessment methods within a module. This can also support their unique assessment preferences and may indeed support the success to which they aspire. However, we need to ensure that the choices we give are procedurally equitable and this chapter explores how this can be achieved in practice. Choice of assessment can support the outcome of an increase in student grades, a key indicator of student success as noted by them (National Forum 2019). However, more inter-stakeholder dialogue needs to take place to explore some solutions to the tension between this aspect of student success and what can be perceived, by some, as "unwanted" grade inflation. Failure to resolve this issue can cause more "social division among students depending on where they stand in the grading hierarchy" (Tannock 2017, 1350).

One challenge to mainstreaming the approach is that we should not take for granted the underlying challenge that some staff, and indeed some students, have towards the adoption of student-centred approaches. Trusting students and giving them more responsibility is one aspect of the emerging concept of assessment for social justice (McArthur 2016, 2021). To support a more widespread use of the approach, institutional polices need to resource, and supports staff in rolling out this approach. Examples of how it has been implemented in practice needs to be showcased and disseminated. This chapter, therefore, concludes with a seven-step process, which describes how I supported the design, implementation, and evaluation of the approach in my institution (O'Neill 2011, 2017).

The chapter highlights the research and practice of students' choice of assessment methods. I hope it will assist in both ensuring the choices given to students are equitable and that it goes some way towards its more widespread use in practice.

Note

1 The term "module" is used in this chapter to refer to a stand-alone unit that is part of a bigger program of study. Sometimes modules are described as a "course". Modules have a defined set of learning outcomes, a set student credit load and aligned teaching, learning and assessment approaches. "Module co-ordinators" is the term used for staff responsible for a module's design and delivery.

References

AHEAD. 2021. "Universal Design for Learning." Accessed 29 September 2021. https://www.ahead.ie/udl.

Armstrong, L. 2014. "Barriers to Innovation and Change in Higher Education." TIAA-CREF Institute. Accessed 29 September 2021. https://www.tiaainstitute.org/publication/barriers-innovation-and-change.

Bennett, C. 2016. "Assessment Rubrics: Thinking Inside the Boxes." *The International Journal of Higher Education in the Social Sciences* 9 (1): 50–72. http://doi.org/10.3167/latiss.2016.090104.

Bevitt, S. 2015. "Assessment Innovation and Student Experience: A New Assessment Challenge and Call for a Multi-Perspective Approach to Assessment Research." *Assessment and Evaluation in Higher Education* 40 (1): 103–119. https://doi.org/10.1080/02602938.2014.890170.

Brown, S. 2015. A Review of Contemporary Trends in Higher Education Assessment. *@tic.revista d'innovacio educative* 14: 43–39. http://doi.org/10.7203/attic.14.4166.

CAST. 2018. "Universal Design for Learning Guidelines Version 2.2." Accessed 29 September 2021. http://udlguidelines.cast.org/.

Cook-Sather, A., Bovill, C., and Felten, P. 2014. *Engaging Students as Partners in Learning and Teaching: A Guide for Faculty*. San Francisco, CA: John Wiley and Sons.

Craddock, D., and Mathias, H. 2009. "Assessment Options in Higher Education." *Assessment and Evaluation in Higher Education* 34 (2): 127–140. https://doi.org/10.1080/02602930801956026.

Easterbrook, D., Parker, M., and Waterfield, J. 2005. "Engineering Subject Centre Mini Project: Assessment Choice Case Project." HEA-Engineering Subject Centre. Accessed 29 September 2021. https://www.advance-he.ac.uk/knowledge-hub/engineering-subject-centre-mini-project-assessment-choice-case-study.

EUA. 2020. "Student Assessment: Thematic Peer Group Report: Learning and Teaching Paper # 10." European University Association. Accessed 29 September 2021. https://eua.eu/resources/publications/921:student-assessment-thematic-peer-group-report.html.

Francis, R. A. 2008. "An Investigation into the Receptivity of Undergraduate Students to Assessment Empowerment." *Assessment and Evaluation in Higher Education* 33 (5): 547–557. https://doi.org/10.1080/02602930701698991.

Garside, J., Nhemachena, J. Z. Z, Williams, J., and Topping, A. 2009. "Repositioning Assessment: Giving Students the 'Choice' of Assessment Methods." *Nurse Education in Practice* 9: 141–148. http://doi.org/10.1016/j.nepr.2008.09.003.

Gibbs, G., and Dunbar-Goddet, H. 2009. "Characterising Programme-Level Assessment Environments that Support Learning." *Assessment and Evaluation in Higher Education* 34 (4): 481–489. https://doi.org/10.1080/02602930802071114.

Hundley, S. P., and Kahn, S. 2019. *Trends in Assessment: Ideas, Opportunities, and Issues for Higher Education*. Sterling, VI: Stylus.

Jordan, L., Bovill, C., Watters, N., Saleh, A. M., Shabila, N. P., and Othman, S. M. 2014. "Is Student-Centred Learning a Western Concept? Lessons from an Academic Development Programme to Support Student-Centred Learning in Iraq." *Teaching in Higher Education* 19 (1): 13–25. https://doi.org/10.1080/13562517.2013.827649.

Kapsalis, G., Ferrari, A., Punie, Y., Conrads, J., Collado, A., Hotulainen, R., Rämä, I., Nyman, L., Oinas, S., and Ilsley, P. 2019. "Evidence of Innovative Assessment: Literature Review and Case Studies." European Commission. EU Science Hub. https://data.europa.eu/doi/10.2760/552774.

Kirkland, K., and Sutch, D. 2009. "Overcoming the Barriers to Educational Innovation: A Literature Review." *Futurelab*. https://www.nfer.ac.uk/publications/FUTL61/FUTL61.pdf.

Leathwood, C. 2005. "Assessment Policy and Practice in Higher Education: Purpose, Standards and Equity." *Assessment and Evaluation in Higher Education* 30 (3): 307–324. https://doi.org/10.1080/0260293050006387 6.

Mavrou, K., and Symeonidou, S. 2014. "Employing the Principles of Universal Design for Learning to Deconstruct the Greek-Cypriot New National Curriculum." *International Journal of Inclusive Education* 18 (9): 918–933. https://doi.org/10.1080/13603116.2013.859308.

McArthur, J. 2016. "Assessment for Social Justice: The Role of Assessment in Achieving Social Justice." *Assessment and Evaluation in Higher Education* 41 (7): 967–981. https://doi.org/10.1080/02602938.2015.1053429.

McArthur, J. 2021. *Creating Synergies between Assessment for Social Justice and Assessment for Inclusion*. Keynote presented at Centre for Research in Assessment and Digital Learning (CRADLE) International Symposium, 21 October 2021. https://www.youtube.com/watch?v=fFE7qxqCVFY.

Medland, E. 2016. "Assessment in Higher Education: Drivers, Barriers and Directions for Change in the UK." *Assessment and Evaluation in Higher Education* 41 (1): 81–96. https://doi.org/10.1080/02602938.2014.982072.

National Forum. 2016. "Profile of Assessment Practices in Irish Higher Education." National Forum for the Enhancement of Teaching and Learning in Higher Education. Accessed 29 September 2021. https://www.teachingandlearning.ie/publication/profile-of-assessment-practices-in-irish-higher-education/.

National Forum. 2017. "Enhancing Programme Approaches to Assessment and Feedback in Irish Higher Education: Case Studies, Commentaries and Tools." National Forum for the Enhancement of Teaching and Learning in Higher Education. Accessed 16 January 2022. https://hub.teachingandlearning.ie/resource/enhancing-programme-approaches-to-assessment-and-feedback-in-irish-higher-education-case-studies-commentaries-and-tools/.

National Forum. 2019. "Understanding and Enabling Student Success in Irish Higher Education." National Forum for the Enhancement of Teaching and Learning in Higher Education. Accessed 29 September 2021. https://www.teachingandlearning.ie/publication/understanding-and-enabling-student-success-in-irish-higher-education/.

National Forum and USI. 2016. "Assessment OF, FOR and AS Learning: Students as Partners." National Forum for the Enhancement of Teaching and Learning in Higher Education. https://hub.teachingandlearning.ie/resource/students-as-partners/.

O'Neill, G. (Ed.). 2011. "A Practitioner's Guide to Choice of Assessment Methods within a Module." UCD Teaching and Learning. Accessed 29 September 2021. https://www.ucd.ie/teaching/t4media/choice_of_assessment.pdf.

O'Neill, G. 2017. "It's not Fair! Students and Educators Views on the Equity of the Procedures and Outcomes of Students' Choice of Assessment Methods." *Irish Educational Studies* 36 (2): 221–236. https://doi.org/10.1080/03323315.2017.1324805.

O'Neill, G. 2018. "Designing Grading and Feedback Rubrics." Dublin: UCD Teaching and Learning. https://www.ucd.ie/teaching/t4media/designing_feedback_rubrics.pdf.

O'Neill, G., and Padden, L. 2021. "Diversifying Assessment Methods: Barriers, Benefits and Enablers." *Innovations in Education and Teaching International*. https://doi.org/10.1080/14703297.2021.1880462.

Pham, T. H. T. 2010. "Implementing a Student-Centered Learning Approach at Vietnamese Higher Education Institutions: Barriers under Layers of Casual Layered Analysis (CLA)." *Journal of Futures Studies* 15 (1): 21–38. https://jfsdigital.org/wp-content/uploads/2014/01/151-A02.pdf.

Stowell, M. 2004. "Equity, Justice and Standards: Assessment Decision Making in Higher Education." *Assessment and Evaluation in Higher Education* 29 (4): 495–510. https://doi.org/10.1080/02602930310001689055.

Tai, J., Ajjawi, R., and Umarova, A. 2021. "How Do Students Experience Inclusive Assessment? A Critical Review of Contemporary Literature." *International Journal of Inclusive Education*. https://doi.org/10.1080/13603116.2021.2011441.

Tannock, S. 2017. "No Grades in Higher Education Now! Revisiting the Place of Graded Assessment in the Reimagination of the Public University." *Studies in Higher Education* 42 (8): 1345–1357. https://doi.org/10.1080/03075079.2015.1092131.

UCD Teaching and Learning. 2022a. *Student Information and Equity Template*. Dublin: UCD Teaching and Learning. https://www.ucd.ie/teaching/t4media/student_information_and_equity_template.docx.

UCD Teaching and Learning. 2022b. *Equity Between Choice of Assessment Evaluation Tool*. Dublin: UCD Teaching and Learning. https://www.ucd.ie/teaching/t4media/equity_between_choice_of_assessment_evaluation_tool.docx.

UCD Teaching and Learning. 2022c. *Students Views on Choice of Assessment Methods (Evaluation Tool)*. Dublin: UCD Teaching and Learning. https://www.ucd.ie/teaching/t4media/students_views_on_choice_of_assessment_methods.docx.

Wanner, T., Palmer, E., and Palmer, D. 2021. "Flexible Assessment and Student Empowerment: Advantages and Disadvantages – Research from an Australian University." *Teaching in Higher Education*. https://doi.org/10.1080/13562517.2021.1989578.

Waterfield, J., and West, B. 2006. "Inclusive Assessment in Higher Education: A Resource for Change University of Plymouth." University of Plymouth. Accessed 29 September 2021. https://www.plymouth.ac.uk/uploads/production/document/path/3/3026/Space_toolkit.pdf.

Witte, A. E. 2011. "Understanding International Grading Scales: More Translation than Conversion." *International Journal of Management Education* 9 (3): 49–59.

19

"HOW TO LOOK AT IT DIFFERENTLY"

Negotiating more inclusive assessment design with student partners

Joanne Dargusch, Lois Harris, and Margaret Bearman

There is increasing impetus to make assessment in higher education more inclusive of diverse student populations. This reflects a broad social movement; for example, Australian higher education institutions are legally obliged to cater for students with disabilities (SWDs) in socially just ways (Australian Government, Department of Education, Skills and Employment 2005). According to Hockings (2010), inclusive assessment is "the design and use of fair and effective assessment methods and practices that enable all students to demonstrate to their full potential what they know, understand and can do" (34). For assessment practices to be inclusive, there is a need for students to be allowed to show learning in differing ways, with options for flexibility and choice (Morris, Milton, and Goldstone 2019). Despite use of tools such as the Universal Design for Learning Guidelines (CAST 2018), designing inclusive assessments in higher education remains a challenge (Grimes et al. 2019; Lawrie et al. 2017). There are real world challenges to creating inclusive assessment practices, with assessment processes at universities often highly bureaucratic and perceived as inflexible, reacting to SWDs' diverse needs through assessment accommodation systems which are sometimes not responsive or make decisions that are not appropriate (e.g., Bessant 2012). Concerns about workloads for staff and the need to align with university and industry expectations impact on assessment design decisions and remain an obstacle to more inclusive and flexible assessment design (e.g., Morris, Milton, and Goldstone 2019). Against, this backdrop of challenge, it is important to look for meaningful processes that can support more inclusive assessment.

It is our contention that real understanding and response to the needs of SWDs is only possible when students have input into the conversation about assessment in ways that influence practice. If assessment is to be designed in inclusive ways that "enable all students to demonstrate to their full potential" (Hockings 2010, 34), teaching staff should be supported to understand the challenges these

DOI: 10.4324/9781003293101-23

students face as they navigate the complexities of higher education assessment requirements and practices. Educators must also be motivated to overcome real and perceived institutional barriers to designing inclusive assessments. Without student engagement, educators must make assumptions about the impact of assessment decisions on students.

Students as partners

Students as partners (SaP) presents a promising way forward in creating a dialogue, where student needs can be better understood and therefore incorporated into assessment design. Described as process-oriented, SaP is "focused on what students and staff do together to further common educational goals" (Mercer-Mapstone et al. 2017, 2). The call for SaP has been growing in strength, with attention turning to how the inclusion of student voice and partnership practices can influence traditional ways of working in higher education, including assessment practices (Dwyer 2018; Healey, Flint, and Harrington 2016; Mercer-Mapstone, Islam, and Reid 2021).

Underpinning successful SaP projects in higher education is what Cook-Sather and Felten (2017, 5) refer to as an "ethic of reciprocity", foregrounding mutual voices and contributions between students and staff with equal importance attributed to all (Mercer-Mapstone et al. 2017). Such a process has the potential to subvert traditional power arrangements and allow participant roles to be renegotiated through dialogue that includes differing perspectives (Matthews et al. 2018). These are worthy and valuable aims, and the outcomes of existing studies have largely been reported positively (Mercer-Mapstone et al. 2017). However, SWDs appear to be seldom included in the small-scale, institutional-level SaP partnerships and projects (Bovill et al. 2016; Mercer-Mapstone et al. 2017) reported in Australian higher education.

Assessment may present particular challenges for a SaP approach, with strong contextual influences on design processes, such as departmental norms (Bearman et al. 2017). However, including SaP in a dialogue may help lecturers better understand how assessment design impacts students and their learning, potentially bringing new ideas and insights into the design process. Likewise, students may feel more invested in assessment processes, understanding that their perspectives are heard and valued. There are, however, tensions between the various stakeholders' assessment expectations, including external accreditation requirements, university rules and processes, and students' understanding of what is fair and reasonable (Tai et al. 2022).

Power inequality is a key challenge for all students. The SaP literature acknowledges the challenge of power imbalances with some researchers describing the "reinforcement of power asymmetries between students and staff" in SaP projects (Mercer-Mapstone, Islam, and Reid 2021, 229), framing these as an obstacle that needs to be overcome (Matthews et al. 2018). SWDs may also be unsure how to articulate their problems/challenges in public forums, in ways that other students understand. Diverse students need to be included in order to address questions of inclusion and equity (Bovill et al. 2016; Mercer-Mapstone, Islam, and Reid 2021). The interactions between staff and students are therefore foregrounded in this chapter, in order to highlight the practical issues that impact on achieving change.

While embracing the potential and necessity for SaP, this chapter examines some of the complex, ambiguous, and inevitable challenges of including diverse student voices in assessment design. While the literature provides a mainly positive view of students as partners, with many advocates discussing benefits (Mercer-Mapstone et al. 2017), existing empirical studies do not clearly show how change is negotiated between participants in SaP research projects. This chapter draws on data from the project Reimagining Exams: How do assessment adjustments impact on inclusion (Tai et al. 2022) to explore how SWDs engaged in workshops and how their suggestions contributed to the more inclusive redesign of exams and other timed assessments. In this project, funded by the Australian National Centre for Student Equity in Higher Education (NCSEHE), students were asked to share their personal experiences of exams and offer suggestions about ways exams could be changed to better suit their needs. We consider instances where students and staff at times struggled to establish a mutuality of purpose and exchange, examining the different outcomes achieved. We present an analysis of these data focussing on the participation process, followed by our reflections on how the aspirational notion of partnership might take account of some of its complexities.

Context of the project

The project took place at two Australian universities, different in physical locations and structures, but both serving diverse student cohorts. In Phase 1, 40 SWDs were chosen to participate in interviews, with those not selected invited to provide a written or oral submission in response to prompts. This chapter draws on Phase 2 data from a series of five "participatory" online workshops conducted at each university, bringing together SWDs, unit co-ordinators/chairs (UCs), accessibility/inclusion staff, and assessment researchers. To explore how exams could be reimagined in more inclusive ways, SWDs were positioned as consultants (Bovill et al. 2016) whose insights might help stakeholders understand the issues and become motivated to change and improve assessments. There were practical goals, including bringing about change within two subject units at each university and the development of a framework to evaluate exam inclusivity and guide change. Students were invited to take part in reflection activities after the workshop series had concluded, designed to elicit their perceptions of the workshop process.

Workshop design

Online workshops were designed to elicit suggestions and recommendations, generating ideas for change. They provided opportunities for participants to speak openly, valuing the mutual voices and contributions that underpin successful SaP projects (Mercer-Mapstone et al. 2017). Participants were sent written materials (e.g., short student narratives), and asked to anonymously reflect/respond in a Microsoft Teams worksheet, allowing alternative forms of interaction and recording thoughts generated outside of each workshop. Workshops 1 and 2 were designed to build relationships and share exam experiences. In workshops 3 and 4, participants considered specific units' exams/timed assessments and discussed potential changes in format, conditions, and mode. Workshop 5 focused on reviewing a draft framework for generating more inclusive exams and future directions.

After workshop 5, students were invited to reflect on their workshop experiences. Set questions were posed about the workshop process and structure, students' level of comfort, workshop resources, and suggestions for other ways to involve students in the work of improving assessment. Additional information about the project's methodology and outcomes can be found in the NCSEHE report (Tai et al. 2022).

Data analysis

The aim of this current analysis was to understand how successfully the SaP had promoted practical dialogue, with all students and staff given pseudonyms. We wished for insight into how participating SWDs, Dalton (Psychology) and Veronica (Psychology) from University 1 (U1), and Pete (Business) and Francine (Allied Health) from University 2 (U2), engaged in workshops designed around SaP principles and how their interactions contributed to the group (see Table 19.1).

Analysis of workshop transcripts was focused on the interactions between participants and the roles of students. We took student utterances, understood here to mean every spoken contribution in the conversation, as our unit of analysis and sought to examine what prompted students to speak, what they said, and how staff reacted to what they said. A general thematic analysis was conducted on the reflection transcripts to gain insights into participating students' perceptions of the process. Table 19.2 lists the codes applied for each different analytical focus.

TABLE 19.1 Workshop student participants

University	*Student*	*Discipline area*	*Workshops attended*	*Completed reflections*
1	Dalton	Psychology	5	Y
1	Veronica	Psychology	5	Y
2	Pete	Business	3	N
2	Francine	Allied Health	2	Y

We employed thematic analysis, with some supplementary counts of prevalence. Data sources were: transcripts of workshop 3 (U1, $n = 8$ participants; U2, $n = 11$) and workshop 4 (U1, $n = 8$; U2, $n = 9$); and written ($n = 2$) and spoken ($n = 1$) student reflections.

TABLE 19.2 Analysis focus and related codes

Analysis focus	*Codes*
How did students join the conversation?	Response to a direct question; unprompted
What contributions did they make and how did staff respond?	Contribution: affirmation/agreement; personal story; comment; suggestion Staff responses: problematise; consider, accept; ignore; revoice
How did they feel after the workshops?	Affordances (e.g., being heard), challenges (e.g., lack of student voice)

How students joined the conversation

Each conversational turn that occurred directly prior to student contributions was coded in order to identify any patterns in how students entered, or were invited to enter, the conversation. Three of the four students (Veronica, Pete, and Francine) responded to questions asked specifically of them in the majority of their turns. These questions were predominantly from the research team, with some questions posed by unit coordinators.

Unprompted contributions were infrequent for three of the four participating students (Pete, Francine, Veronica), indicating the level of hesitancy for these students in entering the conversation uninvited. Dalton's approach contrasted sharply with his peers, and he was confident and willing to make frequent unprompted contributions, responding to questions posed to all students in the workshops, as well as those asked of the whole group. At times, Dalton interrupted staff members and other students, but these interruptions may have occurred due to difficulties arising in the on-line workshop environment where it was sometimes difficult to hear others and see whether other participants were waiting to speak.

Student contributions and staff responses

Data show that student contributions to the workshops were rich and varied, and included pleasantries, affirmations/agreement, personal stories, comments, and suggestions. Pleasantries helped to establish relationships, while affirmations and agreement usually blended into suggestions or personal stories designed to help other participants understand the speaker's feelings about assessment. The following personal story was offered in response to one UC's exploration of the need for shorter exams, including splitting exams into two parts:

> Dalton: The idea of going into a room and sitting there for two or three hours or even doing it … It is painful. Also, because you've got this huge stress that what if something goes wrong, and I get a headache, or I get a nosebleed? Whatever the scenario goes through one's head, you end up, I think, losing so much productive time and effort that you could have been studying effectively, just worrying about concerns that could be addressed in another way, I think, that would eliminate those concerns.

TABLE 19.3 Proposed changes to assessment

Categories of change	*Examples – student suggestions*	*Examples – staff suggestions*
Assessment – structure/content	Break up exams into separate parts/chunks Smaller, interrelated assessment pieces Multiple opportunities to meet the same outcomes	Break up exams into two parts Allow students choice between paper based and computer formats in exam Include scenario-based questions Reduce number of questions Ensure topics are not unnecessarily assessed Changes to task language
Assessment – task type/mode	Replace large exams with weekly tests or one-on-one discussions	Open book exams Option to read questions aloud (practical exams)
Assessment – conditions/timing	Flexible exam start times Breaks between exam parts	Flexible exam start times Give students more time to complete exams Short breaks during exams as a standard feature Additional set up/reading time before exams
Assessment – conditions/access	Different modes of assessment instructions	
Assessment – conditions/use of technology	Use of interactive, automated online quizzes for exam preparation	Automated online quizzes embedded in weekly tutorials
Improvement – study advice	Explicit exam preparation instructions	Completion of practice exams for formative feedback
Assessment design roles		Student input into question design

Students took on the role of expert in the workshop, with weight given to the value of their lived experiences in understanding the challenges SWDs negotiate within assessment. Given this framing, comments like the following were a common contribution:

FRANCINE: I feel like all my assessment tasks have been pretty relevant to what I've had to go out and do.

Students and staff also provided a range of concrete suggestions for changes to timed and other types of assessments, with categories of suggestions shared in Table 19.3. There were some common suggestions from the two groups, with most suggestions related to task structure, types/modes, and conditions.

Illustrative examples of staff responses to student suggestions

Across workshops at both institutions, the group most readily took up student suggestions when they offered easily actionable ideas or when the students were perceived as having discipline-specific insight. Persistent challenges included staff concerns about academic integrity and discipline/accreditation requirements and institutional policy was frequently cited as a roadblock to change. As presented in Table 19.2, staff reactions were coded as: problematise, consider, accept, ignore, revoice. However, these reactions themselves could lead to different outcomes. For example, when ideas were problematised, the student suggestion was debated, leading to a discussion of various possibilities.

Two contrasting excerpts are shown here from the category of problematise. In the first excerpt, the student suggestion for change is listened to, but the ideas are lost in the subsequent discussion:

DALTON. … for one of the level two psych units, … there were 10 or 12 small assessment pieces. I think that in a way works better, because then each piece feeds into the next, and because each piece is fairly small, you get the feedback really quickly. … could you break some of the assessments into smaller pieces, smaller chunks, where the person knows that this is the content for the two weeks they've got to do, and they'll do an assessment on it?

Unit Coordinator 2 considers Dalton's suggestion, indicating she will "think about it, for sure", ultimately, the idea was blocked by other participants, including a comment that "our policy goes against that". While no clear actions for change resulted from this part of the conversation, alterations to the structure of the exam grew from suggestions at other points in the workshops. These changes did not involve major adjustments to assessment across the unit (as suggested by Dalton). Planned possible changes included introducing an exam break and using short answer, rather than essay-style questions to reduce the overall exam time. As was witnessed in many exchanges across the workshops, policy/imposts on lecturers took priority over students' suggestions.

A contrasting excerpt is offered here to illustrate how interactions between students and staff could lead to a more collaborative outcome.

FRANCINE: Sorry, I don't know if this is right, but I know when I was doing my practical exam something that I really wish I could've done was read out that form out loud … I couldn't speak it, it wasn't going into my head.

UNIT CHAIR/COORDINATOR 1: In the past students have gone into a room at the very start and have been able to set themselves up in there. That could possibly be an option.

RESEARCHER 2: I'm wondering, I don't know how the practical exams take place, but the examiner could simply just ask the student if they wanted to read it out loud as well too, the prompt.

UNIT CHAIR/COORDINATOR 1: They're all in, for optometry, they're all in a hallway quite close to each other. If they did read things out, the person next to them will hear it. We can't let that before they go in but definitely when they enter the station, it's an option. They might not be aware that they can do that.

RESEARCHER 1: Yes. I wonder how things will go if there is still a need for more online versions of these things versus face-to-face things because obviously, like what Francine said about reading it out, if you're at home by yourself then there's no barrier to being able to talk through stuff, which there obviously is if you're in a crowded space with other students around.

The participants problematised Francine's practical solution in order to identify how this could be implemented. In contrast with excerpt 1 (above), participants saw possibilities for change that did not compromise the assessment's integrity. In the next offering of the unit, students were permitted to read aloud each practical exam scenario (one of several changes made in response to suggestions).

Staff suggestions

Staff proposed substantive changes to assessment designs during the workshops (see Table 19.3). In three of four units discussed, assessment changes were planned for the next term in direct response to workshop suggestions. In the fourth unit, the UC's concerns about academic integrity meant the exam remained the same, with the approach to exam preparation being the focus of change. In most cases, and particularly at U1, planned changes did not need formal permissions through academic committees, but could be changed by unit coordinators/chairs as part of routine updates.

How did students evaluate their SaP experience?

Students' reflections indicated that they valued the opportunity to have their voices heard, with few feedback mechanisms available for SWDs within the university system. For example, Dalton indicated that in the past, "I have felt voiceless in many ways as a student".

Students commented that there was a need for more sustained focus on student stories, case studies, feedback, and interactions in the workshops, with a strong message that more collaboration with SWDs would provoke change. As Francine asserted, there was a need for:

> More students in meetings. I understand others were invited but did not attend but it seemed trying to fix issues without those who suffer the issues in the room is kind of counter-intuitive, although I also understand the research team does have this information from surveys.

Whilst students indicated that they personally felt comfortable and unintimidated when engaging the workshops, they hypothesised that to get greater participation from a range of SWDs, "other" ways for students to interact would be needed to ensure that workshops were a "safe space" (Veronica).

Reflections on SaP in designing inclusive assessment

The project presented in this chapter had at its core aspirational notions of partnerships promoted in current research (Mercer-Mapstone, Islam, and Reid 2021) and sought to include SWDs as partners to address questions of inclusion and equity (Bovill et al. 2016). The research was underpinned by the understanding that inclusive assessment design is only possible when SWDs are deeply involved in the process in an environment where all participants are committed to change. It was anticipated that SWDs would use their lived experience to help lecturers recognise the impacts of assessment design on students and their learning, bringing new ideas and insights to the design process, helping re-imagine the ways in which assessment could be more inclusive. However, our results show that this aspiration was variably and incompletely achieved.

Power imbalances can create obstacles in SaP projects (Matthews et al. 2018), and structural issues of power were evident in this project at the level of relationships within the group, as well as at a university systems level. Despite trying to create an environment that foregrounded mutual voices and contributions between students and staff, students [with the exclusion of Dalton] predominantly waited for questions/statements to be directed at them from the researchers to enter the conversation. In many instances, teaching staff members problematised student suggestions as a first response. There is a need for more active listening, and a focus on unpacking and understanding, in keeping with Cook-Sather and Felten's (2017, 5) "ethic of reciprocity". At the same time, it may be necessary to recognise the limitations of SaP, that not all partnerships will be fruitful, and it is hard for any educator to open their work for scrutiny.

This study also illustrated how university processes can act as roadblocks to change. The motivation for change was tempered, and often dampened, by long timelines required for approvals, reviews, and committee procedures. It is noted that one of the universities in the study (U1) was more process-driven, with UCs giving heavy emphasis to policy and compliance. It followed, therefore, that the immediate changes that were made to assessments at U1 were restricted to assessment design aspects within the UC's control. System and institutional-level change is necessary to address equity problems; long term changes should not be ad hoc, or exist in discrete units, and tensions between responsiveness and compliance should be acknowledged and rectified. Prioritising equity within assessment, rather than equality (Harris and Dargusch 2020; Tierney 2013), may assist with this shift. It is also worth considering that sometimes staff perceptions of policy may not be the same as the policy itself; departmental engagement may also be necessary (Bearman et al. 2017).

SWDs' substantive and useful contributions in our SaP project demonstrated the importance of their input into assessment decisions if we want to move towards equity. However, when involving diverse SWDs, physical and psychosocial challenges that might exist around their participation must be proactively addressed. The online workshops in this study were scheduled with consideration of students' work and study commitments, and included other affordances (e.g., physical safety during the pandemic, participants' choice to have their camera on or off). Despite these advantages, it is possible that the online environment may have impacted group cohesion. Consideration should therefore be given to how to involve SWDs in ways that allow them to engage comfortably in various modes and spaces/places. This might include, as these students suggested, different ways of interacting (e.g., writing into the chat instead of speaking); it might also mean more flexibility around attendance. Consistent with our SaP methodology, we believe future projects would benefit from student involvement in the project design to ensure that eventual mechanisms for student engagement with staff allow full participation for all within the group.

There are many reasons to continue research into, and use of, SaP processes. The types of discrete, small-scale studies reported in the literature (Mercer-Mapstone et al. 2017) are limited in scope and generalisability. Studies such as this one provide insights into the ways in which SWDs can be invited to help staff overcome assumptions about how assessment design impacts on students, and the ways in which issues of power can influence such exchanges. If, as Dalton remarked, SWDs such as himself are "voiceless" in HE, then partnership practices are a key first step to providing a more inclusive university experience, but all partners must be committed to encourage students' ideas and actively listen to them. To reach this aim, universities must overcome a tendency to generalise about student needs and provide many more opportunities to include diverse student voices in co-generative, dialogic approaches to assessment design.

References

Australian Government. Department of Education, Skills and Employment. 2005. "Disability Standards for Education." Last modified on Thursday 15 April 2021. https://www.dese.gov.au/disability-standards-education-2005.

Bearman, M., Dawson, P., Bennett, S., Hall, M., Molloy, E., Boud, D., and Joughin, G. 2017. "How University Teachers Design Assessments: A Cross-Disciplinary Study." *Higher Education* 74 (1): 49–64. https://doi.org/10.1007/s10734-016-0027-7.

Bessant, J. 2012. "'Measuring Up'? Assessment and Students with Disabilities in the Modern University." *International Journal of Inclusive Education* 16 (3): 265–281. https://doi.org/10.1080/13603116.2010.489119.

Bovill, C., Cook-Sather, A., Felten, P., Millard, L., and Moore-Cherry, N. 2016. "Addressing Potential Challenges in Co-Creating Learning and Teaching: Overcoming Resistance, Navigating Institutional Norms and Ensuring Inclusivity in Student–Staff Partnerships." *Higher Education* 71 (2): 195–208. https://doi.org/10.1007/s10734-015-9896-4.

CAST. 2018. "Universal Design for Learning Guidelines Version 2.2." http://udlguidelines.cast.org.

Cook-Sather, A., and Felten, P. 2017. "Where Student Engagement Meets Faculty Development: How Student-Faculty Pedagogical Partnership Fosters a Sense of Belonging." *Student Engagement in Higher Education Journal* 1 (2): 3–11.

Dwyer, A. 2018. "Toward the Formation of Genuine Partnership Spaces." *International Journal for Students as Partners* 2 (1): 11–15. https://doi.org/10.15173/ijSaP.v2i1.3503.

Grimes, S., Southgate, E., Scevak, J., and Buchanan, R. 2019. "University Student Perspectives on Institutional Non-Disclosure of Disability and Learning Challenges: Reasons for Staying Invisible." *International Journal of Inclusive Education* 23 (6): 639–655. https://doi.org/10.1080/13603116.2018.1442507.

Harris, L. R., and Dargusch, J. 2020. "Catering for Diversity in the Digital Age: Reconsidering Equity In Assessment Practices." In *Re-Imagining University Assessment in a Digital World*, edited by Margaret Bearman, Phillip Dawson, Rola Ajjawi, Joanna Tai, and David Boud, 95–110. Berlin: Springer.

Healey, M., Flint, A., and Harrington, K. 2016. "Students as Partners: Reflections on a Conceptual Model." *Teaching and Learning Inquiry* 4 (2): 8–20. https://doi.org/10.20343/teachlearninqu.4.2.3.

Hockings, C. 2010. *Inclusive Learning and Teaching in Higher Education: A Synthesis of Research*. EvidenceNet, Higher Education Academy. https://www.advance-he.ac.uk/knowledge-hub/inclusive-learning-and-teaching-higher-education-synthesis-research.

Lawrie, G., Marquis, E., Fuller, E., Newman, T., Qiu, M., Nomikoudis, M., Roelofs, F., and Van Dam, L. 2017. "Moving towards Inclusive Learning and Teaching: A Synthesis of Recent Literature." *Teaching and Learning Inquiry* 5 (1): 9–21. https://doi.org/10.20343/teachlearninqu.5.1.3.

Matthews, K. E., Dwyer, A., Hine, L., and Turner, J. 2018. "Conceptions of Students as Partners." *Higher Education* 76 (6): 957–971. https://doi.org/10.1007/s10734-018-0257-y.

Mercer-Mapstone, L., Dvorakova, S. L., Matthews, K. E., Abbot, S., Cheng, B., Felten, P., Knorr, K., Marquis, E., Shammas, R., and Swaim, K. 2017. "A Systematic Literature Review of Students as Partners in Higher Education." *International Journal for Students as Partners* 1 (1): 1–23. https://doi.org/10.15173/ijSaP.v1i1.3119.

Mercer-Mapstone, L., Islam, M., and Reid, T. 2021. "Are We Just Engaging 'the Usual Suspects'? Challenges in and Practical Strategies for Supporting Equity and Diversity in Student–Staff Partnership Initiatives." *Teaching in Higher Education* 26 (2): 227–245. https://doi.org/10.1080/13562517.2019.1655396.

Morris, C., Milton, E., and Goldstone, R. 2019. "Case Study: Suggesting Choice: Inclusive Assessment Processes." *Higher Education Pedagogies* 4 (1): 435–447. https://doi:10.1080/23752696.2019.1669479.

Tai, J., Ajjawi, R., Bearman, M., Dargusch, J., Dracup, M., and Harris, L. 2022. *Re-Imagining Exams: How Do Assessment Adjustments Impact on Inclusion*. Final Report for the National Centre for Student Equity in Higher Education. https://www.ncsehe.edu.au/publications/exams-assessment-adjustments-inclusion/.

Tierney, R. D. 2013. "Fairness in Classroom Assessment." In *SAGE Handbook of Research on Classroom Assessment*, edited by James H. McMillan, 125–144. Thousand Oaks, CA: SAGE Publications.

20

ADDRESSING INEQUITY

Students' recommendations on how to make assessment more inclusive

Shannon Krattli, Daniella Prezioso, and Mollie Dollinger

Introduction

In July 2021, the student co-authors of this project (Shannon and Daniella) saw a job opportunity to become paid student partners on a research project exploring how assessment could be more inclusive and equitable to diverse students. While we all had our own motivations for applying, what struck us was the uniqueness of the job. Staff were asking us – students – to help them understand how to design assessment. And staff were naming us – students – as their partners. Was this real?

As we learned through the project, the topic of inclusion in assessment is increasingly discussed by scholars and educators (Hanesworth, Bracken, and Elkington 2019; McArthur 2016; Nieminen 2022). However, missing from the discussion is students' expertise on how assessment could be improved. Too often, students are seen only as a data source, for example, as attendees in a focus group or participants in a survey. These opportunities do not allow for students to freely, over time, share their ideas and recommendations, and through training and support, become co-researchers in this important topic.

Some readers may ask, why is it important for students to be co-researchers? Our answer is that because as recipients of the education provided to us, we are truly the ones who can evaluate its quality. For example, McArthur (2016) uses an analogy by Nussbaum (2006) to illustrate the importance of moving beyond procedural evaluation:

> ...[imagine] if a cook has a fancy, sophisticated pasta-maker, and assures their guests that the pasta made in this machine will be, by definition, [the best] ...[because] it is the best machine on the market. But surely ... the guests will want to taste the pasta and see for themselves and [judge if they agree].

DOI: 10.4324/9781003293101-24

This analogy highlights how students see learning design. It's not that students don't trust educators to do their best research and use the best practice to design our learning experiences. But just because they have taken their time and tried their hardest does not mean, necessarily, that it is the best experience for students. Only we – students – can taste the pasta and judge for ourselves. And further, it is important to note that we will not all give the same evaluation. It depends on our subjectivities, for example, our preferred study strategies or environments, the topics that interest us, and the varied supports that we need. But by including us as co-researchers, scholars and educators can minimise the gap between what they think is best, and what we need to succeed in our learning.

In this chapter, we will reflect on what we have learned in this students as partners (SaP) research project exploring inclusion and equity in assessment. We will provide an overview of the project and then discuss our three key recommendations. Our recommendations are informed both by the co-design workshops that we facilitated with our peers ($n = 52$), and our own reflections and experiences as students. Finally, we will conclude by advocating for others to embed a SaP approach in their future research.

Background to our project

Our SaP project took place at Deakin University, a research-intensive university located in Australia. The project began when six staff from various central areas (e.g., a research centre for assessment, Office of the Dean of Students, an academic development unit, and a disability resource centre), recruited five student partners (including co-authors Shannon and Daniella) to join the team as paid members. The team then worked together to create a co-design workshop protocol using the CoLab model. CoLabs are one- to two-hour-long co-design workshops, in this case held online, where a range of participatory design methods are used to facilitate dialogue and co-investigate challenges or areas for improvement within the university (Dollinger and Vanderlelie 2021). The aim of the CoLab in this project was to elicit students' participants perspectives on inclusive assessment.

The participatory design activities applied in the CoLab were scaffolded, and ranged from storyboarding, mind maps, role playing, and persona generation. Unlike focus groups, which are primarily aimed at "investigating shared beliefs among cohorts, or trends across participants' experience" (Dollinger, Eaton, and Vanderlelie 2021, 1), CoLabs are designed to support cross-cohort collaboration and idea generation.

After a literature review and group discussions, two CoLab protocols were designed by the team with input from both staff and student partners. Each protocol was conducted three times for a total of six workshops. A total of 52 student participants attended a CoLab, from a range of disciplines and year levels.

TABLE 20.1 Overview of protocols A and B

Scaffolded activity	*Protocol A*	*Protocol B*
Activity 1	Icebreaker activity where students reflect on what words come to mind when they think about assessment	Icebreaker activity where students reflect on their personal goals for completing assessment
Activity 2	Students work in small groups to create a mind map on what they have found challenging about assessment	Students work in small groups to create a mind map on what teachers should consider when designing or implementing assessment
Activity 3	Students work in small groups to co-create a campaign to support students navigating assessments	Students read fictional stories about assessment in small groups and then discuss potential solutions that would have helped the student

Please see the Table 20.1 for an overview of CoLab activities. Note: CoLabs were hosted online, and the team used a combination of Zoom, Mentimeter, and Padlet software to support activities. Student partners were the facilitators of the workshops, while staff attended to take notes.

In each of the above activities, the student participants were allocated Zoom breakout rooms with one student partner to facilitate and one staff member to take additional notes, as some of the feedback may occur outside of the software (e.g., a spoken comment not recorded on the online whiteboard). To analyse the data the team worked in pairs (one student and one staff) and thematically grouped data into overarching ideas, common experiences, or as seen below, recommendations for improving inclusion.

In dialogue: Students' ideas for inclusive assessment

In this section, we will now present three themes which support inclusive assessment for diverse students. To add depth to these recommendations, we will present each recommendation with data drawn from the workshops, as well as student authors' reflections.

1. ***Creating empathetic relationships between staff and students***
   The first theme identified in our data was creating empathetic relationships between staff and students. Teacher empathy for students has been previously defined as "the degree to which an instructor works to deeply understand students' personal ad social situations, to feel care and concern in response to students' positive and negative emotions, and to respond compassionately without losing the focus on student learning" (Meyers et al. 2019, 161). From the workshop data, as well as our reflections, there was a clear message that teachers could do more to acknowledge the challenges faced by students. Diverse students may have multiple priorities, including work, family, and

balancing their health, which means study may not always be their main goal. Rather than treat these other priorities as excuses, students want to be treated with respect as mature adults. An example of this from our data was when students felt uncomfortable having to provide explicit reasons for an extension request for their assessments.

We also recommend from the data and our reflections for staff to feel more open about encouraging their own stressors or challenges as a way to create a friendlier learning environment. One student summarised this sentiment for the workshops with,

> Lecturer-student relationships should go both ways. Lecturers being aware not all students are created equal, different circumstances, living, financial stressors, obligations. As well, back the other way.

In fact, the student co-authors felt that when staff share aspects of their personal or work life, students can also get a glimpse of their lives, and by consequence understand staff's busy schedules.

Another example of the importance of empathy emerged when students shared experiences of when they were put down by teachers when asking for additional clarification or help. One student voiced,

> [My teacher] met me in the practicals and belittled me for not doing something right. Teachers need more empathy – there is a reason student are struggling. The teachers – I feel like they don't care.

Student co-authors also discussed similar experiences and suggested that some teachers may forget that students are often doing practicals or assignments for the first time. Therefore, it's a key recommendation that teachers should reflect on what it must be like for students and approach the topic or assessment with empathy for them.

Finally, students stressed there should be less stigma around failure in their subjects and more support for mental health and wellbeing resources. Failure doesn't mean the student won't succeed and it can be incredibly daunting when teachers begin units with phrases such as "50% of students will fail this unit". Rather than focus on the fail rate, we suggest that teachers focus on educating students on tips and resources and reminding them of alternate pathways to success. One student shared with us their summary of this,

> Encourage students to look after one another, mental health situations are not well explored. Knowing that there are resources out there, but also less focus on failure and the stigma around failing an exam [it doesn't mean you aren't] as good.

Teachers can achieve this through reminders to students about resources available to them (such as study sessions or mental health workshops), not just at the beginning of the subject but throughout. As well as providing students with the confidence that they can succeed despite setbacks they may experience.

2. ***Ensuring assessment instructions, rubrics, and criteria are consistent and clear*** The second theme identified in our data is ensuring assessment instructions, rubrics and criteria are consistent and clear. From the evidence gathered in the workshops and our reflections, students frequently brought up the inconsistencies between assessment instructions, rubrics and other resource materials which made completing assessments more difficult and time consuming. For example, oral instructions in class may not match what was included in the rubric provided on the learning management system or the instructions may be vague or ambiguous. Students expressed this in workshops with,

> Every course is a bit different, and the structure is not very explicit, teachers say things on the fly, which is fine, but they don't say what they actually want. For example, the marking criteria are often vague, this is confusing. Sometimes I have done research and then found out it isn't needed. The assessment criteria needs to be more explicit.
>
> Another challenge is when you get instructions for the assignment, a rubric, FAQs, additional material, notes from a lecture and notes from a discussion board. You end up trying to collate 7 sets of instructions which don't always align. So, lots of time spent/wasted working out what they want.

Student co-authors recommend for a method or guide to be created for the markers to follow to ensure less variation across assessment marking processes. This can be a generalised resource that can be adjusted to the needs of the unit in various courses. This could, for example, be a checklist for teachers to ensure all instructions are consistent and that every tutor follows a similar marking process.

Moreover, the difference between achieving a high distinction (HD) in comparison to a distinction (D) criterion in the rubric was often cited as unclear, and potentially, linking to an inefficient use of students' time as they struggle to make sense of the rubric. As Carless and Chan (2017) have previously noted, students may have a difficult time understanding what "good" work looks like, without examples. Sometimes, as we have personally experienced, the difference in the rubric between HD and D could be as slight as one or two words. We suggest that one way to tackle this issue is for teachers to provide examples of what would meet an HD versus a D and perhaps even commentary to highlight the difference between. If teachers were worried about plagiarism, they could use a different subject topic that the one in question.

3. ***One easily accessible location***
   Finally, the last theme identified in our data was that students preferred to have all learning resources, including any articles, examples, or rubrics, on one easily accessible location, and from the start of the unit. This is particularly pertinent for equity students because students may be balancing health, family, or work commitments and strive to have flexibility around when they complete assessments. Having everything available from the start also recognises that every student learns at their own pace, and by providing resources upfront, some students may be able to learn better. Students in the workshop also expressed a similar recommendation with,

   > All resources on the cloud should be available at the beginning as [this] helps with preparation and planning.
   >
   > The piecemeal information about the assessment drip fed badly. Would be good to have all the pieces well before the due date of the assessment. All information about assessment should be recorded and stored in one place so that all students can access it beforehand for planning.

   Linking to this, students also felt it was important that unit chairs consider which resources to recommend and condense these resources for students, to avoid students feeling overwhelmed. For example, creating one document that links to several key articles that students can use to start their research as well as an FAQ with common questions that students may have. Discussion boards were also seen as critical to support student success because they can support informal dialogue, as well as opportunities to get further clarification.

Additional considerations relating to assessment

In addition to the three key themes listed above, we have several other reflections to share based both on our own experiences as diverse students as well as what we learned from our peers in the workshops. The first reflection is that many of the changes requested by students to make learning more accessible should be quite straightforward for teachers. These include enabling subtitles on Zoom or MS Teams, recording all online lectures, videos, or practicals for later access, having description text for any images, and ensuring file types are compatible with audio readers. These modifications can help improve inclusivity in assessment, for example, if there is a video that the student must watch before taking a quiz, subtitles would help support diverse learners. While these modifications may be time consuming in the first instance, they will ensure that the unit is accessible for students for many years to come.

Another aspect frequently discussed by students was around how flexibility was integrated into the learning design. To illustrate, a student with chronic illness may struggle to participate in a four-hour practical tutorial that is required to complete an assessment task. However, if some of the tutorial could be pre-audio recorded, for example the instructions given beforehand, then the overall duration of the practical could be reduced. As a bonus, by providing the instructions prior it may also reduce anxiety for students. Similarly, quizzes for students should ideally have multiple attempts allowed, to reduce stress for students, and acknowledge that some students may be having a bad day or may have a flare up of their condition. If the quiz must be completed in one take, another option would be to allow for a larger window for which it must be taken and give the student ample time to choose when they would like to complete it.

The student partners involved in this project, as well as the participants we spoke to, also reflected on the importance of learning access plans. Learning access plans (also known as access plans or individual study plans) are study support plans that aim to minimise disadvantages in the learning environments resulting from a disability, health condition, mental health condition or caring responsibility. Typically, students need to declare a disability, and potentially submit medical evidence, to request specific adjustments, such as more time on an exam. These adjustments can vastly support students' learning. Yet many students we spoke to reported not knowing that they qualified for a learning access plan until well into their course. And, more troubling, is that many students indicated the variation of how these plans were accepted by their teaching staff (also see Becker and Palladino 2016). For instance, one teacher might acknowledge the students' access plan unprompted, and email the student that they were supportive and, if applicable, extra time would be given. While another teacher in a different unit may never acknowledge the plan unless a student emails them asking for confirmation, and even then, may dispute giving them extra time. This variation of practice is unacceptable. There needs to be additional training for staff on what an access plan is and how students who have one should be treated. Students with an access plan should not have to "prove" additional hardship to their individual unit chairs.

Lastly, we think it's important to acknowledge that our findings and reflections here arose because the project took a SaP approach. As well documented in literature, there are numerous benefits to SaP, both for the individuals involved but also for the university (Dollinger and Lodge 2020; Mercer-Mapstone et al. 2017). By working with students, we can harness their lived experiences and expertise and get an on-the-ground point of view on what is needed to support student success. More research like this should be undertaken, and teachers should also consider other SaP mechanisms such as user-testing their resources or curriculum with students, and even hosting CoLabs with students to understand issues they may be facing in their teaching practice.

Conclusion

Our findings build on previous literature which has highlighted the importance of staff training and awareness to support inclusive assessment design (Nieminen 2022; Tai, Ajjawi, and Umarova 2021). Yet as we argued, and showcase here, students should play a pivotal role in future work to understand what practical ways teachers can improve inclusion in assessment. Therefore, the value of this project was that it was designed to give diverse students a voice to share their ideas on how to make assessments at university more inclusive and equitable. Engaging students as partners and listening to the students in the workshops provided the opportunity for students to raise concerns and speak to the inequity they have faced. The process also gave students a sense of relief knowing that these important issues are being heard and taken into consideration for further improvement.

CoLabs proved to be a useful model to eliciting students' feedback and generating practical ideas on how assessment design can be more inclusive to diverse students. The three recommendations provided in this chapter, creating empathetic relationships, ensuring consistent and clear instructions and rubrics, and having all assessment information in one easily accessible location are uncomplicated steps any teacher can take to improve inclusion.

Even though the participants of this project were from different academic backgrounds and neurodivergence, we have had similar experiences and are advocating for the same thing – equity. As we showcased in this chapter, it was this common goal, and the leverage of our unique experiences and insights, that helped us uncover how we could make assessment more inclusive. We urge for further projects that involve cross-cohort collaborations between student and staff to make the best out of everyone's academic journey.

Acknowledgements

The authors would like to acknowledge the other research team members who were integral to collecting data and analysing results, including Rola Ajjawi, Sam Bohra, Marina Booth, Harmeet Kaur, Danni McCarthy, Merrin McCracken, Trina Jorre St Jorre, and Joanna Tai.

References

Becker, S., and Palladino, J. 2016. "Assessing Faculty Perspectives about Teaching and Working with Students with Disabilities." *Journal of Postsecondary Education and Disability* 29 (1): 65–82.

Carless, D., and Chan, K. K. H. 2017. "Managing Dialogic Use of Exemplars." *Assessment and Evaluation in Higher Education* 42 (6): 930–941. https://doi.org/10.1080/02602938.2016.1211246.

Dollinger, M., Eaton, R., and Vanderlelie, J. 2021. "Reinventing the Focus Group: Introducing Design Thinking CoLabs." https://unistars.org/papers/STARS2021/03B.pdf.

Dollinger, M., and Lodge, J. 2020. "Understanding Value in the Student Experience through Student–Staff Partnerships." *Higher Education Research and Development* 39 (5): 940–952. https://doi.org/10.1080/07294360.2019.1695751.

Dollinger, M., and Vanderlelie, J. 2021. "Closing the Loop: Co-designing with Students for Greater Market Orientation." *Journal of Marketing for Higher Education* 31 (1): 41–57. https://doi.org/10.1080/08841241.2020.1757557.

Hanesworth, P., Bracken, S., and Elkington, S. 2019. "A Typology for a Social Justice Approach to Assessment: Learning from Universal Design and Culturally Sustaining Pedagogy." *Teaching in Higher Education* 24 (1): 98–114. https://doi.org/10.1080/13562517.2018.1465405.

McArthur, J. 2016. "Assessment for Social Justice: The Role of Assessment in Achieving Social Justice." *Assessment and Evaluation in Higher Education* 41 (7): 967–981. https://doi.org/10.1080/02602938.2015.1053429.

Mercer-Mapstone, L., Dvorakova, S. L., Matthews, K. E., Abbot, S., Cheng, B., Felten, P., Knorr, K., Marquis, E., Shammas, R., and Swaim, K. 2017. "A Systematic Literature Review of Students as Partners in Higher Education." *International Journal for Students as Partners* 1(1). https://doi.org/10.15173/ijsap.v1i1.3119.

Meyers, S., Rowell, K., Wells, M., and Smith, B. C. 2019. "Teacher Empathy: A Model of Empathy for Teaching for Student Success." *College Teaching* 67 (3):160–168. https://doi.org/10.1080/87567555.2019.1579699.

Nieminen, J. 2022. "Assessment for Inclusion: Rethinking Inclusive Assessment in Higher Education." *Teaching in Higher Education*. https://doi.org/10.1080/13562517.2021.2021395.

Nussbaum, M. C. 2006. *Frontiers of Justice*. Cambridge, MA: Belknap Press.

Tai, J., Ajjawi, R., and Umarova, A. 2021. "How Do Students Experience Inclusive Assessment? A Critical Review of Contemporary Literature." *International Journal of Inclusive Education*. https://doi.org/10.1080/13603116.2021.2011441.

21

MOVING FORWARD

Mainstreaming assessment for inclusion in curricula

Rola Ajjawi, David Boud, Joanna Tai, and Trina Jorre de St Jorre

The book has focused on assessment because assessment shapes and directs student learning; it is the assessment system that formally defines what is worth learning. The chapter authors have brought together a diversity of perspectives to explore, conceptualise, and problematise assessment for inclusion as well as showcasing good practice. In this final chapter, we make some concluding remarks and draw themes from across the book to reflect ways forward for assessment for inclusion.

Assessment for inclusion has both pragmatic and conceptual features. Focussing on immediate practical solutions alone is unlikely to be sufficient, given the philosophical roots of inclusion in the promise that education will contribute to a better world for both the individual and society more widely. Concomitantly, only working in abstract or theoretical spaces will not help to change practice. There is a great need to collaborate across disciplinary and organisational boundaries to build upon ideas, rather than operating in silos, if we are to mainstream assessment for inclusion. Given the diversity we seek to acknowledge and support within higher education, there are likely to be many people who can contribute to re-casting assessment for inclusion, from a range of perspectives. Academics, researchers, practitioners, academic developers, industry, professional bodies, and students themselves. The backgrounds, philosophies, theories, and practices, these people bring will also be diverse – beyond those which we have outlined within research fields. At this early stage of considering assessment within a broader goal of inclusion, we should be open to what each can bring, and work on finding resonances and commonalities to make substantial advances in assessment.

It is also important to note that this work cannot exist solely within academic research journals, or handbooks for assessment design, or even student advocacy agendas: it must promulgate across these spaces to achieve change in what happens on the ground. It is of no use to talk about wonderful new types of assessment designs which might improve inclusion, if they are never implemented or proven

DOI: 10.4324/9781003293101-25

to be effective. It is not just wide sweeping changes, due the pandemic, that have made an impact for diverse students already (Tai et al. 2022a). We should also look to our own "backyards" and see what can be done incrementally, since these small things may make the difference between students choosing a different course (or worse – discontinuing study) or persisting with their chosen course/degree. In the end, it is not educators who determine what is inclusive, it is the students and their future trajectories or their absences from them. We need to be observant about not only who is present in our courses, but as importantly, who is absent or under-represented.

Assessment design is often simply an accretion from tradition (Dawson et al. 2013), and yet, academics often justify specific designs by referring to the "real world". Assessment's fabricated constraints, and thus currently allowed adjustments, do not withstand scrutiny when we consider this juxtaposition: after all, the rules are themselves social constructions and can therefore be subject to alteration (McArthur 2016). Therefore, in this book and beyond, we call for engagement and involvement at every level to improve assessment for inclusion.

While the chapters in this book have focused primarily on assessment, we also need to reflect on inclusion in other aspects of the curriculum. We cannot look at assessment independently of what else is happening in the course. The backwash effect of assessment is on learning and all aspects of the curriculum: the intended learning outcomes and learning and teaching activities (Biggs and Tang 2011). So, while we might start our focus on assessment we need to look backwards to learning and teaching activities, the context in which they occur, and the learning outcomes desired. Intended learning outcomes should be formulated in ways that are not so limited that they do not permit students to work on different things and still meet the learning outcomes. They may not need to be so dependent on specific subject content that they exclude equivalent demonstrations of meeting learning outcomes as is currently assumed. Some current learning outcomes may be inappropriately exclusionary and need to be rethought. It is also worth noting that while we have adopted the language of inclusion in this book, inclusion can be tokenistic if a student is merely counted but does not feel like they belong or are active participants with a voice. Inclusion is not just a technical requirement, it encompasses students being part of what is being assessed.

As editors, in reflecting on the various chapters, there are common refrains that we can draw out: 1) that students should take an active and agentic role in assessment; 2) that inclusion needs to become a mainstay of regulatory frameworks that govern assessment from design through to evaluation; 3) that teachers need to adopt ethical reflexivity; and 4) that more diverse discourses need to be embedded to disrupt positivist and ableist discourses of assessment.

1. Students as agentic

   Several chapters in this book showed how students needed to be positioned as active actors in the assessment process in order to be included. This can be as partners involved in the design of assessment (Chapters 19 and 20), as actively choosing the assessment method (Chapter 17 and 18), or as contributing to the evaluation of the effects of assessment (Chapters 15 and 16). Nieminen (2022) argues that it is only when students are positioned in an agentic role within assessment that we can disrupt traditional practices in which assessment may be experienced as being foisted on or done to students.

While feedback has not been explicitly addressed in this book, it often occurs in conjunction with assessment, and we recognise that it has an important role to play in ensuring that assessment is inclusive. Feedback is a key opportunity for tailoring the curriculum to individual student needs and work. If feedback is designed well, then it too should position the student as active in the processes of seeking, interpreting, and taking action on feedback to inform learning. Lambert, Funk, and Adam (Chapter 5) remind us that feedback that acknowledges diversity and culture should not come from a deficit discourse. Johnstone, Ketterlin Geller, and Thurlow (Chapter 12) note that universal design for assessment includes improving the accessibility of feedback through multiple means of delivery.

However, as cautioned by several of the authors in the book, any changes to assessment regimes can lead to student anxiety and stress. We caution about offering too many options to students to avoid inappropriately overloading them. O'Neill recommends offering two options (or alternatives) only. However, that change might cause stress should not stop us from improving assessment. Instead, it behoves us to advise and support students so they understand why changes were made and how their new role in assessment might benefit their learning. Chapters in the book pay attention to specific student groups: Indigenous (Chapter 4), mature age students living in regional and remote areas (Chapter 16), students from low socio-economic status backgrounds (Chapter 13), international students (Chapter 14), and students with disabilities (Chapters 19, 20), showing a diverse range of students and needs. However, we agree with Crawford, Emery, and Baird (Chapter 16) that this is not about stereotyping "types" of students, rather, our intention is to highlight diversity, while also acknowledging that students have complex identities and can belong to other groups that may impact their experiences of assessment.

2. Regulatory frameworks of inclusion

Course handbooks and unit guides prompt teachers to construct defensible descriptions of assessment tasks. If these are not regularly questioned by colleagues, traditional practices are perpetuated. This benign neglect can harm students through unaware exclusion.

Brett and Harvey (Chapter 9), in their policy analysis, show that inclusion is often absent from assessment policy statements and that there are weak accountability and evaluation frameworks for assessment for inclusion. Worryingly, they show that reporting frameworks for equity groups have remained mostly static for the past three decades. These policy frameworks require augmenting "with a more nuanced understanding of how inclusion and diversity play out within the student experience". Beyond this, we must look to how the increasing manifestation of artificial intelligence and educational technology (e.g., proctoring) in assessment are unwittingly embedding bias and exclusion through taking highly selected groups as representing the whole. New forms of accountability and regulation might be needed to prompt ethical decision-making around these new technologies (Chapter 11). These are not simply administrative tasks. We should have more scrutiny of assessment practices that are educational rather than bureaucratic.

Any form of scrutiny can be misused and can perpetuate conservative practices. Whitburn and Thomas (Chapter 7, 76) remind us how "regulatory compliance is at the fore when compelling students to disclose disabilities to institutions, as a way to ensure that they can then expect reasonable adjustments to be made to their programs of learning, rather than to consider the inclusiveness and accessibility of courses". Following the rules is not good enough: ethical reflexivity and flexibility are required alongside regulation.

3. Ethical reflexivity, relationality, and flexibility to influence assessment practices
A broad survey of the higher education landscape suggests that student diversity has increased (Marginson 2016). Assessment philosophy has also changed, moving beyond testing what was taught to include assessment for learning and sustainable notions of assessment (Boud and Soler 2016). This implies that we need a different relationship between students and teachers. Gleeson and Fletcher (Chapter 4) remind us that education is fundamentally relational – it occurs through people working together. Strong student-teacher relationships foster inclusion (Tai et al. 2022b). The big challenge is to get educators to think differently about assessment. And to think carefully about who their students are and who is and isn't being accommodated by current assessment regimes.

Part of the inertia that surrounds the design of assessment is that assessment regimes are set within rigid systems of quality assurance. Decisions about assessment must be made well in advance of knowing which students are enrolled. These early decisions, made without direct knowledge of who will be affected by them, cannot be unmade or revisited and so the main recourse for inclusion are individual accommodations that are peripheral to task design (e.g., extra time, breaks or rooms). We need more flexibility in the system and allowance for professional and ethical decision-making by academic and course teams.

Many authors have argued that assessment should orient towards social justice, including the key proponent of assessment for social justice Jan McArthur (Chapter 2). Working out what social justice might involve requires considerable prompting to encourage conversations about what this might look like in particular disciplines and how this can be embedded in courses. The implication that follows is that this would lead to greater satisfaction for staff as well. Fostering communities of praxis and ethical reflexivity may be needed to reimagine inclusivity not through the lens of deficit but through the collective interrogation of whose knowledges, values and experiences are included and excluded in assessment frameworks (Chapter 8). There is also a need for better education of institutional staff, from academics, support staff, and web designers through to senior managers, on the legislative requirements and moral imperatives of inclusion (Chapter 9).

4. Alternative discourses and ways of knowing
   Many authors in the book sought to disrupt hegemonic ableist discourses of assessment that draw on linear Western models of education (Chapters 2–8), systematically dismantling practices that might on the face of it appear neutral, but that perpetuate systemic disadvantage. The theoretical frameworks invoked include decolonialism, critical disability theories, social justice, Indigenous ways of knowing, ontology, and internationalisation. For example, giving all students a fixed length of time assumes that time itself is equal for all students including those who might have caring or work responsibilities or those with chronic conditions that ebb and flow in severity. The main recourse for these students at present is through individual accommodation to make the system seem fairer. And yet this requires more paperwork, doctor visits and emotional work to disclose and convince what may seem to be unsympathetic ears (Chapter 12). Why have a discourse that creates additional burdens on those students who may already have the greatest burdens to bear? An assessment discourse that starts from the premise that all students should be able to demonstrate how they meet learning outcomes without additional requirements for some is needed.

   Continued adherence to the traditional notions of failure and success as they are presently embedded within institutional processes can restrict the capacity for more nuanced, inclusive assessment and risks further excluding candidates whose understandings fall outside these narrowly defined positions (Chapter 15). Indeed, O'Shea and Delahunty (Chapter 15) critique practices of grading as pinning self-worth to a score – which McArthur (Chapter 2) argues is a degrading act.

   Dawson (Chapter 10) tackles the big question of whether our present exclusionary assessments practices are a fundamental threat to the validity of assessment. If assessment misrepresents what some students are capable of, how can we accept it as valid? He suggests that we need to reconceptualise notions of fairness in assessment in higher education to focus on equity not equality. Are assessments able to judge who and who has not met the learning outcomes of a course rather than who can answer questions oriented to students with certain characteristics? We need to consider whose notion of validity is valid and who contributes to the definition of validity. Alongside this there needs to be reengagement with the discourse of fairness in assessment – beyond procedural fairness (i.e., transparency) and measurement fairness (i.e., absence of bias) to being receptive to diversity (Tierney 2013). Research by Valentine et al. (2021, 2022) suggests that fair assessment should accept subjectivities and privilege a more narrative approach to assessment.

No matter how thoroughly the notion of inclusion is debated and enacted, there will continue to be a need for both universal design for assessment and accommodations for individual students (Chapter 12). However, the balance is currently tipped far towards individual adjustments in our systems (Tai, Ajjawi, and Umarova 2021) and not enough on what will work for all. Critical universal design is an on-going process that takes ableism seriously (Chapter 3).

The book has been mostly silent about the pandemic. That is because the problems with inclusive assessment well and truly predate COVID-19. However, it is likely that the shift to emergency remote teaching and assessment highlighted the multiple sources of inequity arising from difficult home situations and the digital divide (Bartolic et al. 2022). The aftermath of the disruption caused by the pandemic might be an opportune time to challenge that which has been taken for granted in our assessment practices. One prediction that is particularly appealing to us comes from Peters et al. (2020, 720):

> Universities have the possibility to emerge from this pandemic as places of compassion, of wisdom and worthiness. … [to] become places where prior privilege does not give priority in engagement, where international respect flourishes for their students, not for their bank accounts, where recognition of diversity, equality and inclusion are the premises of formalised education and where humanity can flourish with the transdisciplinary humility the rest of our world is owed. The opportunity is a new educative focus not a new business model.

In conclusion, we hope that this book opens new conversations and investigations about assessment for inclusion. We ask educators to take courage in changing assessment and to work with students to take on this challenge. We urge the sector to fund and support continued research and development in assessment for inclusion. Finally, we look forward to the flourishing of new collaborations and conversations about assessment for inclusion.

References

Bartolic, S. K., Matzat, U., Tai, J., Burgess, J.-L., Boud, D., Craig, H., and Archibald, A., et al. 2022. "Student Vulnerabilities and Confidence in Learning in the Context of the COVID-19 Pandemic." *Studies in Higher Education*. http://doi.org/10.1080/03075079.2022.2081679.

Biggs, J., and Tang, C. 2011. *Teaching for Quality Learning at University: What the Student Does*, rev. ed. Buckingham: Society for Research into Higher Education and the Open University Press.

Boud, D., and Soler, R. 2016. "Sustainable Assessment Revisited." *Assessment and Evaluation in Higher Education* 41 (3): 400–413. http://doi.org/10.1080/02602938.2015.1018133.

Dawson, P., Bearman, M., Boud, D. J., Hall, M., Molloy, E. K., and Bennett, S. 2013. "Assessment Might Dictate the Curriculum, But What Dictates Assessment?" *Teaching & Learning Inquiry: The ISSOTL* 1 (1):107–111. http://doi.org/10.20343/teachlearninqu.1.1.107.

Marginson, S. 2016. "The Worldwide Trend to High Participation Higher Education: Dynamics of Social Stratification in Inclusive Systems." *Higher Education* 72 (4): 413–434. http://doi.org/10.1007/s10734-016-0016-x.

McArthur, J. 2016. "Assessment for Social Justice: The Role of Assessment in Achieving Social Justice." *Assessment and Evaluation in Higher Education* 41 (7): 967–981. http://doi.org/10.1080/02602938.2015.1053429.

Nieminen, J. H. 2022. "Assessment for Inclusion: Rethinking Inclusive Assessment in Higher Education." *Teaching in Higher Education*. http://doi.org/10.1080/13562517.2021.2021395.

Peters, M. A., Rizvi, F., McCulloch, G., Gibbs, P., Gorur, R., Hong, M., and Hwang, Y., et al. 2020. "Reimagining the New Pedagogical Possibilities for Universities Post-Covid-19." *Educational Philosophy and Theory* 54 (6): 717–760. http://doi.org/10.1080/00131857.2020.1777655.

Tai, J., Ajjawi, R., Bearman, M., Dargusch, J., Dracup, M., Harris, L., and Mahoney, P. 2022a. *Re-imagining Exams: How Do Assessment Adjustments Impact on Inclusion?* Perth, Australia: National Centre for Student Equity in Higher Education. https://www.ncsehe.edu.au/wp-content/uploads/2022/02/Tai_Deakin_Final.pdf.

Tai, J., Ajjawi, R., and Umarova, A. 2021. "How Do Students Experience Inclusive Assessment? A Critical Review of Contemporary Literature." *International Journal of Inclusive Education*. http://doi.org/10.1080/13603116.2021.2011441.

Tai, J., Mahoney, P., Ajjawi, R., Bearman, M., Dargusch, J., Dracup, M., and Harris, L. 2022b. "How Are Examinations Inclusive for Students with Disabilities in Higher Education? A Sociomaterial Analysis." *Assessment and Evaluation in Higher Education*. http://doi.org/10.1080/02602938.2022.2077910.

Tierney, R. D. 2013. "Fairness in Classroom Assessment." In *SAGE Handbook of Research on Classroom Assessment*, edited by James H. McMillan, 125–144. Thousand Oaks, CA: SAGE Publications.

Valentine, N., Durning, S. J., Shanahan, E. M., van der Vleuten, C., and Schuwirth, L. 2022. "The Pursuit of Fairness in Assessment: Looking beyond the Objective." *Medical Teacher* 44 (4): 353–359. http://doi.org/10.1080/0142159X.2022.2031943.

Valentine, N., Shanahan, E., Durning, M., and Schuwirth, S. J. L. 2021. "Making It Fair: Learners' and Assessors' Perspectives of the Attributes of Fair Judgement." *Medical Education* 55 (9): 1056–1066. https://doi.org/10.1111/medu.14574.

INDEX